TEACH ME ABOUT HEAVEN & ETERNAL LIFE

BY KENNETH E. SULLIVAN, Ph.D.

All rights reserved. Written permission must be secured from the publisher to use or reproduce any part of this book, except for brief quotations in critical reviews or articles.

Unless otherwise indicated, all Scripture quotations are taken from the *Holy Bible, New Living Translation* (NLT), copyright ©1996, 2004, 2007. Used by permission of Tyndale House Publishers, Inc., Wheaton, Illinois 60189. All rights reserved.

Quotations from the King James Version of the Bible (public domain); *New International Version of the Bible* (NIV), ©1973, 1978, 1984, by International Bible Society, used by permission of Zondervan, all rights reserved; *Living Bible*, (LB), ©1971, by Tyndale House Publishers, Inc., Wheaton, Illinois 60189.

Scripture quotations taken from the New American Standard Bible®, Copyright ©1960, 1962, 1963, 1968, 1971, 1972, 1973, 1975, 1977, 1995 by The Lockman Foundation. Used by permission. (www.Lockman.org)

ISBN 978-0-9827553-6-5
©2014 Emerge Curriculum Publishing
www.emergecurriculum.com
Production Consulting:
Vision Communications, *www.visioncomsolutions.com*
Cover Illustration Provided by *Dollar Photo Club ©2014*

Printed in the United States of America

CONTENTS

Introduction	4
Chapter *1* After Death, Life Goes On	7
Chapter *2* Your Best Life After Death	22
Chapter *3* Comforting Facts About the Resurrection	45
Chapter *4* A Brand-new Body and a Brand-new Mind	65
Chapter *5* Home Training: On Earth As It Is in Heaven	87
Chapter *6* A World with One Law	112
Chapter 7 Absolute Peace	131
Chapter 8 Joy and Pleasure Forever	146
Chapter 9 Paradise Heaven	168
Chapter 10 New Heavens and a New Earth	185
Notes & Citations	205
Answer Key	210
Bibliography	216
Other Books by Dr. Sullivan	219

Introduction

Since you have been raised to new life with Christ, set your sights on the realities of heaven, where Christ sits in the place of honor at God's right hand. Think about the things of heaven, not the things of earth.

(Colossians 3:1-2 NLT)

One of the most neglected yet most important subjects in the entire Bible is heaven. One of the things of greatest importance to God is that those who turn to Him should make heaven their primary focus and priority. In these opening verses, the apostle Paul strongly urges us as God's people to set our sights on the realities of heaven. In other words, we are compelled to focus on the fact that heaven is a very real place and the future home and destiny of every believer. Those of us who have placed our faith in Christ are joined to Him. We have been raised to new life in Him. Since this is the case, we should keep this reality squarely in mind and be very deliberate in establishing the habit of meditating on heaven and Christ. Paul makes it clear that even though we cannot see Him, Christ is in heaven, seated at God's right hand. Paul includes this information because he wants us to firmly grasp the reality of heaven's existence. He wants us to realize that heaven is not some imaginary fantasyland, but it is real and tangible. It is visible, touchable, and perceivable through the senses.

To help us avoid losing sight of this fact, Paul urges us to, "think about the things of heaven, not the things of earth." Heaven and our future existence with Christ should not be something we only think about occasionally. We should muse and reflect on the joys, realities, and pleasures of heaven on a daily basis until we get there. Keeping heaven in our thoughts is so important to God that He provides us with a great deal of detailed information about it throughout the

Teach Me About Heaven and Eternal Life

Bible. But when we come to the New Testament, there is a dramatic increase in the information provided about heaven, as well as an increase in the admonitions for us to focus our sights there. We are urged to think and learn about heaven and long for it.

During His time on earth, Jesus spent a great deal of time teaching about heaven and what it is like because He wants us to understand it, see the value of it, and keep our eyes upon it as the ultimate prize of life. When our eyes are fixed on heaven, we are drawn to it. It becomes the treasure that our heart follows. It becomes our life goal and dream.

Jesus also wants His disciples to understand the culture and customs of heaven in order to properly represent it as His ambassadors here on earth. The Bible provides enough descriptive information about heaven for us to examine, study, and commit to memory in order to maintain a focus upon this wonderful place. This information is intended to give us hope, joy, and encouragement as we travel through this life. There is very detailed information about the architectural design of the capital city of heaven, New Jerusalem. There are details about the landscape of heaven, vegetation, animal life, the environment, social life, relationships and activities, glorified human anatomy, diet, and the beauty and splendor of this eternal world. There is more than enough information to fill our minds, lift our spirits, and keep us motivated while we wait for our turn to enter heaven's gates.

Immediately after my wife, Joyce, and I were married, we decided that we wanted to own our own home. We knew that renting was not the best investment, so we began to save money toward our dream house. We lived beneath our means, banking her paycheck and living off of mine. To keep ourselves inspired and encouraged, we sometimes looked at our bankbook to see how much ground we had gained. To really stay inspired, we made a habit of browsing through real estate magazines with pictures of homes in nice neighborhoods that appealed to us. We took weekend drives through some of the neighborhoods we aspired to live in and discussed the subject with friends who were homeowners. This was our way of seeking the thing we had set our hearts on. These exercises helped to make our dream of owning a home more real and tangible. It filled us with hope, possibility, and anticipation.

When we had setbacks in our finances, like having to use our savings to repair the car or meet some other unexpected expense, looking at the magazines and visiting the neighborhoods restored our focus. This exercise made the wait more bearable and the sacrifices seem less of a deprivation. It helped us put everything in perspective and keep our hopes, dreams, and expectations alive. It allowed us to continue believing that we would get there, and thus we were encouraged to continue working and saving.

As I worked overtime hours, I would visualize the homes we had looked at and count how many more weeks of saving we would have to do before the goal of home ownership was within our grasp. Finally, after two and a half years of dreaming, looking, and saving, we had enough for the down payment on our first dream home. It was a brick and stone ranch-style home on about half an acre of land in a very nice neighborhood. The home was in excellent condition, so we were able to move right in.

We were able to achieve our goal by keeping our eyes on the prize. This is the same attitude God wants us to have about heaven. We are urged to keep it fresh in our minds and thought lives. To give food for our imagination to feast on, God has revealed many fascinating details to His prophets and apostles, who then recorded these revelations and experiences and passed them on to us in the Holy Scriptures. We are urged to formulate visual images by reading, re-reading, and memorizing these passages, along with imagining what it will be like to live in that wonderful place. No mortal eye has seen the complete picture of heaven, but a number of eyewitnesses have seen different details of it. Like pieces of a puzzle, these bits of information can be fitted together to create a picture of our future homeland. Throughout human history, God has spoken to the world through His prophets, but in the latter days He sent His own Son to communicate directly with humanity (Hebrews 1:1-2). Jesus has given us more information about heaven than any other person, except the apostle John.

We have taken these many bits of information and fitted them together in such a way as to answer important questions about this mystical place and assist the reader in conceptualizing a fuller view of heaven, our eternal home.

CHAPTER 1
After Death, Life Goes On

From the very beginning of human history, fear has been the common reaction on the part of those facing the prospect of the end of life and familiar things. To be faced with the specter of being suddenly snatched from everything we know and are familiar with and thrust into something completely unknown is justifiably frightening. William Randolph Hearst, the newspaper magnate of yesteryear, so feared death that he prohibited anyone from mentioning the word or speaking about death. Yet Jesus makes the startling statement that we need not fear death (Matthew 10:28).[1]

Since the time of Adam, people have watched friends and loved ones depart this life and enter the realm that Shakespeare refers to as "the undiscovered country." Throughout our lives, we've watched those around us slip away one by one, never to return. Each time someone we know departs this life, we are reminded that at some uncertain point along the line, our turn will also come.

People of every generation have tried to prepare themselves to face the inevitable in various ways. Some have tried to cope with the anxiety of death by confronting it with courage. Others have sought to trivialize or minimize death in their thinking, seeking to render it an insignificant part of life. Still others have simply concluded that death is only an eternal sleep.

Moreover, ignorance about death has worked through the human imagination to produce a great number of religious superstitions and practices. Some imagine that we die and return as either a lower or higher form of life depending upon how good we are. This is the belief system that defines reincarnation. Some religions teach that we become gods. On the other hand, atheism urges us to believe that we simply vanish into nothingness and merely cease to exist.

While there is no denying the fear and terror generated by the thought of leaving this life, most people are also curious about what lies beyond. Many of us hold in tension fear and curiosity about what awaits us after we die. Driven by this need to know the unknown and reconnect with the spirits of the departed, the black art of necromancy arose and has survived throughout the centuries. Some charlatans claiming to have psychic abilities pretend to communicate with the dead. These so-called psychics convince people that those who die are still here on earth and can be summoned by those with a sixth sense.

But what really happens when we die? This curiosity is sparked by our first exposure to death. Every human being is introduced to this enigma as a child. Our first encounter with death may be a lifeless bird or some other tiny creature we happen to stumble upon while playing in the yard. This first introduction to death may be a mild shock delivered by the unfamiliar sight of the stiffened body of something with which we have had no connection and therefore feel no sense of loss. On the other hand, our first encounter may be the heart-rending grief brought on by the death of a beloved pet or even a close relative. We may remember the bitter and sobering sting of death that came when someone explained the loss and separation we would have to learn to live with. It became clear to us that anyone or anything that passes into death will not be returning.

What Happens After Death?

Attached to the understanding that at some point in life everything dies is the fear and dread of our own death. Thoughts about our own mortality have haunted us from childhood. The thing about death that frightens people is the question regarding what happens when we die. Undoubtedly, the apostle Paul had also been curious about this subject while living among people who were also extremely inquisitive. Knowing how important this question was to the early Christians, Paul set aside some time and space to address it in several of his letters to the various churches. In his second letter to the church in the city of Corinth, Greece, Paul spoke in great detail about exactly what happens when a Christian dies. It is important to note that Paul was specifically speaking about the fate of Christians after death—not to the world of unbelievers. (We will deal with the fate of non-Christians later.)

After encouraging the Corinthian Christians not to lose heart over the many troubles they were going through (2 Corinthians 4:16-18), Paul launches into the subject of life after death. With eight powerful verses he drives away the fog that has surrounded the issue of death for the Christian. We will use these eight verses to introduce some of what the Bible reveals about the subject of life after death. These verses are only a small part of all that is written in the Scriptures on this important subject. However, as a very important part of the whole puzzle of information, they are critical for helping us understand what happens immediately after the death of those who place their faith in Jesus Christ. To get the most out of these verses, we will examine each one carefully. Opening the fifth chapter of this important letter, Paul writes,

> For we know that when this earthly tent we live in is taken down (that is, when we die and leave this earthly body), we will have a house in heaven, an eternal body made for us by God himself and not by human hands.

(2 Corinthians 5:1 NLT)

Paul makes several important points in this verse. First he emphasizes the fact that at some point we will all reach the end of this life in these mortal bodies and die. Of course, the Bible points out elsewhere that there is one exceptional generation. The cycle of death will be interrupted in mid-stride for those Christians who are alive when Jesus returns. They will be instantly transformed from mortal to immortal without ever having to die (1 Corinthians 15:51-52). However, Paul makes it clear that this is the exception to the rule, which is that every person has an appointment with death (Hebrews 9:27). Unless the Lord Jesus returns in our lifetime, we will all keep this appointment. It is just a matter of when and how. Paul says, "We know that *when* we die, ..." (emphasis author) not *if* "we die." He wants to convey to us the certainty of death and the subsequent need to prepare for this eventuality.

Secondly, Paul compares the death of Christian disciples with the act of merely leaving a tent. He uses this analogy because, as a tent maker by trade, he was very familiar with nomadic people who lived in tents and moved about from place to place. When they got ready to move on to another location, they simply took down their tent, packed it away, and relocated.

Paul is not the only biblical author who compares the human body to a tent we live in while here on earth. Peter also refers to his body as a tent and speaks of his impending death as departing his tent (2 Peter 1:13-14). The tent is an excellent analogy because, like the human body, it is a temporal place of habitation that is not made to last forever. Indeed, a tent has an expiration date. It grows old with time and wears out or becomes so damaged that it is no longer inhabitable, so it needs to be replaced.

Paul's third point from verse 1 is that dying is not the end of life. We do not cease to exist, nor do we sleep in the grave, trapped in a decaying body throughout the ages as we wait for the day of resurrection. No! We simply move out of the temporal mortal body, no longer capable of housing the spirit, to live in another dwelling and place. Paul makes it clear that when these tents are taken down, or when we escape these bodies, we go immediately from earth to a place called heaven. He goes on to explain that when we depart from these bodies and move to heaven, God Himself will provide every believer with a brand-new body that will never grow old or wear out. We exit the temporal tent we live in on earth to live in what in contrast would be a palace.

Paul's fourth point from verse 1 is that the new body every Christian will inherit in heaven is made by God, not by human hands. In contrast to the temporary nature of the human body that is brought forth by human sexual means the bodies we can expect to receive in heaven are specifically made by the hands of God, just as Adam's body was created in the beginning. Paul says that we will leave this earth for our home in heaven and the bodies we will occupy are eternal ones that will never perish.

Paul continues his conversation about life after death by highlighting some of the difficulties we experience in our present mortal bodies.

We grow weary in our present bodies, and we long to put

on our heavenly bodies like new clothing. For we will put on heavenly bodies; we will not be spirits without bodies.

(2 Corinthians 5:2-3 NLT)

In these two verses, Paul makes two more very important points. First, he reinforces the fact that human beings are spirits that live in bodies. While on earth these bodies are mortal, constructed of flesh and blood and designed to live in the environment of earth for a brief period of time. The duration of life in a mortal body is compared to the brevity of a vapor that appears for a short time and vanishes away (James 4:14). Paul informs us that when death causes a person's body to cease functioning, that person continues to live as a spirit. However, his second point is that we Christians will not be spirits without bodies; instead, we will leave these mortal bodies and put on a new immortal heavenly body as effortlessly as putting on new clothing.

That is exactly how God wants us to look at these bodies we presently inhabit. They are like clothing—earth suits that we use while living on this planet. These bodies are not all there is to us because we only live inside them. When they wear out or are so badly damaged that they can no longer house the spirit, they will be laid aside, and we will be given new eternal ones that will be suitable for living in heaven. When we see the lifeless body of a loved one, we are not looking at the person but at the tent he or she left behind. That's why they are called remains. The body is what the spirit left behind, for the spirit has already departed for another place.

If the person was a Christian, he or she is in heaven with God, the saints, and the angels. Noted evangelist Billy Graham comments on this subject, "Why live in a sea of despair when you can live knowing that, after death, life can be experienced as it was originally intended—in fellowship with our Creator and our Lord? This is the confidence that Christians possess. Death marks the beginning of a new and wonderful life in Heaven with Christ that will last forever. To the believer, death is merely the gateway to eternal life." [2]

In their book entitled *Beyond Death*, Gary Habermas and J. P. Moreland express it this way: "Immediately after death, a person will continue to be truly alive and conscious, even though transformed into a different mode of being. This mode of existence is restful and happy. It is not a period of idleness and inactivity. Far from it."[3]

When I was a child, I loved to play in the woods of west Tennessee. Occasionally while climbing a tree I would stumble upon the remains of a katydid. What I saw was the perfect shape of the little insect, but only the discarded shell. The real living insect, having outgrown its skin, would simply crawl out of it through a little slit and move on with its life, leaving the remains—an empty, lifeless shell—behind. This is similar to what happens when a Christian dies. The person moves on but still lives on, leaving the lifeless remains behind.

We look at the remains with pity, thinking that somehow what we see is the actual person. If anyone is to be pitied, it is the people who are left behind to struggle on through life. The believer who departs the temporal body is to be envied, not pitied. This is extremely important because it dispels the notions of soul sleep and wandering human spirits roaming the earth as ghosts. Paul makes it clear that we will not be spirits without bodies in heaven; instead, we will put on new bodies. But when will we receive these new bodies that Paul is speaking about?

There are two major opinions held by Bible scholars regarding this question. The first is that when we die, we will leave these bodies and go immediately to heaven as spirits without bodies. Scholars of this opinion believe we will wait and rest, fully conscious and comfortable, in heaven for the day of the resurrection of the dead and the transformation of the living saints. They believe that on resurrection day, our spirits will return to earth with Christ and enter the new bodies that Christ will instantly resurrect from the grave or from the site of the remains.

Ron Rhodes is among those who hold this opinion. He comments,

> The state of our existence between physical death and the future resurrection is properly called "the intermediate state." It is an in-between state . . . . It is the state of our existence in between the time our mortal bodies die and the time we receive our resurrection bodies in the future. The intermediate state, then, is a disembodied state. It is a state in which a person's physical body is in the grave while his or her spirit or soul is either in heaven with

Christ or in a place of great suffering apart from Christ. A person's destiny in the intermediate state depends wholly upon whether he or she has placed faith in Christ during his or her earthly existence."[4]

There is a second major opinion concerning the state of Christians in the immediate afterlife. These scholars believe that when Christians die, they receive a body from the Lord immediately upon entering heaven. This second group believes that we will not be spirits without bodies, but rather we will receive some kind of interim body immediately after death. Well-known author Randy Alcorn is among this second group of scholars. He makes the following argument: "It seems possible—though it is certainly debatable—that between our earthly life and our bodily resurrection, God may grant us some physical form that will allow us to function as human beings while in that unnatural state 'between bodies,' awaiting our resurrection."[5] Paul Enns agrees with Alcorn's position. He remarks,

> The Resurrection that the Scriptures describes is the new body we will receive at the resurrection (1 Cor. 15:51-53). But what happens at death, before the resurrection? Recall that at the transfiguration of Christ, Moses and Elijah appeared to James, Peter and John (Matt. 17:3). Three disciples recognized Moses and Elijah. Clearly, those two had physical bodies through which they were identifiable. Peter immediately recognized them in their physical form (Matt. 17:4). They are identified as "men" (Luke 9:30), hardly the designation of a spirit. In heaven, prior to the resurrection, the elders are seen falling down and casting their crowns before the throne (Rev. 4:10), all of which necessitates a physical body. They are also seen holding harps and golden bowls (Rev. 5:8). The conclusion? Though we don't know all the specifics of a believer's resurrection . . . those who die before the resurrection of the dead will have intermediate bodies before they receive their final bodies before the resurrection."[6]

Paul seems to suggest as much when he says, "For we will not be spirits without bodies, but we will put on our new heavenly bodies" (2 Corinthians 5:3). Of course, opponents of this view can plausibly argue that Paul is referring to the time when we will put on our resurrection bodies at the return of Christ for His people.

The possibility of living in heaven as a spirit without a body may be a bit disturbing to some. But it might help to realize that God is a Spirit (John 4:24). Angels are also spirits (Hebrews 1:14).

As spirits they take on human form, eat, talk, see, and hear (Genesis 18:1-8). They wear clothing, experience joy and pleasure, are capable of moving about the universe freely, and have far greater power and intellectual capabilities than mortal, physical human beings.

Regardless to whether we enter heaven and wait as spirits without bodies or have an intermediate body, life in heaven will be far better than what we are now experiencing. In either case we know we will be full of love, joy, and peace and experience great pleasure. We also know that we will rest from all the struggles of life in these present bodies. Even those who believe that we will be disembodied spirits in the interim period agree that life during that time will be far, far better than life as we now experience it.

After positing his theory of a disembodied existence after death, Ron Rhodes goes on to say, "Christians in the intermediate state enjoy a sense of serene rest in the presence of Christ. They have no tedious labors to attend to. All is tranquil . . . . This 'rest' will be a comprehensive rest. There will be rest from all toil of the body, from all laborious work, from all the diseases and frailties of the body, from all outward sorrows, from all inward troubles, from the temptations and afflictions of Satan, and from all doubts and fears."[7]

Land of the Dying

Now let's examine more of what the apostle Paul has to say on the subject of life after death:

> While we live in these earthly bodies, we groan and sigh, but it's not that we want to die and get rid of these bodies that clothe us. Rather, we want to put on our new bodies so that these dying bodies will be swallowed up by life.

(2 Corinthians 5:4 NLT)

In verse 4, Paul makes four very important points. First, he points out the fact that these bodies we now occupy are in the process of dying. Christians often say that they are grateful to be in the land of the living. But the truth is that we are in the land of the dying. Every living thing on earth is in the process of dying from the moment of conception. From the instant of the merger of sperm and egg, we begin moving toward death. Each heartbeat diminishes the number of heartbeats we have left. Each night we lie down leaves us with one less day to live on earth. Our bodies are dying, and we live in a world of dying people and dying things.

As Paul puts it in his second point, "Our dying bodies make us groan and sigh." The process of dying takes a toll on our bodies, even when we are young. Even children and young adults suffer from illnesses, diseases, and the process of wear and tear on a finite body. We sigh and groan with the agony and pain we sometimes experience in these bodies. These periods of suffering are reminders of the temporal nature of our existence in these mortal bodies. We are especially reminded of our mortality when we begin to grow older.

Wise King Solomon warns of the challenges that come with old age and urges young people not to allow the excitement of youth to cause them to forget about God. Describing the aging process, he writes,

> Remember him before your legs-the guards of your house- start to tremble; and before your shoulders-the strong men- stoop. Remember him before your teeth- your few remaining servants- stop grinding; and before your eyes- the women looking through the windows-see dimly. Remember him before the door to life's opportunities is closed and the sound of work fades. Now you rise at the first chirping of the birds, but then all their sounds will grow faint.

(Ecclesiastes 12:3-5 NLT)

Paul the apostle and Solomon the king were all too familiar with the ravages of age and wear upon the human body. We are born into this world with the human spirit somehow encased within our bodies, and we begin marching toward death. As we grow older, our bodies begin to wear out and we experience pain. Our teeth begin to wear down, our eyesight diminishes, our hair falls out, and our skin wrinkles. Also, our energy level wanes, so we require more rest. We slow down, so the reduced activity coupled with a slower metabolism contributes to weight gain for many of us.

In addition to the aging processes that weigh heavily upon us, there is the assault of sicknesses and sometimes terminal diseases that exacerbate the pain and anguish of living as mortals in this problematic world. We fuss and worry over health care issues and rely more and more on our physician's care. We see more and more of our friends and loved ones pass away all around us, constantly reminding us that death is inching closer and closer. All these things tire us out and cause us to begin to grow weary with life in these mortal bodies. The aging process is a reminder to us that we are not designed to live forever in this world in these bodies as they are now.

Along with the physical changes in our bodies, we also grow weary with life emotionally. And with age come fears, phobias, and concerns about things we once paid no attention to. Our deteriorating physical condition makes us less self-sufficient and no longer confident—and more dependent upon others for our well-being. For many elderly people, bouts with loneliness accompany debilitating diseases, as well as a host of other things that are an emotional drain. Our dying bodies also plague us with guilt and condemnation, sinful thoughts, weariness, disappointment, regret, embarrassment, and physical and mental deficiencies. We indeed groan in these bodies.

Paul's third point is that even with all these struggles that we endure in a dying body, we still do not want to die and have no body at all. No, we long to escape the painful torments of living in these dying bodies to enter into the new heavenly ones that God has waiting for us in heaven. This third point seems to support those who believe that we will receive a temporary body immediately after death. Paul says that our bodies are now ready and waiting for our arrival in heaven and we will put on our new body like a new suit of clothes.

Paul's fourth point from verse 4 is that the new bodies we enter will be eternal rather than temporal. These dying bodies will be swallowed up by everlasting life. Life will triumph over death, and we will live forever. We will drink the waters of life freely and be full of energy and vitality in the presence of God, the angels, and the saints (Revelation 21:6).

Prepared to Die

God himself has prepared us for this, and as a guarantee he has given us his Holy Spirit.

(2 Corinthians 5:5 NLT)

In verse 5 Paul makes it clear that we are not left alone in the struggle of life or when we face death. God has prepared us for the transition by giving us His Holy Spirit as the guarantee or the earnest money. Nowadays in our society we practice a universal custom of demonstrating sincerity and good faith when making a major purchase, such as a house or car, by depositing a down payment or earnest money. In the same way, God has deposited His Spirit in us as His guarantee, demonstrating that the process of the transition from this life into eternal life has already begun. In the midst of all the challenges, pain, and weariness of life and in the face of the terror of death, we are encouraged by the fact that God is present with those of us who turn to Him in faith. He has prepared us for the moment of death and for eternal life with Him. In fact, our entire life on earth is a time of preparation for the end of this earthly life and the beginning of life in heaven.

When the time to die finally comes, there will be no reason to fear because no Christian will have to face death alone and unprepared. King David is famous for saying, "Even when I walk through the darkest valley. I will not be afraid, for you are close beside me . . . . Surely your goodness and unfailing love will pursue me all the days of my life, and I will live in the house of the Lord forever" (Psalm 23:4, 6 NLT). God walks with us through life, and He will walk with us through death into the joys and beauty of life everlasting. We are strengthened by His Spirit and presence and filled with inexpressible joy and anticipation because of the future He has in store for us. He infuses us with peace that defies understanding in view of all we face in this world. We enjoy sweet fellowship with God now and anticipate a future of uninterrupted fellowship in a perfect world as we live among perfected people.

But these present blessings are only a foretaste of what is in store for us in heaven. The knowledge of just a tiny fraction of what God has reserved for us is a great part of what sustains us and keeps us looking up and moving forward. As we reflect upon the promises of God, our resolve is strengthened so that we are able to persevere through this life.

Paul continues his discussion of life after death:

> So we are always confident, even though we know that

as long as we live in these bodies we are not at home with the Lord.

(2 Corinthians 5:6 NLT)

In verse 6 Paul makes it clear that because we have the Holy Spirit, we have confidence that God is with us, even though as long as we are living in these mortal bodies "we are not at home with the Lord." The tenor of Paul's words reveals his opinion that living in these mortal bodies is not as good and desirable as being away from them. As long as we live in these bodies, we are away from the Lord. In other words, we are not beholding Him as He is beholding us. We are separated from God by a wall of flesh. Our mortal bodies hold us here in this present world, but when they release us at death, we will instantly be free to go home with the Lord. While we are in these bodies, we cannot see God, but He sees us. We cannot see heaven, but it is real. While we are in these bodies, our physical senses are blind and dumb to the greater reality of heaven and eternal life. Our contact with our God and future home is through the implement of faith. This is exactly what Paul meant when he wrote,

For we live by believing and not by seeing.

(2 Corinthians 5:7 NLT)

Although Paul had witnessed many miracles and on one occasion had even seen heaven, he makes the statement that "we live by believing and not by seeing." As Christians, we have all had personal experiences with God during which He has revealed Himself in some personal way that boosts our belief that He is true to His Word. However, none of us have really seen heaven, so our imagination is limited regarding what the experience of living in a new, perfect, glorified body in heaven will be like. Yet, having not seen, we believe. We follow after Christ and seek to imitate His lifestyle because we believe. We have not seen Him, yet we love Him and fully expect to be with Him someday.

Moreover, we have God's written Word and our own personal experience of how He has kept His promise to transform our own lives. We have experienced the birth of a deep desire to live righteously and please Him, suddenly and immediately after being born again. Additionally, we have seen His work of transformation in the lives of fellow believers. With this evidence and many other infallible proofs of God's integrity, we fully expect Him to keep His promise to take us home to heaven.

No one is perfect, but every true Christian has been changed. From generation to generation, the lives of those who have truly placed their faith in Christ have been transformed. This reality, coupled with God's Word that encompasses the testimonies of the apostles and prophets and God's promises about the future, is what our faith rests upon. We believe and are confident that while we are living in these bodies, we are not at home in heaven with the Lord. So we live our lives believing that when we leave these bodies, we will be at home with the Lord. This faith dictates how we live our lives in this world. Because we have this expectation of living forever in heaven with Jesus, we aspire to live in this world as He lived. This hope and expectation shapes and colors how we conduct business, how we treat others, how we raise our families, and everything we do in this life. We live our lives by believing, not by seeing.

Thomas, one of Jesus' disciples, refused to believe that He had been resurrected from the dead until he had seen Him and felt the wounds in His body. One day Jesus appeared to Thomas and commanded Him to touch Him and feel the wounds that the nails and spear had made. Upon seeing, Thomas believed. Jesus told Thomas he had seen and believed, but those who had not seen and still believe are the ones who are truly blessed (John 20:25-29). Jesus knew that millions upon millions of people, beginning with those who lived during His generation and extending over more than two thousand years, would have to believe without seeing. They would have to rely upon their faith in His written Word, along with their personal relationship and experience with His work in their own lives and the lives of fellow Christians. They would be blessed because they would live their lives based upon their confidence in His promises.

Paul continues his discussion:
> Yes, we are fully confident, and we would rather be away from these earthly bodies, for then we will be at home with the Lord. (2 Corinthians 5:8 NLT)

In verse 8, Paul makes the bold statement that he would rather be absent from his body and at home with the Lord. In essence,

Paul is saying that he is so confident death is the vehicle that will deliver him safely home with the Lord Jesus, he would rather let death have his body and take him home than to continue living in his body and this world. Reading these words from Paul is what inspired Dr. Erwin Lutzer to comment, "Death is the means by which our bodies are put to rest while our spirits are escorted through the gates of heaven . . . . Death in the New Testament is transformed from a monster to a minister. What at first seems to box us in, frees us to go to God."[8] Of course, in this passage Paul is not thinking of terminating his life. This would have been a terrible sin against God. Instead, he is attempting to help us understand that death holds no terror for Christians and life after the death of these earthly bodies, these tents, is far better than the life we are now living. At death we are freed from the difficulties and limitations that these bodies impose upon us, and we will be at home with the Lord in a perfect paradise. This makes it clear that whatever our state in heaven, whether we are given new temporary bodies immediately or whether we will have to wait as spirits until the day of the resurrection, life in heaven will be sweet.

As she felt her spirit begin to pass from her worn-out mortal body, Lady Glenorchy uttered these final words: "If this is dying it is the pleasantest thing imaginable."[9] This understanding of what awaits those who believe in and follow Christ is very liberating.

Chapter 1 | Thought-provoking Questions

1. Why does Paul compare the human body to a tent?
2. When a person dies, does the soul sleep?
3. What happens to a Christian at death?
4. There are two major positions about when the spirit of a departed Christian receives a body again. What are they?
5. Why do they call the body of a dead person "remains"?
6. Why does Paul say he would rather be away from his body (2 Corinthians 5:8)?

CHAPTER 2
Your Best Life After Death

In his letter to the church at Philippi, Paul again conveyed his preference to be away from his mortal body and at home with the Lord. He so looked forward to the day of his death that he actually preferred death to life. Reflect upon his comments:

> For to me, living means living for Christ, and dying is even better. But if I live, I can do more fruitful work for Christ. So I really don't know which is better. I'm torn between two desires: I long to go and be with Christ, which would be far better for me. But for your sakes, it is better if I continue to live. Knowing this, I am convinced that I will remain alive so I can continue to help all of you grow and experience the joy of your faith.

(Philippians 1:21-25 NLT)

In this passage Paul came right out and said that dying is preferable to living. He knew that for Christians, life after death would be much sweeter and far more pleasurable and rewarding than life *before* death. The only thing that gave Paul a bit of pause about wanting to leave his body for heaven and home was his desire to render fruitful service for Christ. The most rewarding thing for the apostle in his earthly life was bringing other people to Christ, building up their faith, and making them fruitful disciples who could also bring others to Christ. But even with this consideration, he was momentarily torn between wanting to continue this life or depart and be with Christ. Paul spoke as if he had a choice. Of course, he did not. He could not end his life whenever he wanted. Yet, with all the perils and life-threatening situations in which he often found himself, he knew that sudden death was a definite possibility. With

Teach Me About Heaven and Eternal Life

the longing in his heart to be with Christ, Paul was not sure whether he should go on resisting death or just surrender to it when it came. Paul had conflicting desires. Sometimes he wanted to depart this life, and other times, because of the love he had for the people he ministered to and his desire to do something significant for Christ, he wanted to stay and continue his work. He realized his selfishness in wanting to leave when so many people needed his ministry. So he concluded that continuing on in his earthly body on earth would be more beneficial to others.

This passage is so telling because it helps us to understand that this life is not the best life. The best life is yet to come. It is so near we can almost touch it. C. S. Lewis makes the following enlightened statement about death for the Christian: "All your life an unattainable ecstasy has hovered just beyond the grasp of your consciousness. The day is coming when you will wake to find, beyond all hope, that you have attained it."[1]

The thing we fear the most, death, is the very thing that God has assigned to deliver us to life that is so good, it is beyond our ability to fully imagine. But it is important to note that we must not be tempted to hurry death along. No matter how difficult this life may be, we must wait on God and bear the burden of life until He dismisses us. Suicide is never an option. Our times are in God's hands (Psalm 31:15). To take them from God would be robbery and murder.

It is interesting to note that Paul was not operating solely on the basis of faith when he longed for heaven. He had been given the privilege of actually seeing heaven, an experience he mentioned in his second letter to the church at Corinth.

> I was caught up to the third heaven fourteen years ago. Whether I was in my body or out of my body, I don't know—only God knows. Yes, only God knows whether I was in my body or outside my body. But I do know that I was caught up to paradise and heard things so astounding that they cannot be expressed in words, things no human is allowed to tell.
> (2 Corinthians 12:2-4 NLT)

This incident that Paul refers to happened fourteen years prior to his writing of this letter to the Corinthians. He was stoned at a place called Lystra, which was located in Turkey. After stoning Paul, the people left him for dead. It is possible that Paul actually did die at this time and was caught up into heaven. The phrase "caught up" denotes being quickly transported.

Paul suddenly found himself in the third heaven. In this verse he mentions "the third heaven" to distinguish it from the other two heavens. The first heaven is the sky or atmosphere directly above the earth, and the second heaven refers to the stellar heavens—what is commonly referred to as the cosmos. The third heaven is possibly beyond the cosmos. Another possibility is that the third heaven is in another dimension altogether. We really do not know the actual location of heaven, so we can only surmise. But we do know that the third heaven is the heaven where God, the angels, and the departed Christians live.

After being caught up to the third heaven, Paul heard and saw things that he was forbidden to reveal, but he never forgot this experience. He could not determine whether he was in his body or out of it. This suggests that when Christians die, it is not some traumatic experience. The transition is so subtle that the person who leaves his or her body behind and is caught up into heaven does not experience any shock during the separation of the soul from the body. Paul could not discern whether God had transported him to heaven in his mortal body or whether his spirit had left his body and traveled to heaven. Of course, we know that Paul's body was still on earth from the account in Acts 14. The New Living Translation says that Paul was apparently dead (Acts 14:19).

While the saints gathered around his body back on earth, Paul's spirit was visiting heaven. Then, after an unknown period of time, his life came back to his body, and he rose up. The trip from earth to heaven was immediate, suggesting that either we will be able to travel at the speed of thought or we simply travel from one dimension to the next in an instant. The fact that Paul could not determine whether he was in his body or outside of it also suggests that when we leave our bodies behind, we will not feel in any way diminished. Judging from Paul's experience, if we are spirits without bodies, it will not be easily discernible to us.

Whatever the case, Paul had been allowed to see into heaven. He was so affected by what he saw and heard that life on this earth lost its luster and appeal. Life in heaven was so exciting, promising, and rewarding that Paul became obsessed with returning there permanently. He knew he could not move to heaven without dying, so he saw death not as something to recoil from but as something to long for. Paul had seen the other side, and because he had seen it, the uncertainty and fear of death had evaporated from him. Because he was not allowed to report what he saw, we can only speculate. But we know from other accounts that heaven has in reserve for its citizens comfort, rest, wealth, peace, joy, and the tranquility of a world without pain or problems.

After seeing all this, Paul had to return to earth with all its difficulties, challenges, and concerns, and it was all probably a big let-down. But Paul saw one thing that was worth living on planet earth for: the opportunity to serve Christ and help others find their way to Christ and eventually to heaven. Proclaiming Christ as the Savior of the world had been clearly pinpointed as his purpose for living. His approach was to point the way to Christ and duplicate his work through the changed lives of those he was able to convince to believe in Christ and become true Christian disciples.

Paul was liberated by what he discovered about the death of a true Christian. He came to realize that for the Christian, death is only a mirage, an empty threat, or a toothless lion with no power to inflict harm. When he finally came to the end of his life on earth, Paul was able to face it boldly—not with fear and dread, but with a sense of expectancy and excitement about his future. He knew that the end of life on earth meant the continuation of life in heaven. While waiting for the day of his execution, he wrote to his spiritual son, Timothy:

> As for me, my life has already been poured out as an offering to God. The time of my death is near. I have fought the good fight, I have finished the race, and I have remained faithful. And now the prize awaits me—the crown of righteousness, which the Lord, the righteous Judge, will give me on the day of his return. And the prize is not just for me but for all who eagerly look forward to his appearing.
>
> (2 Timothy 4:6-8 NLT)

Paul clearly understood that rather than inflicting prolonged pain and terror, death is actually the vehicle that transports us out of this world of pain and difficulty to a world completely void of all discomfort and hardship. Through death we enter into the place of peace and pleasure. We are reunited with our Christian loved ones.

The apostle also knew he would enter heaven the instant the executioner's axe fell. He would wait amidst the pleasures and rest of heaven for the ultimate reward: his crown of righteousness, which he would receive when Christ returns to earth accompanied by every believer who has ever died, along with countless numbers of angels. This sudden revelation of heaven freed Paul from the terror that death once held over him.

In his letter to the church at Philippi, Paul informed them exactly how to go about resisting fear and anxiety, not just at the prospect of death, but in every area of life. He urged them, "Don't worry about anything; instead, pray about everything. Tell God what you need, and thank him for all he has done. Then you will experience God's peace, which exceeds anything we can understand. His peace will guard your hearts and minds as you live in Christ Jesus" (Philippians 4:6-7 NLT).

Most of us will never experience a visit to heaven prior to arriving there permanently. Our strategy for dealing with the fear of death must be what Paul advises: prayer and thanksgiving. We must memorize key verses from the Bible about heaven and life after death for the Christian and then make a habit of daily meditating upon these truths. We must engage in daily times of prayer and meditation, focusing on the biblical realities of heaven and thanking God for them, while rejecting unbiblical thoughts that generate fear about death, dying, and every other issue of life. We should note those false thoughts that cause us fear and worry and replace them with God's true promises about the joys and delights of heaven. Following Paul's advice, we must boldly ask God for what we need and give thanks for all He has done. Habermas and Moreland comment, "Practicing these truths during our roughest moments, whether we feel like it or not, is the key. As Paul says, constantly rehearsing this process until it becomes a habit will lead to peace."[2]

Paul's freedom from the fear of death was partly due to his habit of meditating on heaven and engaging in prayer and thanksgiving in place of worry. It is extremely important to follow

Paul's example and develop the habit of fixating on these peace-giving truths on a daily basis, not just when we are threatened by fear and anxiety.

This freedom from the fear of death that Paul experienced is part of God's plan for every believer. It is part of the reason He sent His Son, Jesus Christ, to earth in human form. The author of the Book of Hebrews brings light to this whole issue of the fear of death and how God dealt with it.

> Because God's children are human beings—made of flesh and blood—the Son also became flesh and blood. For only as a human being could he die, and only by dying could he break the power of the devil, who had the power of death. Only in this way could he set free all who have lived their lives as slaves to the fear of dying.

(Hebrews 2:14-15 NLT)

To be able to die as human beings do, Jesus had to be born into the world in a human body of flesh and blood. He couldn't die in His pre-incarnate state. Since death is merely shedding the body of flesh and blood, it was necessary for Jesus to have such a body to shed. It was only through His death that Jesus was able to pay for the sins of all humanity and pardon us for those sins. By offering His own body to be sacrificed, Jesus paid the penalty for our sins and removed the horror from death. By experiencing death and rising to life again, Jesus was able to destroy the power that Satan had over death, thereby freeing humanity from being slaves to the fear of death. Jesus' defeat of death through His resurrection gives us confidence that He has also defeated death for us.

Offering up His own Son as a ransom to rescue humanity from the consequences of sin, death, and the domination of Satan was God's greatest expression of love for the whole world. We fear death because we fear the consequences of our sins, as well as pain, the unknown, punishment, and discomfort in the next life. By ransoming His Son, God eliminated those consequences. Now there is no pain and punishment for those who believe and accept Christ, only joy and pleasure.

The issue of the unknown is also dealt with because we are given information about what we can expect after death from Christ, who has been there. God has also informed us through the writings of Paul and the other apostles and prophets to whom He has revealed the secrets of the afterlife. We are clearly told what will happen after we die. We need only to build our knowledge, faith, and trust in those promises to combat fear of the unknown.

The Origin of Sin and Death

In his letter to the church at Rome, Paul carefully explains how sin and death came into the world and why Jesus gave His life to overcome both.

> When Adam sinned, sin entered the world. Adam's sin brought death, so death spread to everyone, for everyone sinned...But there is a great difference between Adam's sin and God's gracious gift. For the sin of this one man, Adam, brought death to many. But even greater is God's wonderful grace and his gift of forgiveness to many through this other man, Jesus Christ...For the sin of this one man, Adam, caused death to rule over many. But even greater is God's wonderful grace and his gift of righteousness, for all who receive it will live in triumph over sin and death through this one man, Jesus Christ.

(Romans 5:12, 15, 17 NLT)

Everything that is wrong with the world today is the result of Adam's sin in the garden of Eden. Every sin committed by every human being in the world today, from the seemingly minor swiping of a cookie by a toddler to heinous crimes such as robbery, rape, and murder, all result from Adam's disobedience and sin. Every war, every disease, and every experience of drought, famine, and starvation are attributed to Adam's sin. When Adam committed sin in the garden, sin latched on to him like a communicable disease. Sin became part of his nature, and like a terminal disease, sin resulted in death. When Adam and Eve had children, the sin in Adam was passed on to them.

Since every human being is a descendant of Adam, every human being inherited his sin. To break the cycle of sin and death, God intervened in human history by sending Jesus Christ into the world. To avoid corrupting Jesus' body with the sin of Adam, the Spirit of God impregnated Jesus' virgin mother, Mary. So Jesus was born into the world as the sinless Son of God for the express purpose of offering His body as a sacrifice for the sins of all humanity.

In obedience to the will of His Father, Jesus took the punishment for the sins of the whole world upon His own body. Adam brought sin and its consequences into the world through his disobedience, but through His obedience Jesus brought forgiveness of sins to everyone who believes. By placing their faith in Christ, those who were unrighteous are made righteous and granted the gift of eternal life. Paul puts it this way, "For the wages of sin is death, but the free gift of God is eternal life through Christ Jesus our Lord" (Romans 6:23 NLT).

God's bountiful gift to the world was forgiveness of our sins, extended to us through the death of His Son. Through His death, Jesus experienced all the horror that we would have had to suffer upon our death. It was only through His own death that He was able to rescue us from the terrible suffering that God, the judge of all the earth, would have inflicted upon us for our own sins. Without the forgiveness of our sins, we face a death that will deliver us to hell, a world of suffering and pain. Since Christ paid for our sins with His own life and blood on the cross, death safely delivers us from life on planet earth, with its mixture of joys and sorrows, to the sweet pleasures of life in heaven.

If we accept the gift that God extends to us through this sacrifice of His own Son, we have no reason to fear death. Death holds no terror for those who place their faith in Christ. Taunting death that once held him in terror and dread, Paul exclaims, "O death, where is thy sting? O grave, where is thy victory?" (1 Corinthians 15:55 KJV).

The Departed

To help us better understand what happens when a person dies, the Bible gives us a look into the lives of the departed. In various places in the Scriptures, we are given very direct and poignant information about the lives of two particular categories of people: the wicked and the righteous. In every instance there is a stark contrast between the two groups. The wicked people are tormented in flames, but the righteous people are comforted in paradise. Luke records the words of Jesus Himself as He described the death and afterlife of a certain wicked rich man and a poor beggar named Lazarus. In life the rich man had been cruel and selfish, while Lazarus suffered from hunger and sickness. The rich man ignored Lazarus' plea for even the crumbs that fell from his table. Jesus explained what happened to them both:

> "The time came when the beggar died and the angels carried him to Abraham's side. The rich man also died and was buried. In hell, where he was in torment, he looked up and saw Abraham far away, with Lazarus by his side. So he called to him, 'Father Abraham, have pity on me and send Lazarus to dip the tip of his finger in water and cool my tongue, because I am in agony in this fire.' "But Abraham replied, 'Son, remember that in your lifetime you received your good things, while Lazarus received bad things, but now he is comforted here and you are in agony. And besides all this, between us and you a great chasm has been fixed, so that those who want to go from here to you cannot, nor can anyone cross over from there to us.'"

(Luke 16:22-26 NIV)

Jesus said that after Lazarus died, he was carried by angels to Abraham's side. Abraham's side, or Abraham's bosom, is a place of peace and comfort. Drawing from the Old Testament prophet, Isaiah, John MacArthur declares that the righteous man who dies "is taken away from calamity; he enters into peace (Isaiah 57:1-2)"[3] This place of peace is also referred to as paradise.

But Jesus said the rich man also died and was found in hell. Both men departed from their bodies, but they ended up in very different places. This information adds to the weight of biblical evidence demonstrating that upon death we continue to exist. Neither of these men lost consciousness. Both were fully knowledgeable and aware of their surroundings. Both men were able to move, see, hear, speak, and feel. One felt pain and the other felt pleasure. The fact that the rich man wanted Lazarus to dip his finger into water and cool his tongue certainly implies that both men had fingers and tongues. This also suggests that they had form and substance with which to contact their environment. Although both men were dead, their bodies were very similar to the way they were when they were alive.

However, one man was tormented, while the other man comforted. From the rich man's experience, we note that their memory was also intact. This proves that people in heaven and hell can remember what went on while they lived on earth. In his book,

Life Promises for Eternity, Randy Alcorn remarks, "Memory is a basic element of personality. If we are truly ourselves in Heaven, there must be continuity of memory from Earth to Heaven. We will not be different people, but the same people marvelously relocated and transformed."[4]

These were the same people (the rich man and Lazarus) who once lived in the world of mortals. Both these men remembered the past and anticipated the future. Abraham reminded the wicked man that their positions were the reverse of what they were during their lifetimes on earth.

However, the rich man's condescending attitude toward Lazarus had not changed, as evidenced by the fact that he wanted Lazarus to come and serve him. Why didn't he ask Abraham to come and cool his tongue, rather than Lazarus? At any rate, the point of this account is that life continues on after we die. Those who follow Christ and His righteousness are given rest, comfort, and peace from the struggles of this life. On the other hand, those who reject Christ and follow the path of wickedness suffer great torment. It is important to mention that it was not Lazarus' impoverished condition that gained him entrance into paradise, but his faith in Christ. Although not mentioned in the preceding passage, the Bible is very clear throughout its pages that eternal life in heaven can only be obtained through faith in Christ.

The Scriptures provide additional evidence of what happens to believers immediately after death in the crucifixion account recorded in Luke 23. Jesus was hanging on a cross between two thieves who were being crucified for the crimes they had committed. At first, both thieves mocked and criticized Christ as they hung on either side of him. But as the hours passed and death was approaching, one of the thieves had a change of heart. With only hours of life left in his mortal body, he confessed his guilt and asked the Lord to remember him when He entered into His kingdom, thus placing his faith in the Christ. Jesus turned to the repentant thief and told him that they would be in paradise together that very day (v. 43).

Notice that Jesus did not say, "After you take the long sleep of death, you will be with Me." Nor did He say, "After I return with My angels, you will be with Me." Instead, Jesus said, "*Today* you will be with me in paradise" (emphasis author). This could only mean that the same day a Christian believer dies, he or she enters into paradise. The thief would not have to sleep in death until the resurrection of his body, but rather he would enter paradise the very day of his death. A few hours later, both Jesus and the thief left their bodies behind and entered paradise.

The Bible mentions paradise in both after-death accounts, although in the account of the rich man and Lazarus, it is referred to as the bosom or side of Abraham. Paradise refers to the garden or park of heaven. It is a place of perfect comfort, peace, and rest from toil and struggle. Some scholars believe that paradise was originally within view of hell itself before being relocated to heaven—after Jesus rose from the dead (Ephesians 4:8). This argument is debatable. The most important point is the fact that life continues after death. But there is a great contrast between the fate of those who place their trust in God and those who do not.

Heaven Revealed

The one man who was actually allowed to visit heaven and write about it was the apostle John. Because God wants us to gain a greater understanding of what happens after this life, he revealed this information to John within the context by which it will unfold in the future. In addition to wanting us, His people, to understand that we do not cease to exist after the death of these mortal bodies, our Lord wants us to understand what will happen in the end times. John was an eyewitness of future events both in heaven and on earth. He was commanded to write down what he heard and saw so that anyone could read it later.

John's writings were canonized and became the last book of the Bible. It is the book of the apocalypse or unveiling, so it is thus commonly referred to as the Book of Revelation. This is the final book of the Bible because it tells of the conclusion or completion of all things. Although most of the things John saw and recorded are prophecies about the future, they provide us with pertinent information about what heaven is like in its present state and what happens to Christians after they pass from this life.

The very first verse of the book describes its contents: The "revelation from Jesus Christ, which God gave him to show his servants the events that must soon take place."

(Revelation 1:1 NLT)

John wrote this book while in exile on a small Greek island called Patmos located in the Aegean Sea. He was imprisoned in this desolate place as punishment for preaching the Word of God and testifying to people about Jesus Christ. The things John saw add greatly to our understanding of heaven and the lives of the people who live there.

> Then as I looked, I saw a door standing open in heaven, and the same voice I had heard before spoke to me like a trumpet blast. The voice said, "Come up here, and I will show you what must happen after this." And instantly I was in the Spirit, and I saw a throne in heaven and someone sitting on it. The one sitting on the throne was as brilliant as gemstones—like jasper and carnelian. And the glow of an emerald circled his throne like a rainbow. Twenty-four thrones surrounded him, and twenty-four elders sat on them. They were all clothed in white and had gold crowns on their heads. From the throne came flashes of lightning and the rumble of thunder. And in front of the throne were seven torches with burning flames. This is the sevenfold Spirit of God. In front of the throne was a shiny sea of glass, sparkling like crystal. In the center and around the throne were four living beings, each covered with eyes, front and back.

(Revelation 4:1-6 NLT)

John was permitted to see the royal court of heaven and the throne room of the Almighty. This record from John provides some vital information about the heart and center of heaven. The throne room is God's seat of authority, heaven's central place of power and rule. While John's description is limited in detail, there is enough information to give us a snapshot of this important point of heaven's rule and power.

John begins by describing God's glory and brilliance. The first thing he saw was God sitting on His throne. He gazed in awe at the bright and brilliant light that emanated from God. The brilliance of God's glory was dazzling, but the light was not simply white. Instead, it was like the multicolored brilliance of sparkling jewels that shone light from within, rather than reflecting it. Circling the throne was the intensely bright emerald- green light, or glow, which had the appearance of a rainbow.

Just as the furnishings and décor we choose for our homes reflect our values and taste, God's throne room reflects something of who He is. It was designed to express something of His majesty, power, and glory. The throne room portrays certain elements of His form and appearance. In this passage God is described as having jewel-like qualities and features. While there may be some symbolism in this description, it is more than symbolic. God actually possesses these gemstone qualities in His appearance. He dwells in unapproachable light (1 Timothy 6:16). We now know that this light is sometimes displayed in spectacular colors.

Then John describes a crystal sea in front of the throne that probably captures and reflects the brilliant light, casting it all around the throne room. God's throne room resembles a magnificently beautiful light show, the likes of which we have never seen and can scarcely imagine. Accenting this splendid celebration of light are rumbles of thunder and flashes of lightning also emanating from the throne. These may be expressions of the awesome power that God exudes.

John mentions seven lighted lamp stands in front of the throne that represent the seven Spirits of God, which are believed to be seven attributes of the Holy Spirit (Isaiah 11:2). He also mentions four intelligent creatures that are full of eyes. According to the apostle's report, there are created intelligent beings in heaven that are completely different from anything we have seen on earth. We would certainly be frightened if one suddenly appeared before us. But in heaven, things we would now consider extremely unusual are actually a common sight.

John saw twenty-four other thrones occupied by twenty-four elders. These elders foretell the truth that God's redeemed people will rule and reign with Him. It is probable that these elders represent the heads of the twelve tribes of Israel and the twelve apostles (Matthew 19:28). They all are wearing white garments and gold crowns on their heads, conveying that they are righteous kings who serve and reign under the King of Kings. This presents us with a picture of structure, organization, and government in heaven. God is a God of order. His whole creation reflects that order, so we can be sure that there is no chaos in heaven.

It is important to note that these elders are people who once inhabited the earth but are now in heaven. It may be deduced that they lived out their lives on earth, their mortal bodies had died, and they departed earth for heaven. These people are fully conscious and aware of themselves and their surroundings. They see, think, speak, and worship God. They are given a high place of honor, as demonstrated by the placement of their thrones surrounding the throne of God. The fact that they wear crowns also indicates that they are held in high honor. Even though this scene takes place before the resurrection of the dead, these elders have form or some type of bodies upon which they put their clothes. They sit upon thrones and have heads upon which they wear crowns.

In Revelation 5 these same elders are seen holding harps and singing along with millions of angels and other angelic creatures (vv. 7-12). From this information we are informed that people, angels, and intelligent angelic creatures will all unite in heaven and coexist together in one family relationship under God. This is confirmed by the words of the apostle Paul in his letter to the church at Ephesus: "And this is the plan: At the right time he will bring everything together under the authority of Christ—everything in heaven and on earth" (Ephesians 1:10 NLT). Heaven will be joined with the coming new earth.

Souls in Heaven

In chapter 6 John records the great and terrible calamities that will come upon the earth during the last three and a half years of history. This will be a terrible time when God releases His judgment upon this planet. In this chapter, John records that he saw the souls of those who had been killed for preaching and teaching the Word of God, as well as sharing their testimony about Jesus Christ.

> When the Lamb broke the fifth seal, I saw under the altar the souls of all who had been martyred for the word of God and for being faithful in their testimony. They shouted to the Lord and said, "O Sovereign Lord, holy and true, how long before you judge the people who belong to this world and avenge our blood for what they have done to us?" Then a white robe was given to each of them. And they were told to rest a little longer until the full number of their brothers and sisters—their fellow

servants of Jesus who were to be martyred—had joined them.

(Revelation 6:9-11 NLT)

These people had died on earth but were very much alive in heaven. They could speak. In fact, they shouted in a loud voice for justice. They asked God how long it would be before He would avenge them by bringing judgment upon those who continued to dwell upon the earth and were guilty of murdering them. They were given robes and told to wait a little while longer until the number of their fellow servants and brothers who were to be killed, as they had been, could be completed.

This account of life in heaven provides more evidence for the argument that people in heaven are not asleep as they await the resurrection of their bodies. These people are aware, at least to some degree, of what is going on upon the earth. We see that they have desires because they desire justice along with an end to the injustices and brutalities that take place on the earth. These martyred saints, like the twenty-four elders, have form and substance upon which they are able to wear clothes. They are given robes to wear. To make it clear that these people were killed, John states it twice: once in verse 9 and again in verse 11. It is conclusive that these people died on earth but were alive in heaven, even before the resurrection of the dead—a future event to them and us.

In verse 11 God told those martyred saints who were calling for justice to wait a little while longer until the rest of the saints who were yet to be martyred could be completed. This telling bit of information allows us to glean from the vantage point of heaven the insight that the death of God's saints, even those who suffer martyrdom, is encompassed in His plan for their future. Although God sees and shares the pain and anxiety that His people feel when they face persecution and sometimes even death, He knows that those who suffer and die only have to endure it for a short time. Immediately afterward, they enter into the blessings that God has waiting for them.

Right Perspective on Present Troubles

The eternal blessings of heaven far outweigh the momentary suffering of earth. Like the apostle John, Paul clearly understood this, and it is evident in his letters. To the saints at Rome he writes, "For I reckon that the sufferings of this present time are not worthy to be compared with the glory which shall be revealed in us." (Romans 8:18 KJV)

Paul's second letter to the saints at Corinth is even more revealing about his understanding of the temporal nature of what we suffer here and now, in comparison with the overwhelming blessings that await us just beyond death's door. He writes, "For our present troubles are small and won't last very long. Yet they produce for us a glory that vastly outweighs them and will last forever! So we don't look at the troubles we can see now; rather, we fix our gaze on things that cannot be seen. For the things we see now will soon be gone, but the things we cannot see will last forever" (2 Corinthians 4:17-18 NLT).

When Paul says the present troubles we face are small, it is important to understand that these are the words of a man who had suffered immeasurable pain and discomfort. His back had been lacerated with thirty-nine lashes on five different occasions. He had been beaten with rods three times. He had been stoned and left for dead. He had been shipwrecked three times and had spent a whole day and night adrift at sea. He had suffered from hunger and thirst and had gone without proper clothing. He had been thrown in prison numerous times. On top of everything else, he carried the burden of the welfare of the churches God had used him to help establish (2 Corinthians 11:24-28). When we consider all that Paul had suffered, we become acutely aware that he is not being cavalier when he says the things we now suffer are small. Paul knew that no matter what we suffer in this life, it cannot compare to the glory and blessings that await us in heaven.

John and Paul were colleagues in the work of educating God's people about the blessings of heaven. Through the special revelation of Jesus Christ, the apostle John was seeing some of those wonderful blessings that Paul had promised. Among other things, he saw people who had overcome the suffering of this present world. Although these people had not yet received their resurrection bodies and John referred to them as the souls of those who had been martyred, they were not without form and substance nor diminished in their capacity to think, feel, move about and express themselves (Revelation 6:9).

Life and Diversity in Heaven

In Revelation 7, John was allowed to see a special scene in heaven's future. He records seeing a great multitude that was so vast, the people were innumerable.

> After this I saw a vast crowd, too great to count, from every nation and tribe and people and language, standing in front of the throne and before the Lamb. They were clothed in white robes and held palm branches in their hands. And they were shouting with a great roar, "Salvation comes from our God who sits on the throne and from the Lamb!"

(Revelation 7:9-10 NLT)

From this brief snippet of what John saw and wrote, we learn that the population who comprise heaven's citizenry will include people from every nationality, ethnic group, and tribe, representing every language group on earth. The people John saw were not separated by race but were all mixed together and standing in front of the Lamb, Jesus Christ, who was crucified for the sins of this great multitude as well as the whole world. These people wore robes, had hands, held palm branches in their hands, and shouted loud praises to God and Jesus Christ with their own voices. If they were disembodied spirits, their spirits were very similar to living bodies and seemed to function in a similar manner. These people were not formless ghosts.

John was told that this multitude of people would come out of the great tribulation period. One of the elders explained that they would die and enter heaven during this terrible period that would come upon the earth in the last half of the final seven years of human history (vv. 14-18). When the elder mentioned those who came out of the tribulation, it is possible that he was including saints of every age who have suffered a martyr's death for Christ. However, special emphasis is placed upon the coming tribulation. The elder further explained that they would wash their robes in the blood of the Lamb, which simply means that they would place their faith in Christ and become disciples of His. The fact that there were too many of these people to count suggests that many people will turn to Christ in the final few years of history and be willing to die for their faith in Him. It is important to note that John is seeing these future events as though they had already transpired, so in some places he records this information as if it was in the past tense. Referring to this great company of martyrs, John records the words of the elder who was his tour guide:

> They will never again be hungry or thirsty; they will never be scorched by the heat of the sun. For the Lamb on the throne will be their Shepherd. He will lead them to springs of life-giving water. And God will wipe every tear from their eyes."
>
> (Revelation 7:16-17 NLT)

Like the beggar Lazarus who died and was carried into paradise, this great company of people will also be comforted. These tribulation saints will never again be hungry or thirsty or in any way made uncomfortable. They will not be scorched by the heat of the sun, and although John does not mention the cold, it is reasonable to assume that they will not experience discomfort because of cold weather either. The elder further informed John that they will be led to streams of living water by the Lamb, Jesus Christ, and that God would personally wipe away their tears of sorrow, which will be turned into joy forevermore.

Once we reach heaven, every care or worry evaporates. We unload all earthly burdens at death's door. They do not follow us into the abundant life that God has prepared for us. The fears and struggles of this life will release us as completely as when we awaken from a bad dream. We will be relieved beyond measure when we escape from the cares and concerns of this present surreal world into the reality of eternal bliss. In his book, *Angels: God's Secret Agents*, evangelist Billy Graham shares the story of his grandmother's death experience: "She sat up in the bed and almost laughingly said, 'I see Jesus. He has His arms outstretched toward me. I see Ben (her dead husband) and I see the angels.' She slumped over, absent from the body but present with the Lord."[5]

The Happy Dead

In Revelation 14 John says that a voice he heard from heaven instructed him to specifically inform his readers of what awaits us.

> Then I heard a voice from heaven say, "Write: Blessed are the dead who die in the Lord from now on." "Yes," says the Spirit, "they will rest from their labor, for their deeds will follow them."
>
> (Revelation 14:13 NIV)

This passage adds to the mounting biblical evidence that proves death is nothing to fear for those who die in the Lord. It agrees with the words of Jesus, as well as those of the apostles and prophets. The voice that John heard especially reminds us of Paul's statement declaring that to depart this life and be with Christ is far better than to remain here (Philippians 1:23). For those who are true Christians, death is actually something to look forward to, not something to dread. When the life of a Christian ends on earth, his or her retirement really begins.

The voice that John heard declared that those who die in the Lord are blessed. The word "blessed" means *happy*. Happy people are not to be pitied, but envied. To be happy is to be filled with pleasure, contentment, and joy. To be happy is to be satisfied. The reason the dead are happy is because they are with the Lord, and for them the struggle has ended. The cares and worries have all ceased. They no longer have to care for themselves. Instead, they are fully assured that God will take care of them.

The voice that John heard also declared, "They will rest from their labor, for their deeds will follow them." The word "rest" means "freedom or escape from trouble and labor or toil." Long before John's time, the prophet Isaiah spoke of this rest into which the righteous dead enter. Speaking by the Spirit of God, he declared, "Good people pass away; the godly often die before their time. But no one seems to care or wonder why. No one seems to understand that God is protecting them from the evil to come. For those who follow godly paths will rest in peace when they die" (Isaiah 57:1-2 NLT).

There is a common saying: "The good die young." The aforementioned verses explain why the good sometimes die young. From our perspective, those who die are being done a disservice. We think it is unfair that good people often die young, while the wicked are sometimes allowed to live on and on. However, the truth is that death for the righteous is really an act of mercy from the Lord. The righteous dead enter into rest and peace. Once we pass over, all the trouble stops. Trouble cannot follow us beyond death's door.

The rest that God's people enjoy encompasses release from burdens but also refreshment. The notion of rest does not mean to be inactive for all eternity. Instead, it means to be loosed from the evils and stresses of this present world and to have the energy and freedom to engage in the joyful activities of heaven.

We only want to rest when we are tired. Only when our energy is depleted do we need inactivity to replenish ourselves. When we are full of energy, we want to do things, experience things, see things, and accomplish things. Sitting around is boring when you are full of energy. Just ask any healthy child. Eternity affords plenty of time for leisure if we need it or want it. But the rest we enter is more about engaging in activities that refresh us, fully satisfy us, and fulfill our God-given capacities and desires.

When we die in the Lord, we have the satisfaction of knowing that our time on earth has been fully served and our labor is done. We will enter heaven fully refreshed, fully energized, and eager to begin doing the things we most enjoy and were created to do (Ephesians 2:10). We will enter into the Lord's rest, into a world of people who were made just and righteous on earth, but have been made perfect in heaven.

Concerning these departed Christians, the author of the Book of Hebrews writes,

> You have come to the assembly of God's firstborn children, whose names are written in heaven. You have come to God himself, who is the judge over all things. You have come to the spirits of the righteous ones in heaven who have now been made perfect.

(Hebrews 12:23 NLT)

The author, believed by many to be Paul, is speaking about a real company of people—Christians who are now in heaven. He is also talking about a very real place, heaven. He wants us to know that when we become Christians, although we may still live on earth, we become members of something much larger and grander than we can imagine. We become members of the "assembly of God's firstborn children." In Christ every Christian has been granted the status of a first-born son. Ancient Jewish custom favored the first-born son. He was heir to most of his father's possessions, and he would have the privilege of being the successor of his father and becoming the chief authority in the household. The writer of the Book of Hebrews is using the analogy of first-born son status to describe the position of every person who becomes a follower of Jesus Christ, whether male or female. When we place our faith in Christ, we enter into the family of God, become citizens of heaven, and are treated like first-born sons.

Moreover, we enter into the presence of God Himself, "the judge of all people," and become a part of the family of all the saints on earth, as well as those who have passed out of this life before us. They now exist in heaven, but not as imperfect mortal Christians who struggle with sin and the desires of the flesh. They are now spiritual human beings who have been made perfect. When Jesus returns to the earth, He will bring those people who have been made perfect with Him, and they, along with us, will receive new glorified bodies that are like the glorified body of Christ Himself.

The author describes those Christians who have departed life on earth and entered into heaven as "the spirits of the redeemed in heaven who have now been made perfect." The King James Version describes them as "the spirits of *just* men made perfect" (emphasis author). The important point is that on the earth, we Christians are redeemed from our sins and declared to be righteous (or just) simply because we place our faith in Christ, who paid the penalty for our sins with his own blood (Romans 4:5), even though we are not perfect while on earth. We strive for perfection but will never completely attain it while living on this planet in these bodies that are tainted with sin and resistant to obedience. God challenges us to strive to be perfect as he is perfect (Matthew 5:48). That means we are to put forth the greatest effort to live a holy and blameless life, despite the weakness of our flesh. God helps us in this process and works in us through His Spirit. We experience dramatic changes in our lives as we allow God to work in us. However, we will never reach absolute perfection in this world.

But when we depart these bodies, we are immediately made perfect in the presence of God. At death we will be freed from the sinful body that held us captive all our mortal lives. The tug-of-war against sin will finally be over. We will finally be free from the thing that caused us so much pain and grief. We will be free from the manipulation of our flesh and Satan's enticements. We are not holy enough to enter heaven now, but when we die, or when Jesus comes, He will complete the job in an instant. That is exactly why Paul refers to departed Christians as "the spirits of the redeemed in heaven who have now been made perfect." Perfection is attained the moment we die. Upon death the bonds of sin—and even temptation—are broken for the Christian. The instant death occurs, our sanctification is completed, and we enter the presence of God and the saints in the beauty of perfect holiness.

As these perfect spirits in heaven, we will be like the angels who are referred to as ministering spirits. The author of Hebrews conveys it this way: "Are not all angels ministering spirits sent to serve those who will inherit salvation?" (Hebrews 1:14 NIV). We will not be angels; we will be *like* the angels! This distinction is very important.

Angels are referred to as spirits, but we know that they are able to assume physical form. They wear clothing as the saints in heaven do. They appear as men. They can walk, talk, eat, appear, and disappear just like Jesus did in His resurrection body (Genesis 18). So when the author of Hebrews speaks of the spirits of the redeemed in heaven, he is speaking about Christians who are real and tangible. At the time of the resurrection, the spirits of all God's people who have died will return to earth with Christ. Their resurrection bodies will rise from the dust. They will enter these brand-new, glorified bodies and ascend into the air with Christ, all in a flash of time.

The apostle Jude speaks of the promised return of Christ with those saints who have died and gone to heaven. Quoting the words of ancient Enoch, who lived during the seventh generation from Adam, he says, "Behold, the Lord cometh with ten thousands of his saints" (Jude 1:14 KJV). This is very exciting stuff! With all that has been said in the Scriptures about the future of the believer, we have much to encourage ourselves with. We have much to look forward to with joy and expectation. No matter what happens to us on this earth, we can look beyond it all with anticipation and the awareness that the best is yet to come.

Chapter 2 | Thought-provoking Questions

1. Why does Paul say he would rather die than live on?
2. Why is suicide never an option to escape this life?
3. Why does the knowledge of heaven relieve Christians from the fear of death?
4. How did death enter the world?
5. What happens to the wicked when they die?
6. The apostle John saw the spirits or souls of Christians who had been martyred. What is revealed to us about those saints, based on what John saw?
7. What does John's report about the population in heaven tell us about diversity there?
8. Why does the Bible say that those who died in the Lord are blessed?
9. When will Christians be made perfect?

CHAPTER 3
Comforting Facts About the Resurrection

And now, dear brothers and sisters, we want you to know what will happen to the believers who have died so you will not grieve like people who have no hope. For since we believe that Jesus died and was raised to life again, we also believe that when Jesus returns, God will bring back with him the believers who have died. We tell you this directly from the Lord: We who are still living when the Lord returns will not meet him ahead of those who have died. For the Lord himself will come down from heaven with a commanding shout, with the voice of the archangel, and with the trumpet call of God. First, the believers who have died will rise from their graves. Then, together with them, we who are still alive and remain on the earth will be caught up in the clouds to meet the Lord in the air. Then we will be with the Lord forever. So encourage each other with these words.

(1 Thessalonians 4:13-18 NLT)

In straightforward, no-nonsense language, Paul addresses the perplexing question: "What happens to Christians after they die?" He is not describing here the interim period between death and the resurrection of our bodies. We carefully examined this after-death interim period in chapter 1, pointing out various passages written by Paul and other apostles and prophets.

In this particular Bible passage, Paul skips over the interim period completely and addresses the issue of the resurrection from the dead. The resurrection takes place after millions upon millions of people have died over the entire history of the earth and have gathered in heaven, awaiting their return to earth with Christ to reunite with their bodies that were left behind. Let's carefully examine each of these verses to see how Paul sheds light on this important subject of the resurrection of the saints.

> And now, dear brothers and sisters, we want you to know what will happen to the believers who have died so you will not grieve like people who have no hope.
>
> (1 Thessalonians 4:13 NLT)

One of Paul's reasons for addressing this question was to comfort and soothe away the pain and sorrow of those Christians bereft of loved ones who had passed away. Those left behind were full of questions about what had happened to their departed loved ones. Rumors and superstitions about the afterlife had left some of them hurt, confused, and without hope of ever seeing those loved ones again. Paul did not want the saints to suffer such needless sorrow and the hopelessness that many unbelievers were experiencing. So he realized that he needed to take the time to clear up any misconceptions about life after death for Christians. With this important piece of information, Paul knew he could alleviate their sorrow and fill them with joy and the expectation of being reunited with their departed loved ones.

Paul wants Christians to know exactly what has happened to our Christian loved ones who have passed on and what we can expect to happen to us. He begins by citing the resurrection of our Lord Jesus Christ.

> For since we believe that Jesus died and was raised to life again, we also believe that when Jesus returns, God will bring back with him the believers who have died.
>
> (1 Thessalonians 4:14 NLT)

The apostle refers us back to the very foundation of the Christian faith: belief in the resurrection of Christ. Our belief in the future resurrection of the saints is directly linked to our belief that Jesus rose from the dead. Subsequently, we also believe His promise to raise everyone who died in the Lord. The Bible declares that Jesus was the first to be resurrected from the dead and His resurrection is our guarantee that we will also be raised (1 Corinthians 15:23). Paul also informs us that "God will bring back with Jesus all the believers who have died." This is an extremely important point to remember.

Paul continues to enlarge on the subject of the resurrection in the next few verses:

> We who are still living when the Lord returns will not meet him ahead of those who have died. For the Lord himself will come down from heaven with a commanding shout, with the voice of the archangel, and with the trumpet call of God. First, the believers who have died will rise from their graves. Then, together with them, we who are still alive and remain on the earth will be caught up in the clouds to meet the Lord in the air. Then we will be with the Lord forever.
>
> (I Thessalonians 4:15-17 NLT)

Paul emphasizes the fact that the information he is providing here is directly from the Lord Himself. Since he was not among the other twelve apostles but was specially called to be the apostle to the Gentiles, Paul had spent a considerable amount of time with the Lord being personally instructed about many things. He received many revelations directly from Christ and by the Holy Spirit. The information he is sharing here is from the instructions he received from the Lord.

In verse 15, Paul lets us know that there is order to the resurrection. The very first thing he wants to divulge is the news that our departed loved ones will not be left behind. In fact, we will not precede them; instead, they will precede us when Christ returns to gather His people (I Thessalonians 4:15). We know that Christ was the first to rise from the dead with an eternal glorified body over two thousand years ago. He ascended into heaven and abides there upon His throne at the right hand of the Father. As we have seen from the Scriptures, when Christ comes again, those Christians who have died will have their old bodies re-created into eternal glorified bodies. They will be raised from the dead and rise up to meet Christ in the air. Then the Christians who are still alive when Christ returns will have their living bodies transformed into eternal, immortal, glorified bodies. They will also rise to meet Christ and the resurrected saints in the air. This whole transformation will take place in a flash of time.

A very revealing point from this passage in 1 Thessalonians 4 is Paul's statement that Christ will bring those departed saints back with Him when He comes again (v. 14). If we compare verse 14 of this chapter to verses 15 and 16, there seems to be a contradiction.

Verse 14 says all the Christians who have died will return with Christ from heaven when He comes. But verse 15 says Christ will come back to earth to get all those saints who are in their graves. How can these Christians come from heaven with Christ but also rise from their graves when Christ comes? How can they be alive and alert in heaven with Christ and the angels while at the same time sleeping the death sleep in their graves? As we have seen in the Scriptures, the saints who died are in heaven and are fully alive, awake, and alert, yet their bodies are still on the earth. Some are in graves, some were lost at sea, and some may even have been cremated and had their ashes scattered. Whatever the case, the bodies remained on earth, but the spirits went to heaven. The answer to this seeming contradiction is simple: When Christ returns from heaven, He will bring the spirits of those saints who have died with Him. He will then re-create and glorify each person's body, and each spirit will reenter his or her own body, which will give it life. Then each resurrected person will immediately ascend into the air.

This agrees with Jude's prophecy mentioned in the previous chapter: "Behold, the Lord cometh with ten thousands of his saints" (Jude 1:14 KJV). These verses inform us that when Paul makes mention of the saints or Christians being in their graves, he is speaking about the bodies that were left behind—not the souls or spirits that went to heaven.

It is important to note that in several places in the Bible, the dead are referred to as those who are asleep. Paul even uses this terminology. However, a misinterpretation of these references is how the concept of soul sleep originated. These references to being asleep in death refer to the body, not the spirit. A favorite verse used by proponents of soul sleep is, "The living at least know they will die, but the dead know nothing" (Ecclesiastes 9:5). This quote from King Solomon does not refer to the spirit or soul of the dead person, but the body. Once the spirit departs, the body becomes as dumb as a stick of firewood. The body knows nothing, but the spirit is fully aware with much greater knowledge and intelligence than it possessed when limited by the body.

Because the human body is no longer animated when it dies, it takes on the appearance of sleep. But we know that the body is really degenerating and decomposing back into the dust from which it came. The spirit cannot remain in the body in a state of sleep because in time there is no body in which to remain. Given enough time, even the bones return to dust. These bodies eventually become part of the soil, but the human spirit moves on, either to heaven or to hell, to wait for the day of resurrection.

Paul makes it clear in these few verses that for the Christian this whole issue of death and dying is not a threat, but a promise of instant joy and ecstasy as well as a brand-new glorified body. He writes,

> So encourage each other with these words.
>
> (1 Thessalonians 4:18 NLT)

After carefully explaining that separation by death for the Christian is only temporary and there will be a great reunion of the living Christians and our deceased loved ones, Paul urges us to comfort each other with these words. I served as a pastor for twenty-one years, and whenever I was called upon to preach the funeral of a departed Christian and soothe the aching hearts of the bereaved, I would rely heavily upon these comforting words from the apostle Paul. It is indeed comforting to know that death is not final after all. It is comforting to know that no matter what happens in this world, our faith in Christ guarantees us a seat at the reunion table with our departed Christian loved ones. It is reassuring to know that a little time is the only thing that separates us from them. We are indeed comforted by the knowledge that mothers and daughters, fathers and sons, husbands and wives, along with other relatives and dear friends who have died in Christ, will be reunited the instant we cross over from this life to the next.

But the greatest encouragement of all is the knowledge that both the living and the dead will be changed from mortal to immortal and be gathered together with God and His holy angels. We will live forever in a perfect world with perfect people, never to die again. This is the hope and expectation that Christians must reflect upon regularly, especially during times of bereavement.

Dry Bones

The Book of Ezekiel provides a great illustration of how God is able to gather the scattered bones and particles of human remains and raise them to life again. The prophet Ezekiel shares an unusual and frightening experience that would fit nicely into a modern-day horror movie.

> The Lord took hold of me, and I was carried away by the Spirit of the Lord to a valley filled with bones. He led me all around among the bones that covered the valley floor. They were scattered everywhere across the ground and were completely dried out. Then he asked me, "Son of man, can these bones become living people again?" "O Sovereign Lord," I replied, "you alone know the answer to that." Then he said to me, "Speak a prophetic message to these bones and say, 'Dry bones, listen to the word of the Lord! This is what the Sovereign Lord says: Look! I am going to put breath into you and make you live again! I will put flesh and muscles on you and cover you with skin. I will put breath into you, and you will come to life. Then you will know that I am the Lord.'" So I spoke this message, just as he told me. Suddenly as I spoke, there was a rattling noise all across the valley. The bones of each body came together and attached themselves as complete skeletons. Then as I watched, muscles and flesh formed over the bones. Then skin formed to cover their bodies, but they still had no breath in them. Then he said to me, "Speak a prophetic message to the winds, son of man. Speak a prophetic message and say, 'This is what the Sovereign Lord says: Come, O breath, from the four winds! Breathe into these dead bodies so they may live again.'" So I spoke the message as he commanded me, and breath came into their bodies. They all came to life and stood up on their feet—a great army.

(Ezekiel 37:1-10 NLT)

Ezekiel was transported by the Spirit of God to a valley that was full of the unburied remains of an army of soldiers who had obviously been slain in battle and left to decompose. There was nothing left of this slain army but dried-up bones. These bones had been scattered all over the valley and all mixed together by animals and vultures that had feasted upon the carcasses. The bones were so thoroughly jumbled together that it was impossible to tell which group of bones belonged together.

God told Ezekiel to walk back and forth through this valley of dry bones as if to get a closer look at them. After asking Ezekiel if the bones could live again, God told him to prophesy to the bones and command them to hear the word of the Lord. Ezekiel prophesied that God would cause flesh to come upon them, cover them with skin, give them breath, and they would know that the Lord is God.

As Ezekiel prophesied these things to the bones, the valley began to shake, and there was the terrible, eerie sound of the bones rattling together. The bones knocked against each other as each one slid across the valley to join its rightful place with the other bones from the same body. It must have sounded to Ezekiel like "The Dance of the Skeletons." The hair on the back of his neck probably stood up in terror as he continued to watch and listen. Before his eyes, the bones joined together to make a valley full of human skeletons. Then he could see the tendons appear and fasten the bones securely together, the flesh as it covered the bones, and skin as it covered the flesh. The bodies were now complete, lying on the valley floor, but there was no life in them. They were the completely restored bodies of lifeless corpses. Ezekiel prophesied to the four winds as God commanded him. Breath entered these corpses, and they came to life and stood upon their feet as a great army.

What Ezekiel saw was a vision. God gave Ezekiel this experience to illustrate to the nation of Israel, who were then in exile, that He would gather them from their captivity, restore them back into the land, and breathe life into their nation again.

For our purposes, this strange occurrence provides a picture of how God can gather the remains of the departed saints, reunite their spirits with their bodies, and bring them back to life again. God knows exactly where each particle of every dead body is located. He is able to bring every atom back together to its rightful place. However, God will probably not need to re-gather all the atoms in a human body when He does His work of re-creation and resurrection.

God only used one tiny fertilized cell that began to divide and multiply to make the individual body that you now have. It is possible that one cell is all He will use to make your new body as well. If the thought of God creating a new body for you somehow seems like science fiction, think about the body you now have. Most of the body that you now inhabit is not the same body you were born with. In fact, most of that old body has been secretly replaced with a new one.

In August 2005 *The New York Times* published an article by

Nicholas Wade entitled "Your Body Is Younger Than You Think." Wade cites the ground-breaking research of Dr. Jonas Frisén, a stem cell biologist who has discovered a method of measuring the amount of carbon-14 enrichment in a cell to determine its age. Basing his comments on Dr. Frisén's research, Wade comments, "Whatever your age, your body is many years younger. In fact, even if you're middle aged, most of you may be just 10 years old or less . . . most of the body's tissues are under constant renewal . . . .Jonas Frisén believes the average age of all the cells in an adult's body may turn out to be as young as 7 to 10 years."[1]

Genesis 2:21 says that God used one of Adam's ribs to create Eve's entire body. Until the last half of the twentieth century, the thought of creating an entire body from a rib seemed inconceivable until scientists discovered cloning. Today a number of different animals have been cloned using a single cell. How much of each dead body will God use to create a whole glorified body?

A swab of saliva provides enough DNA to determine the identity of the person who donated it. Before undergoing a biopsy on a certain portion of my anatomy, a nurse asked me to allow her to swab the inside of my mouth to collect a DNA sample to go along with the tissue samples from the biopsy to avoid getting my tissue samples mixed up with someone else's. Upon my consent, she quickly used two cotton swabs and made a couple of gentle swipes inside my mouth. What she collected was a tiny bit of saliva containing epithelial cells that could not even be seen with the naked eye.

If finite human beings can identify a person by a swab of saliva and clone an animal from a cell, how hard would it be for God to use one strand of DNA left from our human remains and with it create a complete human body and then change that body from mortal to immortal in a moment, in the twinkling of an eye? I am not suggesting that this is the way God will go about resurrecting the dead; I am merely stating possibilities. God is sovereign, possessing all knowledge. He has ways of doing things that we cannot even begin to comprehend. Although we do not know how God will go about raising the dead, we are assured that He will.

Teach Me About Heaven and Eternal Life

What Kind of Body Will We Have?

In his first letter to the church at Corinth, Paul provides some vital information about the new bodies we will receive and the resurrection of the dead. He gives a complete lesson on this subject to the curious Corinthians, answering a number of questions that had not been fully addressed.

> But someone may ask, "How will the dead be raised? What kind of bodies will they have?" What a foolish question! When you put a seed into the ground, it doesn't grow into a plant unless it dies first. And what you put in the ground is not the plant that will grow, but only a bare seed of wheat or whatever you are planting. Then God gives it the new body he wants it to have. A different plant grows from each kind of seed. Similarly there are different kinds of flesh—one kind for humans, another for animals, another for birds, and another for fish.

(1 Corinthians 15:35-39 NLT)

In these verses Paul gives the clearest, most detailed description of the resurrection process than any other passage in the entire Bible. Paul was either responding to a direct question or anticipating the question that any inquisitive person might naturally ask: "How will the dead be raised up, and what kind of bodies will they have?" He launched into this subject with the skill of a master teacher. He called the question foolish because he is also addressing those who have claimed that there was no such thing as a resurrection. However, this would not be a foolish question for anyone who asked out of a sincere heart.

Paul answers the question about the resurrection experience by using the illustration of a seed that goes into the ground in one form but rises out of the ground in a completely different one. The seed is tiny when it is planted in the ground, where it dies and decays. Yet from this dead seed comes a much larger and stronger plant or tree. It is vastly different from the tiny, little seed that was planted.

The apostle makes it clear in these verses that different seeds produce different kinds of plants. An acorn seed produces a giant oak tree, while a corn seed produces a corn stalk. By mentioning the diversity between seeds and the plants they produce, Paul aids us in our visualization of the continuity and contrast in the resurrection of our bodies. Even though there will be a definite connection between our mortal bodies and glorified resurrected ones, there will be a vast difference between the way they are now and the way they will be then. By pointing to the wonder of how a seed produces a tree or plant that is much more voluminous and beautiful than the seed, Paul helps us imagine how much more glorious our resurrection bodies will be in comparison with these mortal bodies. Well-known biblical scholar Warren Wiersbe explains it this way:

> When you sow seed, you don't expect that same seed to come up at the harvest. The seed dies, but from death there comes life . . . . You may sow a few grains of wheat, but you will have many grains when the plant matures. Are they the same grains that were planted? No, but there is still continuity. You do not sow wheat and harvest barley. Furthermore, what comes up at the harvest is usually more beautiful than what was planted. This is especially true of tulips. Few things are as ugly as a tulip bulb, yet it produces a beautiful flower."[2]

The seed-to-plant illustration also helps us realize the wonders and mystery of God's creative capability. When we think of a tiny seed and realize everything that God has encoded in that seed, we are amazed and mystified. However, we know that if God can produce an entire apple tree from an apple seed, an oak tree from an acorn, or a watermelon vine with multiple melons from a single watermelon seed, He can produce a glorified body from one single cell of a mortal body. If we slice a seed open, we are not able to see what causes it to perform all the feats it performs in the process of developing into a plant or tree. Somehow, this little seed is given the ability to extract the correct chemicals from the soil in the correct amounts and convert them into the molecules and cells that make up the body of a plant. God has encoded in each tiny, little seed the information and ability to carry out a huge number of functions on the way to becoming what it was designed to become.

First, the seed dies and decays. Then, the dead, decayed seed draws out of the soil what it needs to create roots that extend deeper down into the ground in all directions, and anchors itself. It also draws what it needs from the soil to create a shoot or little trunk that will extend upward and break through the soil. The seed is encoded to do everything in the proper sequence. First, the root system grows. Its job is to fasten the plant to the ground and suck in the nutrients that feed the plant everything needed to carry on each stage of its growth cycle. Then, the shoot extends above the ground, where it can take in the sunlight and continue to grow and develop.

Encoded in the seed is every stage of the plant's development. Trees grow a trunk with bark, limbs, branches, leaves, blossoms, and buds. The blossoms are pollinated and grow fruit, pods, or nuts that ripen with more seeds inside to repeat the cycle. There are many different kinds of plants, but they all begin with some kind of seed. The plant or tree is a continuation of the seed. Jesus uses this same analogy while speaking about His own death and resurrection (John 12:23-24). This seed-to-plant process in nature was probably designed in the beginning of creation as part of God's plan to perfectly illustrate the resurrection from the dead.

God placed all this growth information into a seed. Even though scientists can manipulate this process, they still cannot duplicate it. When we think about the fact that God does all this with a tiny, little seed, we are better able to imagine and believe that He will do something much more wonderful in transforming our human bodies from mortal to immortal.

Paul transitions from the analogy of plant life to different forms of animal life to give us an even clearer illustration of the resurrection of the human body. God created a variety of animal life, all with different kinds of bodies. Just as there are differences in the bodies of animals, so also will there be a vast contrast in our mortal bodies and resurrection bodies. If God made all these different kinds of bodies for animals, from the bodies of great whales to those of tiny, little ants, it should be easily conceivable that He is able to make glorified bodies for us that are vastly different from what they are now.

The apostle continues his explanation in verses 40 and 41:

> There are also bodies in the heavens and bodies on the earth. The glory of the heavenly bodies is different from the glory of the earthly bodies. The sun has one kind of glory, while the moon and stars each have another kind. And even the stars differ from each other in their glory.

(1 Corinthians 15:40-41 NLT)

To illustrate the diversity that will be brought about through the resurrection, Paul uses the familiar imagery of the sun, moon, planets, and stars. There are vast individual differences between the glory and beauty that emanates from the sun, moon, and stars. The idea here is that there will be individual differences in the brightness and beauty of our resurrected bodies. Paul is conveying to us that when the resurrection takes place, the kingdom of God will be populated with resurrected saints who possess varying degrees of beauty and brightness, or brilliance. The resurrected saints will be radiant, emanating bright light that will likely be similar to the brilliance Christ emanated on the Mount of Transfiguration (Matthew 17:2). The differences in glory may be based on the degree and quality of our work, service, and sacrifice for God here on earth.

Author Sally Walker defines bioluminescence as "light made by living things."[3] Animals found in nature that generate light fascinate us. A firefly is able to produce cold light from its abdomen by combining certain chemicals in its body. Bioluminescent animals in nature may serve as examples of how our new bodies will also emanate light. Of course, it is unlikely that God will use the same processes as those involved in the way fireflies produce light. However, the very fact that these insects are able to light up whenever they desire provides us with food for the imagination. It is a scientific fact that our bodies emit a very low level of light, even now. When we are transformed and glorified, we will emit a much greater level of light.

The resurrected bodies of us Christians will be radically different from what they are now, yet there will be continuity extending from what we are now to what we will be then. For example, although our bodies and intellectual capacity will be vastly superior to what they are now, we will still keep our identities. We will simply possess new bodies with much greater mental and physical capabilities. Just as a butterfly is the continuation of a caterpillar, a frog a continuation of a tadpole, and a mature adult a continuation of an infant, our immortal, resurrected bodies will be a continuation of our mortal, earthly bodies. Despite the transformation of our bodies, the Bible indicates that we will still know each other (1 Corinthians 13:12). Judging from Jesus' resurrected body, it is likely that our new bodies will in some way resemble our original bodies, but they will be perfected, glorified, and beautified.

> It is the same way with the resurrection of the dead. Our earthly bodies are planted in the ground when we die, but they will be raised to live forever. Our bodies are buried in brokenness, but they will be raised in glory. They are buried in weakness, but they will be raised in strength. They are buried as natural human bodies, but they will be raised as spiritual bodies. For just as there are natural bodies, there are also spiritual bodies.
>
> (1 Corinthians 15:42-44 NLT)

In preparation for our existence in the kingdom of heaven, our bodies must undergo this transformation. Let's reflect back for a moment upon Paul's illustration of the frailty and simplicity of a tiny seed. This might help us better grasp the concept of this transition within our bodies from small to great and weak to strong. An acorn seed is a perfect example. It begins as a very small and insignificant thing that can be held in the palm of a hand or dropped on the ground and crushed underfoot. After the acorn is planted in the ground or buried, it dies and decays, and from it springs a tall, strong oak tree. By itself, the seed is small, weak, frail, and insignificant. The oak, on the other hand, is huge, strong, and glorious.

Our bodies in their present human form are like the acorn seed—weak and frail. In fact, Paul says that "they disappoint us." We have to carefully manage them by constantly watching what we eat, trying not to gain too much weight or do harm to them by eating the wrong kinds of food. As we age, we become weaker. We run out of energy before the day is complete. There is much we want to see and do, but the frailty of our bodies prohibits us. Our bodies disappoint us, and finally they wear out and die.

When the resurrection takes place, our bodies will be transformed from frail, weak, and powerless natural bodies into strong, powerful, beautiful, glorious spiritual bodies. They will be as different in power and glory from our present bodies as an oak tree is from an acorn. Paul writes that the Lord Jesus would take our vile, weak, mortal bodies and transform them into glorious bodies like His own.

We now inhabit physical bodies that are designed to function in this present physical world. Paul informs us that there are natural, physical things, but there are also spiritual things that are just as real, tangible, and material as the present physical world we see all around us. There are natural bodies suited for life on this earth, but there are also spiritual bodies that are suited for the spiritual universe we cannot see at this time. When Jesus appeared to His disciples after His resurrection, He had a spiritual body that could be touched and handled. Likewise, when we are resurrected, we will have spiritual bodies that can also be touched and handled. But these new bodies will be designed to live forever in heaven and the new universe.

Drawing from the words of the apostle Paul and other biblical writers, Bruce Barton suggests that "the transformation that will take place in our bodies to prepare us for habitation in heaven . . . will require a 'spiritual' body (*soma; pneumatikon*). Paul did not mean that this will be 'spiritual' as opposed to physical or material . . . . Believers will not become 'spirits.' Instead, 'spiritual' refers to a body that suits a new, spiritual life."[4]

Paul goes on to explain the order and sequence of natural and spiritual things:

> The Scriptures tell us, "The first man, Adam, became a living person." But the last Adam—that is, Christ—is a life-giving Spirit. What comes first is the natural body, then the spiritual body comes later. Adam, the first man, was made from the dust of the earth, while Christ, the second man, came from heaven. Earthly people are like the earthly man, and heavenly people are like the heavenly man. Just as we are now like the earthly man, we will someday be like the heavenly man.
>
> (1 Corinthians 15:45-49 NLT)

Because Adam, the first man, was created with a natural physical body, all of his descendants were also born in natural bodies. Adam was the father and first representative of the human race. As descendants of Adam, we are all sentenced to spend our earthly lives in natural bodies like his. Our natural bodies are frail and flawed by the sin that Adam brought into the world.

However, Jesus Christ came into the world in a body that was similar to ours in that it was natural, but different from ours in that it was sinless. After He died on the cross for our sins, His body was placed in a tomb for three days and was raised to life an indestructible, glorified spiritual body. Jesus is referred to as the last man because He came to reverse the sin and death that Adam, the first man, brought upon the earth. Jesus began a new race of descendants who would live forever and be free from the curse of sin and death. Through His death and resurrection, Jesus brings life to everyone who believes. By confessing faith in Christ, every Christian will be resurrected with a body like His.

Adam's body was beautiful and healthy but very limited in comparison to a spiritual body. Although he was created with a body that could live forever, Adam, along with his mate Eve, became mortal after they committed sin and brought sin into the world. They imposed the sentence of death upon themselves and all of us through their sin. In contrast to Adam's sin that brought mortality, Jesus' obedience and sacrifice of His own life brought immortality. So even though we are born into the world with the image and likeness of Adam, when we are resurrected from death or transformed in the rapture, we will not have a limited mortal body like Adam. Instead, we will bear the image of the glorified Christ. We will have an immortal, spiritual body like His—a glorious body that is strong and powerful, able to pass through walls and appear and disappear, and having no pain, weakness, or frailty. Indeed, our spiritual bodies will be perfect in every way.

In anticipation of being freed from her paraplegic life in a wheelchair to experience the glory of her new body, Joni Eareckson Tada comments, "I will bear the likeness of Jesus, the man from heaven. Like his, mine will be an actual, literal body perfectly suited for earth and heaven. Whether flinging a Frisbee or flying past Ursa Major. Scaling walls or walking through them. Speaking with friends or conversing with angels."[5]

Will transformed believers really possess the power of flight? It is entirely likely. We know Jesus ascended into heaven. According to the Scriptures, the angels are also able to defy gravity. If we will be like Jesus and the angels, it is not unreasonable to believe that we will also be able to defy gravity. In his commentary on the Book of Revelation, Dr. J. Vernon McGee has this to say about the effects of gravity on our new bodies: "I believe that we will have entirely different bodies, and the law of gravity will not affect us; that is, the law of gravity of this earth or of any other planet."[6]

Dr. Erwin Lutzer goes even a step further when discussing the mobility of our new bodies. He enthuses, "All you would need to do is decide where you would like to be and you will be there!"[7] I think most scholars would agree that transportation will definitely not be a problem for a glorified Christian in the new heaven and the new earth.

Paul also says that our mortal bodies cannot enter heaven:

> What I am saying, dear brothers and sisters, is that our physical bodies cannot inherit the Kingdom of God. These dying bodies cannot inherit what will last forever.
>
> (1 Corinthians 15:50 NLT)

From our present frame of reference, the prospect of living forever can be distressing and even downright depressing. Life without end in our current physical condition, in this world as it is now, would be unbearable. In this existence there is pain, sickness, disease, fear, disappointment, struggle, fatigue, exhaustion, crime, cruelty, injustice, racism, poverty, starvation, and the constant threat of war and destruction. It is very difficult to imagine living forever without associating eternal life with the negative experiences of our present existence in this troubled world while living in a mortal body. We have no frame of reference for an existence in a perfect body that does not plague us with physical or mental illnesses, pain, and fatigue. Nor can we imagine a perfect world with no trace of the curse that we are so accustomed to living under.

Paul probably considers this when he explains that these mortal, perishable bodies we now inhabit are incapable of living forever. In other letters, he and some of the other apostles make it clear that we will live in perfect bodies in a perfect world of complete joy, happiness, peace, pleasure, and goodwill. This helps us to understand how it is possible to face the prospect of living forever with enthusiasm and anticipation. The word "transformed" says it all. Paul lets us know that the transformation of our bodies will prepare us to live forever. Absolutely emphatic about this truth, he boldly declares to us just how it will all take place.

> But let me reveal to you a wonderful secret. We will not all die, but we will all be transformed! It will happen in a moment, in the blink of an eye, when the last trumpet

Teach Me About Heaven and Eternal Life

is blown. For when the trumpet sounds, those who have died will be raised to live forever. And we who are living will also be transformed.

(1 Corinthians 15:51-52 NLT)

It is difficult to imagine, but one day a whole generation of Christians will suddenly be transformed from mortal to immortal in an instant, in the blink of an eye, without ever experiencing death. They will then be taken up to where God is. It will not be a gradual transformation but an instant one. Suddenly, all the Christians will be changed and caught away. These living saints will have their natural bodies changed into glorious spiritual bodies without ever tasting death. There will be the powerful blast of a trumpet from the sky, and all this will take place instantly. The dead saints will be raised first. Then, the living saints will be transformed and instantly follow the upward procession into heaven.

This will not be some secret event. Every eye will see Jesus when He returns (Revelation 1:7). To those left behind, this spectacular event will cause fear and consternation. People who are unprepared will be seized with terror. But to those who place their faith in Christ, this will be a time of great joy and celebration.

Everyone will be going about their business as usual when the living saints will suddenly be transformed and taken up into the air. As believers, we will find ourselves with the Lord Jesus, the angels, and a great company of other glorified saints of all the ages. This sudden catching-away and transformation of Christians from mortal to immortality is commonly referred to as the rapture of the church. It will be over in a moment, and we will forever be with the Lord. This will be the beginning of our new eternal life in our glorified bodies with the Lord and the saints. What a wonderful day that will be!

> For our dying bodies must be transformed into bodies that will never die; our mortal bodies must be transformed into immortal bodies. Then, when our dying bodies have been transformed into bodies that will never die, this Scripture will be fulfilled: "Death is swallowed up in victory. O death, where is your victory? O death, where is your sting?" For sin is the sting that results in death, and the law gives sin its power. But thank God! He gives us victory over sin and death through our Lord Jesus Christ.

(1 Corinthians 15:53-57 NLT)

In preparation for life in a totally different environment, our flawed bodies will be replaced with spiritual bodies that will never break down, die, or decay. The moment we are changed from mortal beings with mortal bodies to immortal beings with spiritual bodies, the Scripture promising that death would be swallowed up by victory will be fulfilled (1 Corinthians 15:54). For the Christian, life will consume death.

Paul mentions the fact that the Law of Moses, including the Ten Commandments, gives sin its power because the Law brought the knowledge and awareness of sin but could not deliver people from their sins. On the other hand, Jesus Christ came and fulfilled all the demands of the Law and imparted righteousness to all those who believe in Him and follow Him. We Christians were freed from the power of sin and death through the sacrifice of Christ on the cross. He fulfilled the Law in His life of complete obedience and righteousness. He then paid the penalty for the sins of all humanity by giving His body over to death on the cross. He paid for our sins with His own blood so that we stand righteous before God. He purchased righteousness and gave it to us without charge.

When the resurrection takes place, death will have finally lost all its power over God's people. We will live forever to enjoy the pleasures and blessings of our new heavenly bodies in a paradise that is unimaginable to us now. The will of God will finally be done on the new earth, just as it is now being done in heaven.

Paul ends this portion of his letter with the following words of encouragement:

> So, my dear brothers and sisters, be strong and immovable. Always work enthusiastically for the Lord, for you know that nothing you do for the Lord is ever useless.

(1 Corinthians 15:58 NLT)

We should always keep our heavenly destiny in view. This wonderful knowledge of what is in store for Christians should have a positive influence on the way we live life. Knowing that whatever happens on this earth we have a glorious future ahead of us should give us great joy and enthusiasm, even in the face of difficulties, because we know that the best is yet to come. We should constantly remind ourselves that we will be handsomely rewarded for every little thing we do for the Lord. When we become disheartened and discouraged by the struggles of this life, we should stop and take a few minutes to remind ourselves that the day is surely coming when we will soar above it all. We should take time to reflect upon the details of the promises of God to those who have faith in Him. We should encourage ourselves by filling our minds with thoughts about heaven and eternal life with Christ.

Chapter 3 | Thought-provoking Questions

1. What is the proof or guarantee we have as believers that we will be raised from death?
2. What is the order of the rapture and the resurrection, as outlined by Paul?
3. Explain how the departed saints will come back with Christ but also rise from their graves.
4. What does Paul mean when he says the departed saints sleep?
5. How is a planted seed similar to the resurrection?
6. Describe what our glorified new bodies will be like.
7. Although our new bodies will be radically different, we will still be us. Give some examples of things that go through radical transformation without losing their identity.
8. The Bible says, "Just as we are now like Adam, we will one day be like _____."
9. The Bible says, "Just as there is a natural body there is also a _____ body."
10. Why are we encouraged to meditate on heaven?

CHAPTER 4
A Brand-new Body and a Brand-new Mind

> *For we know that all creation has been groaning as in the pains of childbirth right up to the present time. And we believers also groan, even though we have the Holy Spirit within us as a foretaste of future glory, for we long for our bodies to be released from sin and suffering. We, too, wait with eager hope for the day when God will give us our full rights as his adopted children, including the new bodies he has promised us.*
>
> (Romans 8:22-23 NLT)

The promise of redemption from God is not limited to humanity. According to Paul, all of creation waits in anticipation for the day when it will join God's children in being freed from death and decay. Along with all creation, we are awaiting the end of death and a time when everyone and everything will live without end. But the crowning moment will be the unveiling of the children of God in all of our immortal glory. Paul says that we groan to get out of these mortal bodies and into our immortal ones.

There are things on earth that reveal the transformation process Christians will undergo when Jesus returns. The seed that produces a plant or tree, the sperm buried inside the egg that produces a person or animal, the caterpillar that produces a butterfly, and the tadpole that becomes a frog are just a few examples of the many things in creation that illustrate the glorious change God will bring about in us and all creation.

As we have discussed previously, a butterfly begins life as a stubby, little caterpillar with many limitations. The caterpillar undergoes a transformation process that Bobbie Kalman describes in her book, *The Life Cycle of a Butterfly*. She explains,

> While the caterpillar hangs upside down it molts for the last time. Its skin splits from head to tail. The caterpillar wriggles free of its skin without letting go of the button. Good by stripes! Hello pupa! Once the caterpillar is free of its old skin, a hard case forms around its body. The case is called a chrysalis. The insect inside the chrysalis is now called a pupa. The caterpillar's body changes. It dissolves, or breaks down, into a green liquid. Butterfly parts such as wings start forming in this soupy mixture. The chrysalis protects the changing pupa. At first the chrysalis looks green because the caterpillar is dissolved inside. By the second week, the chrysalis is clear. Look carefully! You can see the pupa starting to change into a butterfly. When the chrysalis becomes totally clear, the butterfly is ready to emerge, or come out of its case.[1]

After undergoing a metamorphosis, the butterfly becomes a vastly different creature, completely unrecognizable from the way it began its life. At precisely the right time, the butterfly begins to struggle to escape from the chrysalis that has been its home during the stage of transformation. After a brief time of struggle, it emerges totally different from the awkward earthbound creature that entered the chrysalis a few weeks earlier. After freeing itself, this glorious little creature spreads its new wings, gracefully ascends into the sky, and disappears into the distance.

It is interesting how the life cycle of a butterfly parallels that of a Christian. We begin life as mortals limited to walking the earth. At death we are placed in a tomb or coffin or simply buried in the ground where our bodies break down, not into liquid like the butterfly, but into powder. Somehow, God will use some of the elements from this powder to form a new body for us that will be vastly different from the body we had before the transformation. In His wisdom God created the chrysalis to symbolize a tomb from which Christ and every believer rises from death. He created the butterfly to symbolize the transformation and resurrection of these once dead believers.

Like a butterfly struggling to escape a chrysalis, we groan to be released from these frail human bodies that have housed us during our time of transition. As the time for our departure grows closer, this world becomes less and less bearable, and the new life that awaits us becomes more and more attractive and compelling. We groan, yearning to escape this mortal existence to enjoy the wonderfully free existence that is ahead of us. In addition to the physical and emotional struggles that we experience in this life of mortality, there is a constant struggle to think the right thoughts, conduct ourselves in the right way, and resist the pull of sin and degradation all around us. Our desire is not to die but to be swallowed up by life. The new life that will engulf us will be life as we have never known it. It is life that the Bible describes as "abundant life" (John 10:10). It holds for us indescribable joy, unheard-of peace, boundless power and energy, higher intellect and goodwill toward everyone. The life that Paul describes is life free from the struggles of sinful thoughts and feelings. It is a life without selfishness, suspicion, resentment, malice, disdain, disrespect, and distrust. It is a life free of worry, anxiety, or care. In the life to come, we will have absolutely nothing to hide. There will be no secrets to keep. We will be fully known and fully loved for exactly who we are. We will need no façade to hide the things we are ashamed of because there will be nothing to be ashamed of.

Christian radio talk-show host Hank Hanegraaff addresses the sinless nature of transformed believers:

> No longer will our bodies be simply natural. Instead, they will be supernatural . . . our resurrection bodies will be gloriously dominated by the Holy Spirit rather than by hedonistic sensations. In place of 'sexual immorality, impurity and debauchery; idolatry and witchcraft; hatred, discord, jealousy, fits of rage, selfish ambition, dissensions, factions and envy; drunkenness, orgies, and the like' (Galatians 5:19-21), we will faithfully manifest the fruit of the Spirit, which is 'love, joy, peace, patience, kindness, goodness, faithfulness, gentleness and self-control' (vv. 22-23). Put another way, our spiritual bodies will be supernatural, Spirit dominated, and sin free.[2]

In agreement with Hanegraaff, noted pastor and author John MacArthur adds, "What will the perfected be like? The most obvious truth is that it will finally be perfectly free from evil forever. We will never again have a selfish desire or utter useless words. We will never perform another unkind deed or think a sinful thought."[3]

This wonderful knowledge of what awaits us sometimes causes us to groan within, desiring to be clothed with our new bodies and enter into the new world. These will be bodies that can touch and be touched, see and feel, and be controlled in a way that is far superior to the functioning of the ones we now possess. But these spiritual bodies will never experience pain, fatigue, the propensity to sin, or vulnerability to the ravages of time and wear.

This is indeed comforting when we consider the dying processes of these bodies that we now inhabit. We are provided with the quiet confidence and deep assurance that even though we do not yet see these promises, we can be sure of them. With this confidence we are able to cope with the temporary arrangement of living in these bodies and away from the Lord as we wait for our change to come.

What We Shall Be

> Dear friends, we are already God's children, but he has not yet shown us what we will be like when Christ appears. But we do know that we will be like him, for we will see him as he really is.
>
> (1 John 3:2 NLT)

We have examined some of the biblical evidence in the attempt to convey what we will be like when Christ returns. Paul deals with this subject extensively in his first letter to the Corinthian church. But the Bible provides a great deal more information about what our bodies will be like after we are transformed from mortal to immortal.

Like Paul, John understands the interest that every Christian has in this important subject about our future existence. While John confirms the fact that we are already God's children, he admits that from our present point of reference it is beyond our ability to fully imagine exactly what we will be like. But he does provide some information that gives us some idea of what it will be like to inhabit a glorified body. John informs us that when Christ appears, "we will be like him, for we will see him as he really is."

Presently, our knowledge and insight about Christ is somewhat sketchy. We sometimes misrepresent Him because we don't know

Him well enough. Sometimes we are harsh and abrasive when He would be patient and kind. We know Him, but not as He really is. When He appears, however, the gaps in our knowledge will be filled. John says that we will see Him as He really is, and we will be like Him as He really is.

In a letter to the Christians living in Philippi, Paul adds his words to those of John, confirming the fact that when Jesus returns He will make us like Himself.

> But we are citizens of heaven, where the Lord Jesus Christ lives. And we are eagerly waiting for him to return as our Savior. He will take our weak mortal bodies and change them into glorious bodies like his own, using the same power with which he will bring everything under his control.

(Philippians 3:20-21 NLT)

After reading the verses in John along with what Paul states here, we are able to determine that we will be like Christ both in character and in nature, both physically and morally. In his book, *What the Bible Reveals About Heaven,* Daniel Brown comments on this likeness of Christ: "He, Himself, is 'the first fruits' of God's new order—a prototype for how everything in all of creation will once again be exactly as God intended it to be from the beginning. When Jesus comes again to Earth, those who are His will become like Him and the next fruits of the renewed order."[4] In other words, Jesus is not only our prototype or the model from which our new bodies and character will be developed, but He is also an example of the kind of perfection that all of the new creation will inherit.

As we have discussed, the human body in its present form is weak. Even those who pride themselves in being in the best physical shape are weak and frail. But because we live in a world of weaklings, we may not be aware of that fact until we either encounter an illness or the ravages of age begin to take its toll. Paul makes the point that Christ will transform these weak mortal bodies that we now inhabit into glorious bodies like His own. After we undergo this transformation, we will have tremendously powerful bodies and enjoy perfect health and vitality. We will be more like the superheroes of the comic books and movies than the weak and frail human beings we are now. Compared to our present state, we will be a race of perfect super beings.

In his book, *A Travel Guide to Heaven*, Anthony DeStefano makes the following interesting comment:"If you really want to understand what this means and are not afraid of feeling a little silly, pick up a comic book and read about the various superheroes with their incredible superpowers. These invincible, make-believe men and women provide as good an example as any theology textbook can give of the powers we will have in heaven."[5]

In comparison to our present mortal state, we may be like the fictional comic-book character Superman. We will have "powers and abilities far beyond those of mortal men." Dr. John MacArthur also addresses the subject of these powerful new bodies that await us. He declares,

> All this is to say that in heaven we will have real bodies that are permanently and eternally perfect ...You will never have a day of sickness. You won't be susceptible to injury, or disease or allergies . . . . We will no doubt have otherworldly abilities in heaven. Remember that the heavenly city is fifteen hundred miles high. Don't think you'll have to wait for elevators to get you to the top. You'll no doubt have the ability to take flight—or if you desire, simply be transported there in an instant—in the same way that Christ's resurrection body could seemingly disappear and reappear in another place at will.[6]

Note MacArthur's statement that the future heavenly city, New Jerusalem, is fifteen hundred miles high. Some translators, like those who produced *The New Living Translation*, suggest that it is fourteen hundred miles high. Although there is a difference of opinion on this point, most scholars agree that the city will be fourteen or fifteen hundred miles in height, length, and width. We will deal with the heavenly city in greater detail in chapter 10. At any rate, the important point MacArthur makes here is that Christians will have super-powerful bodies with supernatural abilities.

When Jesus comes, the time of our weakness and frailty will be past. Remember that Paul says, "We will be raised in power" (1 Corinthians 15:43). We will surge with power and energy. We will no longer suffer periods of weakness, fatigue, or listlessness. This sounds incredible and too wonderful to be true but God who cannot lie has promised all this and more.

Paul's description of our resurrection bodies encompasses strength as well as beauty and splendor. Our new bodies will be super strong as well as aesthetically appealing. It is entirely possible that our transformed bodies will be either restored or advanced to the prime of life. We will not possess the body of an elderly person or that of a child. In heaven the old will be young again, and it is very likely that those who died as infants will be fully grown young adults. Just as Adam and Eve were prime adults from their very first day of life, it is highly probable that those who die old or very young will be brought to the prime of life.

Hank Hanegraaff makes the following interesting observation from Scripture:

> First, when God formed Adam and Eve in the garden of Eden, he created them in the prime of life and with apparent age (apparent age, not appearance of age—there is no warrant for supposing that the parents of humanity were created replete with calluses on their feet, belly buttons, or childhood memories). Additionally, Jesus died and was resurrected at the prime of physical development. Thus we are justified in believing that whether we die in infancy, in the prime of life, or in old age, we will be resurrected physically mature and perfect, as God originally intended.[7]

Our transformed bodies will have perfect physiology. Although the Bible does not specifically state this, it is possible that our new bodies will be totally efficient. If this is the case, then it is also possible that we will be able to completely consume whatever we eat without having to pass any solid waste material. We can only speculate about this, but it is conceivable. We do know that we will not be troubled by obesity resulting from excess storage of fat because obesity is both unhealthy and unsightly and we are emphatically promised that we will be in perfect health and glorious to behold.

Many of us look at our present form with some degree of dissatisfaction. We see wrinkles or bulges. We feel that parts of our body are out of proportion. People spend billions of dollars each year on diet foods and drinks, cosmetics, cosmetic surgery, and clothing designed to change or hide the things we don't like about ourselves. But when Jesus returns, we will receive a body that is perfectly proportioned and splendid to behold. We will be completely satisfied with what God does when He provides us with the glorified bodies we will have throughout eternity.

Super Intellect

> When I was a child, I spoke and thought and reasoned as a child. But when I grew up, I put away childish things. Now we see things imperfectly, like puzzling reflections in a mirror, but then we will see everything with perfect clarity. All that I know now is partial and incomplete, but then I will know everything completely, just as God now knows me completely.
>
> (1 Corinthians 13:11-12 NLT)

According to the apostle Paul, when Christ transforms our bodies, we will experience an explosion of knowledge and intelligence, and our character will be like that of Christ. We will love effortlessly. We will delight to do what is right. There will be no more questions or conflict between right and wrong and no more struggles within. Everything will be crystal clear. We will be fully mature physically, spiritually, and intellectually. We will love, care, share, serve, and identify with every other saint and the angels, with Christ as our head.

When the transformation takes place, we will suddenly know and understand things we could never have known before. Yet, there will still be much to learn. Joni Eareckson Tada exclaims, "We will have the mind of Christ. No need to worry about feeling dumb or not knowing the answers. 'We will know as we are known,' and our present knowledge shall increase beyond belief. What's more, the shine of our best thoughts and memories will be made more resplendent as they are magnified through our new mind."[8]

Also, learning will not be the frustrating struggle that it sometimes is for us now in these mortal bodies. We will be given the intellectual capacity to grasp ideas and truths that we are not able to grasp now. We will be able to understand the most complex concepts and realities with ease. There will be no struggle to recall the information we have taken in. We will learn and never forget any of the information we learn. Every minute detail of information we consume will be added to our store of knowledge and retained forever. We will accumulate new knowledge and new experiences, along with the awareness of new and exciting things throughout eternity. We will be forever growing in knowledge.

The mortal human brain has far greater capacity than we realize. According to some researchers, "To utilize the entire storage capacity of just one human brain we would have to learn something new every second for the next three million years."[9] Not only will we have millions of years to learn new things, we will have a perfect immortal brain with which to learn it all.

Habermas and Moreland comment, "Believers will be living in God's newly created universe, which will be at our fingertips to explore and learn about. And we will never come to the end of examining it either. Believers will also be changed and glorified, and so will have an increased capacity to continue to learn . . . . We will never cease to learn more and more about each other nor cease to enjoy the continuing fellowship that such knowledge will bring."[10]

There will be a continual accumulation of fresh and new discoveries building up our store of knowledge of new and exciting things. Imagine how much knowledge and information a person could accumulate if he lived a thousand years with just average intelligence and the desire to learn. Now, imagine that same person with the mind of a super genius and a million years of learning and never forgetting any of what has been stored in his brain. That person would be light-years ahead of where we now stand. Regarding our future intellectual capacity, our present mental state will be beyond the comparison between the intelligence of an infant to that of an Einstein. I believe that this is partly why Jesus said that although John the Baptist was the greatest man who ever lived, the person who is least in the kingdom of God is greater than John (Luke 7:28). As great as John was during his time as a mortal human being, he was still inferior to the least among the immortals residing in heaven.

When we cross over into the realm of the immortals, our Lord will lead us into discoveries as well as new and exciting things throughout eternity. We will have the opportunity to use our acquired knowledge to benefit the new creation. Christ Himself, the great Teacher and Counselor, will be our guide and instructor. We will explore the wonders of the universe under His tutelage. Anthony DeStefano remarks, "There will be so much to see and investigate, so much to enjoy—and so much time to do it in. We'll be able to go on sightseeing excursions to a million different countries, cities, planets, galaxies, and universes."[11]

A common saying among mature adults is, "I wish I knew then what I know now." We sometimes think of all the wiser and better decisions and actions we would have taken if we'd had the wisdom and experience that only comes with age and maturity. When we reach our adult years, we think of how much better our lives would have been if we'd had the wisdom that only comes toward the end of life. In heaven we will have abundant wisdom and knowledge and all the time we need to apply it to life. We will also have the health, energy, and vigor to do the things we know to do.

DeStefano expresses it this way, "God, in a sense, gives us back our dreams. Indeed, he gives us back *childhood* itself. The difference is that in heaven, the goals, that we set for ourselves will be real, and the time we have to achieve them truly infinite. Instead of youth being 'wasted on the young,' it will be lavished on the most wise and appreciative of God's creatures—us!"[12]

As we have learned from Paul's writings, the bodies of resurrected Christians will be radically different from what they are now, yet there will be continuity extending from what we are now to what we will be then. We will simply possess new bodies with vastly greater mental and physical capabilities.

As a senior adult, I am actually the same person I was as a three-year-old child. I am a continuation of that child. I carry the memories and the experiences of the child I once was. Many of those memories have faded with time, and many more memories and experiences have been added to my store, but I am the same person today that I was nearly six decades ago.

When I was that three-year-old child, my physical, mental, and intellectual makeup was that of a three-year-old. I was fascinated by the towering stature of fully grown people. I desired to be big and tall like the giants who towered over me. Because I was clumsy and awkward, I fell down a lot. I couldn't run as fast or jump as high as my older brothers. I felt limited by a body that was incapable of performing the kinds of feats and wonders that I saw adults performing. I was so limited by physical and mental capabilities that it was frustrating. I wanted to hurry and grow up. I wanted to know more than I knew. I wanted to do more than I was capable of doing. Without fully understanding it, I wanted the freedom and independence that I thought adults enjoyed. Intellectually, I saw through a child's eyes and thought with a child's limited intellect.

Paul explains that in our present mortal condition we see things imperfectly because we only have partial and incomplete knowledge. His exact words are, "All that I know now is partial and incomplete" (1 Corinthians 13:9 NLT). Even great minds like Albert Einstein, George Washington Carver, and Sir Isaac Newton knew only a little in comparison with the intelligence of the angels and the level of intelligence we will enjoy after the transformation of our bodies. When Jesus returns for us, we will see everything with perfect mental clarity. We will know things completely, just as God knows us now. Included in our clear understanding of things is our recognition of fellow saints. We will know each other in heaven.

In his commentary on First Corinthians, David Prior makes the following comment:

> These physical bodies of ours simply are incapable of coping with the glory of God. If we are going to be resurrected in Christ, we need also to be transformed into his likeness. Only Christ-like people will be suitable for such a quality of life. Yet, however radical and total such a transformation must inevitably be . . . there is nevertheless a clear continuity between Christians now and Christians then . . . . This continuity guarantees the fulfillment of such natural desires as being able to recognize and enjoy those whom we have known here in this life.[13]

When we get to heaven, we will have transformed bodies, along with minds that are clear enough to know the people we knew on earth, who will be our eternal brothers and sisters. Paul says, "I will know everything completely, just as God now knows me completely" (1 Corinthians 13:12 NLT). If we will know everything completely just as God knows us, included in that complete knowledge will be knowledge of ourselves, other Christians we knew on earth, and those Bible characters we have read about.

Evidence of this is presented in Matthew 17 and Luke 9. Jesus and three of His disciples were on a high mountain when Moses and Elijah suddenly appeared and began talking to Jesus. It is important to note that all three of the disciples—Peter, James, and John—recognized Moses and Elijah, whom they had never seen and who lived on earth centuries before their time. They knew without being told exactly who these two men were.

After the transformation of our bodies, we will suddenly know things without being told about them. There will be much to learn, but there will also be a sudden infusion of knowledge and awareness beyond anything we can now imagine in our present mortal state. In our transformed state we will put away childish, immature ways of seeing things. We will lay aside misinformation, false notions, and misunderstandings and walk in the light of the knowledge of God.

To Be Like Christ

John confirms that we are already children of God (1 John 3:2) and Paul confirms that we are already citizens of heaven (Philippians 3:20). Despite these two important facts, we have not seen Christ as He really is. Although we have yet to see Christ in all His splendor and glory, the apostles did see Him after His resurrection and wrote about it for our knowledge and benefit. Of course, our Lord did not reveal Himself in all His splendor and glory, as He will when He returns. Nevertheless, the post-resurrection encounters and experiences that the apostles had with Christ provide some valuable insight into what our Lord was like after rising from the dead. By examining what Christ revealed to the apostles after His resurrection, we can build some kind of picture regarding what we will be like.

Luke records that our Lord has a resurrection body of flesh and bone and He is able to eat, just as He did before His resurrection. In the twenty-fourth chapter of his Gospel, Luke informs us that on one occasion while the apostles were assembled together, Jesus appeared among them. Because He appeared suddenly, seemingly out of nowhere, the apostles were filled with fear and terror. (People tend to draw wrong conclusions when they encounter strange and unfamiliar sights.) In this case, the disciples made the assumption that what they were suddenly seeing was a ghost.

To calm their fears, Jesus assured them that He was not a ghost. He spoke in His familiar voice and reassuring tone to quiet them. Then, He invited them to touch and handle His body to demonstrate that He was not a spirit but a tangible, physical person. Imagine the excitement that must have filled their hearts and minds as they were allowed to carefully examine the first body that had ever been resurrected to immortality. It is possible that they could feel and sense the power and strength that coursed through Jesus' glorified body. Their excitement must have been heightened even more as they imagined that one day they would also possess a body like this.

Jesus showed them His hands and feet because the holes made by the nails were still present and visible but no longer raw and painful. Jesus' resurrection body will always bear the scars as emblems that represent the price of our salvation. The gaping wounds that once caused people to wince in empathetic agony are now ornaments that represent the depth and beauty of God's love for us.

Jesus mentioned the fact that His body had flesh and bone (Luke 24:39). This informs us that while our new bodies will have flesh and bone, it will not be the weak kind of mortal flesh and bone that we now have. The flesh and bone that will make up our heavenly bodies will be powerful, glorious, and perfectly suited to any environment we might live in or want to travel into. This reminds us of Paul's words declaring that there are natural bodies and spiritual bodies (1 Corinthians 15:44). Jesus possesses a spiritual body. Remember that Paul also said, "Just as we are now like Adam, the man of the earth, so we will someday be like Christ, the man from heaven" (1 Corinthians 15:49). In our new glorified bodies, we will not be all-powerful as Jesus is, but we will be extremely powerful as the angels are.

The fact that Jesus suddenly appeared in their midst without having to walk at a normal human pace using bipedal motion suggests that we will also have the capability to transport ourselves in a way that is now completely unknown and impossible for us. Imagine being able to suddenly appear and suddenly disappear. From the human point of view it looks as if Jesus materializes and dematerializes when He wants to travel from one place to another. This may or may not be the case. Perhaps He simply moves in and out of different dimensions that we are not aware even exists. Perhaps He is capable of traveling at such speeds that He is able to move about without being seen. Because we are now limited by incomplete knowledge, we can only surmise about the many possible ways Jesus and the angels are able to transport themselves. What we can be sure of is that we will be absolutely fascinated when we find ourselves in a body like Jesus' glorious one and capable of doing many of the things He is able to do.

Despite all of the supernatural capabilities Jesus displayed in His glorified body, there are some aspects of His body that did not change. Luke records that after Jesus allowed the disciples to examine His body to prove that He was not some ghostly apparition, He gave them another demonstration. He wanted them to know that He was able to eat just as He did before the resurrection. So, He asked them for some food, and they gave Him a piece of broiled fish and a piece of honeycomb. He took it and ate it while they watched (Luke 24:42-43). These few verses of Scripture open up a world of insight as to what we can expect to be like after the resurrection. We will not be ghostly figures floating about in the breeze; instead, we will be powerful, wonderful, immortal beings with supernatural capabilities but with the best human qualities still intact. We will love and feast and travel and increase forever and ever.

Jesus demonstrated great care and concern for His disciples. He wanted them to know what His resurrected body was like and hence, what ours will also be like. After greeting them warmly, He realized that His sudden appearance frightened them, so He took immediate action to allay their fears by comforting and teaching them. He demonstrated the same kind of tender care for them that a mother exhibits toward her children. We can expect to have this same kind of tender care for each other when we are freed from these mortal bodies and transformed into the image of Christ. We will be like Him, not just in form but also in feature, character, and love.

John also writes about the resurrected Christ in his Gospel record to add his testimony as an eyewitness and provide more information about what we can expect when we are resurrected or transformed. John adds a few details that Luke omits in his report. In chapter 20, John informs us that the disciples were assembled behind closed doors, hiding out because they feared the Jews who were responsible for having Jesus crucified. Jesus appeared in their midst and presented Himself for examination. John adds that Thomas, who was not present when this occurred, refused to believe unless he could see and touch the nail wounds in Jesus' hands and feet. Eight days later, Jesus appeared again in the midst of the disciples who were again behind closed doors. This time, Jesus went straight to Thomas and presented Himself for examination. He told Thomas to come examine the nail holes in His hands and feet and even urged him to thrust his hands into the hole the spear had made in His side (John 20:24-28).

The added information that John provides makes it clear that after His resurrection, Jesus was able to move through walls or somehow appear inside spaces that were completely closed off, without using an opening to gain access. Since we will have a body like His glorious one, it is possible that we will possess the capability to pass through solid objects, just as He is able to do. Of course, this is not to suggest that we will be able to do everything Jesus is able to do.

There is no promise in the Bible that we will be gods, but we have already examined promises that emphatically state that we will be like Jesus (1 John 3:2). Paul said, "we will someday be like the heavenly man" (1 Corinthians 15:49 NLT). Jesus Himself said that those who are resurrected from the dead will be as the angels (Matthew 22:30; Mark 12:25; Luke 20:34-36). Of course, Jesus was speaking specifically about the fact that angels do not marry and neither will we. But in addition to that fact, I believe we will be like the angels in terms of power and glory. If we will judge angels, as Paul declares (1Cor. 6:3), it logically follows that we will be at least equal to them. Angels are not gods, but they are certainly able to do some of the things Jesus did after His resurrection. Since the Bible teaches that we will be like Christ and the angels, we can be sure that we will share many of the similarities that exist between them.

The Power and Glory of Angels

Angels can appear and disappear (Luke 2:8-15). Angels can eat (Genesis 18:1-8). Angels can defy gravity, ascend and descend into heaven, and are not harmed by fire. The angel who announced the birth of Samson to his parents made his departure back to heaven by leaping into a blazing fire and ascending up and out of their sight (Judges 13:20). Angels are very powerful beings. We stand in awe of them because of their supernatural abilities, powerful personas, and mysterious ways. They are able to conceal their presence and control physical objects at will. They appear, carry out the mission assigned to them, and then disappear. Their words are few, and they are focused on their task. Following is the account of an angel who appeared in Peter's jail cell after he had been arrested by King Herod and was awaiting execution:

> Peter therefore was kept in prison: but prayer was made without ceasing of the church unto God for him. And when Herod would have brought him forth, the same night Peter was sleeping between two soldiers, bound with two chains: and the keepers before the door kept the prison. And, behold, the angel of the Lord came upon him, and a light shined in the prison: and he smote Peter on the side, and raised him up, saying, Arise up quickly. And his chains fell off from his hands. And the angel said unto him, Gird thyself, and bind on thy sandals. And so he did. And he saith unto him, Cast thy garment about thee, and follow me. And he went out, and followed him; and wist not that it was true which was done by the angel; but thought he saw a vision. When they were past the first and the second ward, they came unto the iron gate that leadeth unto the city; which opened to them of his own accord: and they went out, and passed on through one street; and forthwith the angel departed from him.

(Acts 12:5-10 KJV)

Notice the power and capabilities of this angel. He suddenly appeared in Peter's locked cell, invisible to the guards posted at the cell door. A light shined in the prison that was probably the light of the glory exuding from the angel. What is even more amazing is the fact that Peter was chained to two other guards and sleeping between them. The angel awakened Peter and raised him up while preventing those guards from being alerted to all this activity. The angel told Peter to get dressed, preparing him for his escape.

This angel had evidently cast some kind of dreamlike state over those in proximity to him because even Peter was not sure that what he was experiencing was really happening. He thought he was seeing a vision. This dreamy effect upon Peter, who was wide awake, had an even more powerful effect upon the guards standing at the door. They seemed to be in a trance that prevented them from seeing what Peter and the angel were doing. This suggests that angels have power over the minds of mortals. The angel caused Peter's chains to fall off, probably without even touching them. Peter and the angel walked right past the guards on post, who were likely wide-awake but unable to see or hear them.

It is interesting to note that when Peter and the angel approached the iron gate leading into the city, it opened without being touched by either of them, much like the gates in a modern gated community that swing open electronically. This demonstrates the power that angels have over inanimate objects. We can only speculate about how they are able to perform such feats. Perhaps they are able to use the power of their minds to manipulate objects without touching them, a kind of telekinesis. Perhaps they are able to control the elements around them by the sheer power of their will.

We cannot be sure at this time exactly how angels do what they do, but God will reveal all these fascinating things to us in the future when we will know just as we are known. The fact that we will be as powerful, intelligent, and glorious as these awesome beings provides us a great deal to look forward to. With great anticipation, we live out our lives as mortals confined to planet earth.

A similar incident is recorded in Acts 5:17-23, when Peter and the other apostles had previously been thrown into prison for preaching the gospel and had been released by an angel later that same night. The Bible does not mention the number of the apostles who had been arrested. We are just told that the angel was able to unshackle them, somehow transport them past the prison guards without their being seen or heard, and walk them out of the prison. When the officials came to get the prisoners, they found the guards standing at the doors fully alert and awake; but when they opened the prison doors, Peter and the other apostles were gone.

The superior strength and power that angels possess is also revealed in the Book of Isaiah and a corresponding passage in 2 Kings. One angel is sent to rescue the nation of Israel from invasion by the Assyrian armies that had besieged the city of Jerusalem. This lone angel destroyed one hundred and eighty five thousand soldiers in a single night (Isaiah 37:36; 2 Kings 19:35).

Angels exude such power and glory that mortals sometimes wilt in their presence. There is one example in Scripture when an angel appeared in his glory in Daniel's presence (Daniel 10). The experience was so traumatizing that Daniel was sick and bedridden for several days. The glory exuding from the face of this angel was like lightning.

Angels often appeared as men, somehow concealing their power and glory from people. At other times they appeared and lit up everything around them with their glorious radiance. This light and glory is something that Jesus and the angels have in common. However, it is important to note that the angels receive their glory from Christ. His is the light and glory of almighty God, the creator and sustainer of all things. While He lived on earth, Jesus stripped Himself of His power and glory as God, but on one occasion He revealed it to three of His disciples. Jesus was on the Mount of Transfiguration talking to Moses and Elijah when He was suddenly transfigured. His face shined as brightly as the sun, and His clothing became dazzling white and were as radiant as a very bright light (Matthew 17:2).

There were a number of possible reasons that Jesus allowed Peter, James, and John to see His glory and radiance. One reason may have been to illustrate that our transformed immortal bodies will also shine brightly reflecting God's glory. Since we will have glorified bodies like His, it is possible that we will also be capable of radiating light or at least to absorb and reflect His light. Jesus briefly mentioned this fact when He told His disciples what would happen in the future.

> The Son of man shall send forth his angels, and they shall gather out of his kingdom all things that offend, and them which do iniquity; And shall cast them into a furnace of fire: there shall be wailing and gnashing of teeth. Then shall the righteous shine forth as the sun in the kingdom of their Father.
>
> (Matthew 13:41-43 KJV)

The gentle Jesus issues a grim warning to those who persist in their wickedness. His angels will gather every single one of them and cast them into a furnace of fire. This furnace of fire is described in Revelation 20:15 and 21:8 as the lake of fire. John issues the same grim warning that Jesus did to those who practice wickedness. He also informs us that those who turn to Christ have their names written down in a book referred to as the Book of Life. Those whose names are not included in this Book of Life will be cast into the lake of fire.

There is no denying that the future of those who refuse or neglect to turn to Christ for salvation will be terrible. But for those who call upon Him, the future is extremely bright, both figuratively and literally. Jesus promised that after the wicked are removed from God's kingdom, the righteous will shine like the sun. Certainly this is a reference to the righteousness, glory and honor of the saints, but I believe it also denotes the light we will radiate or reflect. The transfiguration of Christ on the mountain was a foretaste of the glory that will be revealed in us.

This is not a promise that originated in the New Testament. The promise of the resurrection and radiant glory of the saints is an ancient one. Five hundred years before Christ came to earth, the prophet Daniel also foretold of the day when the Lord would send His holy angels and the resurrection would occur. After fasting and seeking God about the future of the Jewish people, who were in captivity at the time, Daniel was visited by an angel who gave him detailed information about the future of his people and the end of the world (Daniel 10-12). Daniel listened and recorded what he was told.

> "At that time Michael, the great prince who protects your people, will arise. There will be a time of distress such as has not happened from the beginning of nations until then. But at that time your people — everyone whose name is found written in the book — will be delivered. Multitudes who sleep in the dust of the earth will awake: some to everlasting life, others to shame and everlasting contempt. Those who are wise will shine like the brightness of the heavens, and those who lead many to righteousness, like the stars forever and ever."
>
> (Daniel 12:1-3 NIV)

Daniel mentioned that Michael is the most powerful among the angels. He is referred to in other places as the archangel (1 Thessalonians 4:16; Jude 1:9). But our focus is upon the fact that Daniel foretold a time that is yet future. At that time those who are wise enough to seek God and trust in the righteousness of Christ will receive eternal life and possess transformed bodies that shine with brightness and glory like the light of the sun and stars. So, like Christ we will have powerful, glorious bodies that consist of flesh and bone. We will be full of the glorious, brilliant light of God. We will eat, drink, and celebrate throughout eternity, and we will experience the love of God, angels, and fellow redeemed human beings.

Daniel was not the only Old Testament prophet to foretell the day of the resurrection and the transformation of the saints from mortals to immortals. The prophet Job, believed to have lived nearly a thousand years before the time of Daniel, spoke in specific detail about possessing a new body even after the death and decay of the body he was born with.

> "But as for me, I know that my Redeemer lives, and he will stand upon the earth at last. And after my body has decayed, yet in my body I will see God! I will see him for myself. Yes, I will see him with my own eyes. I am overwhelmed at the thought!"

(Job 19:25-27 NLT)

Job spoke with complete confidence and a great deal of insight about his expectations to survive the death of his mortal body. He knew that at the end of time and after his body had decayed, he would look upon God in his own body. This informs us that Job understood that although he would have a new body, there would be continuity between his new body and the old one. His statement, "After my body has decayed, yet in my body I will see God," leaves little room for debate. Job was certain that he would see God with his own eyes after he was resurrected from the dead in a glorious new body, and he was *overwhelmed* when he thought of his wonderful future.

Paul adds these encouraging words to those from Job: "Therefore we do not lose heart. Though outwardly we are wasting away, yet inwardly we are being renewed day by day" (2 Corinthians 4:16 NIV). We are encouraged not to allow the degeneration of our physical bodies to cause us concern because the degenerative processes only affect our bodies. They have absolutely no effect upon our spirits that are being renewed day by day. Our spirits are being regenerated every day, even while our bodies are wearing out with age and use. Every redeemed human spirit will continue to live and occupy a new body.

The prophet Isaiah also testifies about this truth: "But your dead will live; their bodies will rise. You who dwell in the dust, wake up and shout for joy. Your dew is like the dew of the morning; the earth will give birth to her dead" (Isaiah 26:19 NIV). These Old and New Testament prophets died in anticipation of being raised to life again. They knew that death was not the end of life. For the believer, it is only a transition from mortality to immortality. God has revealed all these promises of the resurrection of the dead and sudden transformation of living believers as a means of encouraging us and strengthening our faith. Through these many promises we are able to enjoy great confidence that what God has promised, He will also perform. "This hope is a strong and trustworthy anchor for our souls. It leads us through the curtain into God's inner sanctuary" (Hebrews 6:19 NLT).

Chapter 4 | Thought-provoking Questions

1. When Paul describes our new bodies as glorious, what are some attributes that are included?
2. Will Christians know each other in heaven?
3. The Bible says we will be like Christ. What are some things Christ did after His resurrection?
4. We will be equal to the angels. What are some things angels are able to do?
5. Job declared that after his body had decayed, yet in his body he would ____God.
6. What does Job's words suggest about what he believed?

CHAPTER 5
Home Training: On Earth As It is in Heaven

Thy kingdom come. Thy will be done in earth, as it is in heaven.
(Matthew 6:10 KJV)

    This quote is taken from what is commonly known as the Lord's Prayer. This portion of the Lord's Prayer is so important in the plan of God that Jesus placed it right at the beginning of what He taught His disciples to pray for. They were instructed to ask God for His kingdom to come and His will to be done, in earth as it is being done in heaven. In other words, the prayer is for earth to be like heaven. Of course, it is the plan of God ultimately to bring forth new heavens and a new earth and to bring earth and heaven together as one. To prepare us for that eventuality, He spent a great deal of time teaching those who would be His followers how they were to begin the practice of living on earth now, as people in heaven live.

    I grew up during a time when proper manners and respect for elders was a given. In the African-American community, if a child was rude, ill-mannered, disrespectful, or got out of line in some other way, adults would ask, "Boy, ain't you got no home training?" This question was presented in the form of a rebuke because the ill-mannered child shamed his parents by violating the social mores of the community. The home training that most children received in a time referred to today as "old school" was evidenced by good manners, moral character, and respect for other human beings, especially the elderly. Most parents were embarrassed, regardless of their social or economic status, if they heard that one of their children had violated these community standards and given the impression that the family was just a bunch of heathens.

The following passage from Matthew 5 is a perfect example of Jesus providing His disciples with some home training. Recorded are the instructions He used to begin training His followers for the time when they would live in heaven. As we examine some of the teachings of Jesus and those of the apostles, we are presented with a picture of how people in heaven relate to each other and how we are compelled to live our lives in anticipation of joining them.

> "You have heard the law that says, 'Love your neighbor' and hate your enemy. But I say, love your enemies! Pray for those who persecute you! In that way, you will be acting as true children of your Father in heaven. For he gives his sunlight to both the evil and the good, and he sends rain on the just and the unjust alike. If you love only those who love you, what reward is there for that? Even corrupt tax collectors do that much. If you are kind only to your friends, how are you different from anyone else? Even pagans do that. But you are to be perfect, even as your Father in heaven is perfect.

(Matthew 5:43-48 NLT)

Jesus instructs His followers to get rid of aggression and violence and instead practice living in peace. This is how people live in heaven. We are not only supposed to love our friends but to practice love and kindness toward our enemies as well. People in heaven do not have to deal with the issue of loving enemies since there are no enemies in heaven. However, we do have enemies here on earth. Therefore, we are instructed to practice loving others under the difficult circumstances in which we now find ourselves.

These verses are just a few of the many words of instruction woven throughout the Bible that are designed to acclimate us to the culture of heaven and lead us toward absolute perfection. Although it is certain that we will not attain the goal of perfection in this life, we are challenged throughout the Scriptures to keep striving toward it. Even the great apostle Paul admitted that he had not attained perfection. But he quickly added that he would continue to press toward the mark for the prize of that higher calling. That higher calling will include perfection and is the final destiny of every true believer (Philippians 3:11-14).

Since these early believers had been adopted into God's royal family, they were expected to act in a way that truly represents God and His family in heaven. We are actually referred to as ambassadors for Christ (2 Corinthians 5:20). The assignment of an ambassador is to represent his native country while living in a foreign land. Jesus began training His ambassadors by correcting some ideas that had been advanced by the teachers of the Mosaic law. Some of these ideas were presented in a way that ran counter to the ways and values of the kingdom of heaven.

Through His teaching, Jesus is presenting a higher standard and a higher way to live, a way that is completely foreign and contradictory to this planet. Jesus teaches us how things are done in heaven. The culture of heaven is so different and far removed from that of earth that when some people hear Jesus' teachings, they may think they are not meant to be taken seriously.

The common misconception about this particular part of Jesus' teaching is that His words are just a set of high ideals that sound good but are certainly not practical in this corrupt, selfish, and violent world we live in. But what Jesus is attempting to do is prepare His disciples for eternity in a place that is not corrupt, selfish, or violent. In heaven, people do not retaliate. Heaven is a place that is ruled by love. It is a place where there is no violation of the peace by anyone and everyone acts in the interest of everyone else. There is no thought about retaliation because every citizen of heaven is full of the perfect love of God. There is no selfish and offensive behavior that results in injustice, and consequently, there are no reasons for retaliation.

When Jesus commands us to do good to evil people, feed and pray for our enemies, and respond to persecution with love and kindness, He is commanding us to practice the ways and culture of heaven in a hostile environment. Aside from the fact that evil can often be overcome with good (Romans 12:21), the more important point is that as children of God and citizens of heaven, we are commanded to act like God and do things the way they do them in heaven. Jesus says, "In that way, you will be acting as true children of your Father in heaven" (Matthew 5:45). Dr. Martin Luther King

Jr. put it this way: "The church must continually say to Christians, 'Ye are a colony of heaven.'

It's true that man has a dual citizenry. He lives both in time and eternity, both in heaven and on earth. But he owes his ultimate allegiance to God. It is this love for God and devotion to His will that casteth out fear."[1]

Hatred, evil, and injustice are temporal realities, but love is an eternal reality. Despite the fact that God's children on earth live in an environment that is filled with hate, we are expected to be true to who we are: children of God and children of the kingdom. This is why we are referred to as salt and light. In the end hate, evil, and injustice will pass away, but love will last forever.

God wants us to represent Him and the eternal realities of heaven, especially in this corrupt environment, because our conduct defines us and makes people aware of the fact that there is a higher way to live. In her book, *Everything the Bible Says About Heaven,* Linda Washington summarizes the whole matter: "Those trusting in Christ as Savior no longer belong to the earth. Therefore, they should act like citizens of heaven."[2]

God is preparing us to fit into our family in heaven—a family that is completely united with absolutely no dysfunction. Our heavenly family is perfectly knit together in love. It is a family that cares for each other and serves each other. It is a family that shares a common identity and bond that far exceeds the bond of the "kin-by-blood" relationships that bind us together on earth. This perfect family in heaven is complete, with God as Father and head over all. There are no sibling rivalries, petty jealousies, strife, or division. When one family member receives a blessing, everyone genuinely shares it, owns it, celebrates it, and feels the joy and excitement of it.

Concerning the love and unity among the people we will one day enjoy in heaven, Anglican theologian Harry Blamires concludes, "There will be neither motive nor reason for envying what another has or can do. Delight in what others can do will be as natural as delight in what we can do ourselves . . . . every Christian soul is a limb of the Lord, . . . The head doesn't feel resentful or spiteful if there is a bracelet on an arm or a ring on a finger."[3]

Teach Me About Heaven and Eternal Life

The biblical teachings that challenge us to live on earth as they live in heaven is part of God's assimilation program. The Bible is unequivocally clear about this: "All Scripture is inspired by God and is useful to teach us what is true and to make us realize what is wrong in our lives. It straightens us out and teaches us to do what is right" (2 Timothy 3:16 NLT). Everything recorded in the Bible is designed to prepare us for assimilation into the culture of heaven. We Christians are already part of the family of heaven, but we need a great deal of home training. Much more work has to be done on us and in us before we are ready. Peter Kreeft, a professor of philosophy at Boston College and King's College, describes this preparation for assimilation: "Our business here is a process of thickening, becoming more real, learning to endure more light."[4]

God begins this work in every true Christian here on earth and will instantly complete what is lacking when Christ comes for us. This fact is confirmed by the words of Paul the apostle. Writing to the saints at Philippi, he says, "And I am sure that God, who began the good work within you, will continue his work until it is finally finished on the day when Christ Jesus returns" (Philippians 1:6 NLT).

These words are encouraging because we are sometimes greatly discouraged by our own failures and shortcomings, even after we have tried our best. To know that God will perfect what is lacking in us when He comes for us releases some of the pressure. It is reassuring to know that the task of attaining perfection is not left to us to accomplish within ourselves. God will help us grow up into Christ in all things (Ephesians 4:15). We now bear a vague resemblance of Christ, but when He is done, we will be like Him in image and character (2 Corinthians 3:18). As we read and study God's Word and yield to the work of the Holy Spirit within us, and as He works on us through His ministers who teach, coach, and urge us forward, we are gradually becoming more and more like Christ, and He will complete the job when He comes.

What better way to prepare His disciples to live in heaven than to have them embrace these values of love and peace in a world that often does not respect them, is hostile to them, and sees them as weaknesses rather than strengths. Having us practice living a heavenly lifestyle in this corrupt world, with all its abuses and injustices, is an excellent way to heighten our awareness of heaven while shaping our attitudes and conduct so they are more in harmony with those of heaven. Certainly it is challenging when most of the people around us are going in the opposite direction. In such a world we are often tempted to believe that we are the ones out of step and out of sync. We are sometimes even chided by other Christians not to take our walk too seriously when we seek to live precisely as Jesus commanded us to live. But we are being home trained to practice love and obedience in this arena of violence and unbelief.

Jesus said, "My sheep hear my voice, and I know them, and they follow me" (John 10:27 KJV). Hearing His voice and following Him simply means that His disciples follow His ways and teachings and seek to imitate His lifestyle. They refuse to conform to the world around them. To be a follower of Jesus means to seriously adopt His teachings and values. Jesus is training His followers to act like their Father in heaven and all the other inhabitants of heaven who have been made perfect (Hebrews 12:23). Those of us living on the earth are pressing toward perfection. And when Jesus returns or we make the trip to heaven via the vehicle of death, we will finally attain perfection along with those who have already gone ahead.

While we are undergoing the process of moving toward perfection, Jesus wants us to represent Him and the kingdom of heaven as faithful and true ambassadors. As the salt and light of the world, we influence and teach the world about the kingdom of God through our conduct. If we act as if we have no home training, we misrepresent Christ and heaven. If we neglect to follow His teaching, we exert a negative influence upon those around us and give the wrong impression about the love and peace of God.

But because the culture and values of heaven run counter to that of this world, when we are true to them, our conduct will likewise run counter to the way the citizens of this world conduct themselves. When this happens, we tend to stand out—not in some artificial, superficial way, such as the decision to wear or not wear make-up or our choice of clothing. Instead, we represent Christ on a much deeper level through our Christian character, demonstrated by virtues such as joy, honesty, humility, integrity, justice, compassion, and concern for the poor. We shine brightly through the love and peace that we exhibit, as well as our courtesy and respect we extend toward other people. We have an especially positive impact upon people when we respond to injustices with forbearance and forgiveness.

When we display this kind of home training, people tend to take notice and ask why we live as we do. Some may ask why we have such hope and optimism when others do not, thus presenting us with opportunities to glorify Christ. We are admonished to always be ready to give an answer to those who ask for the reason of the hope within us with *gentleness* and *respect* (1 Peter 3:15 NIV).

Ideals or Reality?

As stated earlier, the teachings of Christ and the apostles are perceived by many to be just high-sounding ideals. But what are often deemed ideals on earth are the realities in heaven, and it is God's intention to make them the realities of earth as well. Remember, Jesus prayed, "Thy will be done in earth as it is in heaven" (Matthew 6:10 KJV). We can be sure that Jesus' prayer will be answered. But it is the responsibility of each of us who claim the name of Christ to strive to make His prayer real in our own lives. It helps when we realize that the holy Scriptures are not designed to be something we worship but something we live by.

We live in a world of darkness. There is so much ignorance and confusion about what is the right and proper way to live. Adding to the confusion is the fleshly bent toward greed and selfishness. The light of God's Word shines into this dark place and provides clear instructions about how we are supposed to live our lives on this planet as we wait for Jesus' return.

These instructions are handed down from heaven as a pattern for us and are drawn directly from the culture and values of heaven. What we are taught in the Scriptures is exactly how people live and interact with each other in heaven. The teachings in the Bible are not some unrealistic set of rules and regulations; instead, they are representative of that country where we aspire to spend eternity. Another excellent example of biblical instruction that is designed to help us think and act like the people of heaven is found in Paul's letter to the church at Ephesus.

> Therefore I, a prisoner for serving the Lord, beg you to lead a life worthy of your calling, for you have been called by God. Always be humble and gentle. Be patient with each other, making allowance for each other's faults because of your love. Make every effort to keep yourselves united in the Spirit, binding yourselves together with peace. For there is one body and one Spirit, just as you have been called to one glorious hope for the future. There is one Lord, one faith, one baptism, one God and Father of all, who is over all, in all, and living through all.

(Ephesians 4:1-6 NLT)

These words from Paul sound strikingly like the teachings I received from my parents. Their words may not have been as eloquent, but they conveyed the same values of humility, patience, and forbearance. We were taught to get along with each other and people outside the family. We were instructed to maintain family unity and other values that Paul taught elsewhere. In these verses Paul is teaching those of us who have been converted from the world of darkness how we are now to conduct ourselves as members of the royal family of God. First, he reminds us of who we are: We are now the called-out ones. We have been called out of the world of darkness and are now children of light, children of God. He begs us to lead a life that is worthy of this high calling. Next, he instructs us on how to behave as children of God. Rather than living the kind of prideful lives that we have been accustomed to, Paul urges us to begin to practice humility. That's the way people live in heaven— completely humble because everyone in heaven knows that no one has anything to boast or be prideful about. They know that every possession is a gift from God.

People in heaven are gentle toward each other, so Paul instructs those of us who have been prone to violent conflict to instead begin to exercise gentleness in our interactions with others. We are exhorted to replace harsh and abrasive words and actions with gentleness. Then Paul urges us to be patient with each other and make allowances for each other's faults because of our love for one another. We are gently reminded in this verse that because we all have faults, we must recognize that fact and make room for the faults of our brothers and sisters, just as they adjust to our own faults. This means that we are to bear offenses in our effort to live like the people of heaven. Of course, those who now live in heaven have a great advantage over us because they have no faults.

Nevertheless, God wants us to exercise these virtues while we are here on earth in preparation for our transition to heaven. Obeying these instructions while here on earth is the way we express our desire and aim to live in heaven. It is also a way of shining the light of heaven into this dark world, as well as a means of demonstrating our love and submission to God. Living this way also expresses our faith in God and His promises.

In verses 4 through 6, Paul seeks to help us internalize the idea of family unity. The church, which includes the citizens of heaven and all the true Christians on earth, is one body, with one head over us all. Paul wants to help us realize that we are part of this one body right now, not at some time in the future. We are one with the saints and angelic hosts of heaven now, with God as the head of the family. Paul says that we are of the same Spirit and have been called to the same glorious future.

The most important bonds we share are the Spirit of God and blood of Christ. These bonds draw us into a relationship with each other that far exceeds the bond of blood kinship and even that of holy matrimony. Regardless of racial or ethnic background, Christians are members of the same family, bound together by the Spirit and blood for all eternity. Earthly family relationships are temporal and eventually broken by death, except in cases where family members are fellow Christians. But even then, the superior heavenly family relationships will supersede earthly family relationships. Our heavenly family relationships are eternal and will never be broken or interrupted. They are made possible by the sacrificial blood of Christ and established by the Holy Spirit who enters us when we receive Christ and never leaves us, even when we die.

This is an extremely relevant point, especially when we consider how race and ethnicity has divided the people of God for centuries and continues to this day. Addressing this issue, Dr. Anthony T. Evans comments, "We are going to have to stop ignoring Christ's teaching on the responsibility of people to tangibly demonstrate our love for our neighbor even if our neighbor is from a different culture (Luke 10:30-37)."[5]

A World of Diversity

Today both secular society and the church are negatively influenced by past and present practices of racial division and the exploitation of one race of people by another. The world and the church have long been deceived by the myth of racial and ethnic inferiority and superiority. These beliefs were developed largely by the sins of greed and pride that prompted people to dehumanize and devalue their fellow human beings in order to exploit and oppress them. The prize was free or cheap labor, along with free land and natural resources, which translated into wealth and power. Religion has even served as a tool to perpetuate false ideas about the superiority of one group of human beings over another.

At any rate, past practices of separation and exploitation of one ethnic group by another has resulted in the continued separation of those groups. This is due to the continued influence of false ideas about racial inferiority and superiority that were forged in the past but have proven to be very difficult to discard. Stereotypical beliefs about the value of one race above another are handed down from one generation to another. These beliefs effectively maintain the separation of racial groups, even after laws have been passed abolishing practices such as segregation and discrimination.

In ancient times, God did divide two groups of people: Jews and Gentiles. The Jews were the descendants of Israel, and the Gentiles were all the other people on earth of all ethnic origins. God's reason for separating these two groups had nothing to do with race but everything to do with religion. Because the world was overspread with idolatry, false religions, and misleading and destructive religious beliefs, God selected a small group of people to whom He would reveal Himself. Through this group, He chose to teach the truth about Himself and His creation.

The father of this chosen group was Abraham. Abraham's grandson Jacob, whose name was later changed to Israel, had twelve sons who became the heads of the twelve tribes that made up the nation Israel, a nation of people that came to be known as the Jews. To preserve the knowledge of the one true God in the minds and lives of this small remnant of people, God gave them laws forbidding them from mixing with people outside their Jewish group.

God imbedded in their customs and culture certain practices

that were designed to separate them from others. Their dietary laws were very strict and forbade them from eating many of the foods that those outside their group were accustomed to eating. Many of the kinds of animals commonly used for food by Gentiles were labeled unclean by Jewish law. In time, people who ate unclean animals became detestable and repugnant in the eyes of the Jews. Additionally, Jewish religion taught that there was only one God and they were only supposed to worship Him, while the people around them practiced polytheism—the worship of many gods. Jews were forbidden to practice incest, bestiality, sorcery, witchcraft, human sacrifices, consorting with demon spirits, and other dark religious and superstitious activities that were widely practiced by the nations around them.

God allowed them to intermarry with people outside the Jewish race and religion, but only if those people were willing to renounce these pagan practices, accept Him as the one true God, and embrace the Jewish way of life. Jewish men circumcised their male children when they were eight days old as a sign of their covenant with God and their commitment to follow His way of life, while rejecting the ways of the pagans outside the Jewish nation. Those desiring to embrace the Jewish God and way of life were also required to circumcise the male members of the family, just as the Jews did. This was God's way of effectively separating the Jews from the rest of the world.

It is important to remember that God was not separating people on the basis of race. He has never declared one race of people better than another. Anyone of any race could assimilate into the Jewish nation by separating themselves from the pagan way of life and embracing the Jewish God and Jewish laws and customs. This separation of Jews from Gentiles was only temporary. It was put in place until Christ could come and present Himself to the world, bringing the full knowledge and plan of God's salvation for all people, not just the Jews (Luke 2:10). Christ came and ended the separation between Jews and Gentiles, uniting the two into one new family. We enter this new family of God by putting our faith in Jesus Christ and accepting Him as the savior of the world. God will go even a step further and unite everything in heaven and on earth together into one family and kingdom under Christ (Ephesians 1:10).

To prepare His people for a heavenly society that is absolutely free of racial prejudice and division, God inspired Paul to provide some very important home training. The apostle conveys it through some special instructions in a letter to the church at Ephesus.

> For Christ himself has brought peace to us. He united Jews and Gentiles into one people when, in his own body on the cross, he broke down the wall of hostility that separated us. He did this by ending the system of law with its commandments and regulations. He made peace between Jews and Gentiles by creating in himself one new people from the two groups. Together as one body, Christ reconciled both groups to God by means of his death on the cross, and our hostility toward each other was put to death. He brought this Good News of peace to you Gentiles who were far away from him, and peace to the Jews who were near. Now all of us can come to the Father through the same Holy Spirit because of what Christ has done for us. So now you Gentiles are no longer strangers and foreigners. You are citizens along with all of God's holy people. You are members of God's family.

(Ephesians 2:14-19 NLT)

Paul makes it clear that there is absolutely no justification for division among God's people on the basis of race or any other reason. The reality is that all people of all races who accept Jesus Christ as Lord are members of one great family, with no reason for division. Since there is no racial division in heaven, it is time for the people of God to realize that fact on earth and begin to live their lives according to the reality of heaven rather than the delusion of earth. To have this knowledge and continue to separate along racial lines is to reject God's truth and plan for all His people and cling to a lie.

To help His Jewish disciples begin to rid themselves of the racial prejudices that had developed as a result of their history of God-imposed segregation and to illustrate how people live in heaven, Jesus told them a story about a Samaritan. The Jews had a special hatred toward the Samaritans because many of them were Jews who had intermarried and intermingled with Gentiles and had established a separate site for worshipping God. They had abandoned much of Jewish law and customs as well. The Samaritans were part Jewish and part Gentile, so the Jews who prided themselves in their Jewish blood and heritage looked down on the Samaritans as inferior. Being fully aware of this deep

Jewish disdain of the Samaritans, Jesus shared a story with them that presented a Samaritan as the hero. The story is recorded in the Gospel of Luke:

> One day an expert in religious law stood up to test Jesus by asking him this question: "Teacher, what should I do to inherit eternal life?" Jesus replied, "What does the law of Moses say? How do you read it?" The man answered, "'You must love the Lord your God with all your heart, all your soul, all your strength, and all your mind.' And, 'Love your neighbor as yourself.' "Right!" Jesus told him. "Do this and you will live!" The man wanted to justify his actions, so he asked Jesus, "And who is my neighbor?" Jesus replied with a story: "A Jewish man was traveling from Jerusalem down to Jericho, and he was attacked by bandits. They stripped him of his clothes, beat him up, and left him half dead beside the road. "By chance a priest came along. But when he saw the man lying there, he crossed to the other side of the road and passed him by. A Temple assistant walked over and looked at him lying there, but he also passed by on the other side. "Then a despised Samaritan came along, and when he saw the man, he felt compassion for him. Going over to him, the Samaritan soothed his wounds with olive oil and wine and bandaged them. Then he put the man on his own donkey and took him to an inn, where he took care of him. The next day he handed the innkeeper two silver coins, telling him, 'Take care of this man. If his bill runs higher than this, I'll pay you the next time I'm here.' "Now which of these three would you say was a neighbor to the man who was attacked by bandits?" Jesus asked. The man replied, "The one who showed him mercy." Then Jesus said, "Yes, now go and do the same."

(Luke 10:25-37 NLT)

The Samaritan was the perfect example of what it means to love our neighbors as we love ourselves. This man was doing God's will on earth as it is done in heaven. Despite the fact that the injured man was Jewish and considered to be an enemy of the Samaritans, the Samaritan man treated him as his neighbor and as he would want someone to treat him if found in a similar set of circumstances. The other two men who passed without helping were examples of a religious system that had failed to embrace the fundamental value of heaven—love. To love the Lord our God with all our heart and love those around us as we love ourselves is the summation of all the laws and commandments in the Bible. It is the way people live in heaven, and it is what those of us who claim to be Christians must aspire to. This story was a challenge to the Jews and Samaritans, and by extension, to us—to break with traditions and cultural norms that oppose the teachings and ways of Christ. It challenges us to live as people live in heaven.

Jesus prayed that we would all be united as one, just as He and the Father are one (John 17:21). It is not certain that Jesus' prayer will be answered on this side of heaven. It may not happen until he sets up His kingdom here on earth. Yet, we can be sure His prayer will be answered. Those who reside in heaven no longer have to struggle to live as one. But, because we live in a corrupt world in corrupt mortal bodies that have a bent toward sin and selfishness, we are compelled to strive to bring ourselves into harmony with the majority of the family of God in heaven.

I Hear a Symphony

> After this I beheld, and, lo, a great multitude, which no man could number, of all nations, and kindreds, and people, and tongues, stood before the throne, and before the Lamb, clothed with white robes, and palms in their hands; And cried with a loud voice, saying, Salvation to our God which sitteth upon the throne, and unto the Lamb.

(Revelation 7:9-10 KJV)

A symphony is the blending of many different instruments that harmonize together to create one pleasing sound. Each instrument is different in appearance and the sound it produces. This is by design so that all the different sounds can merge into one. There are times when all the sounds blend. But there are also times when all the instruments are silent except for one particular instrument or section of instruments that goes solo, and then the others join in again. All the instruments harmonize and unite, even in silence, in order to present a symphonic sound. This is the way the different races harmonize in heaven. There are people from every nation, language, and ethnic background, but their love for each other is so complete that there is symphonic harmony. All that God has been striving to teach us through the Bible on earth is being fulfilled and completely realized in heaven and will one day be realized on earth, just as it is in heaven.

Another great example of the beauty and harmony in diversity that exists in heaven can be seen in the variety of flowers on earth. Imagine a world without the beauty and fragrance of these wonderful plants. Flowers are among God's most breathtakingly beautiful creations. Jesus said that even Solomon in all his glory was not adorned like one of the lilies in a field (Matthew 6:28-29). God, the ultimate master at creative design, uses just the right balance of contrasting and complimentary colors in the design of each flower He makes. In the part of the country in which I live, daffodils are the first to herald the advent of spring. They bring joy and anticipation of a season of warm sunshine after a long gray winter by breaking through the snow-chilled soil, opening themselves, and flashing their green stems and beautiful yellow or white blossoms.

Each kind of individual flower in nature exudes its own unique beauty and fragrance to be appreciated and enjoyed by the beholder. But when an assortment of these beautifully designed flowers are gathered together and arranged into a bouquet, they become the decorative centerpiece of any setting, commanding the attention and admiration of everyone. The various colors, shapes, and smells mingle together to create an intoxicatingly delightful sight and fragrance. The distinctiveness of each flower and the richness of variety make the arrangement so breathtakingly beautiful.

This is an important part of what makes heaven so appealing—people of every race, language, and nation mingled together (Revelation 5:9; 7:9). The distinctiveness of each people group united together presents beauty like nothing that can be seen on earth. In our new existence there will be absolute acceptance of everyone by everyone else, regardless of ethnicity. Speaking of the reality of this unity between the various people of God, Paul says,

> For you are all children of God through faith in Christ Jesus. And all who have been united with Christ in baptism have put on Christ, like putting on new clothes. There is no longer Jew or Gentile, slave or free, male and female. For you are all one in Christ Jesus.

(Galatians 3:26-28 NLT)

The reality in God's kingdom is that we are no longer identified by race, ethnicity, or even gender. Instead, we are identified by our membership in the family of God. The word that identifies and defines us is "Christian"—not Christian Jew or Christian Greek or Christian

American or even Christian man or woman, but Christian. This is not meant to suggest that there will not be distinctions of ethnicity or gender in heaven but that the distinctions will not be points of division. Our distinctions will accentuate the qualities inherent in each of us, not divide us. This is heaven as it exists today. It is the new earth as it will exist when God's will is being done on earth as it is in heaven. As we come to understand this reality, we will come to embrace it in our daily lives as we move closer to imitating life in heaven.

Out with the Old

After providing us with pertinent instructions designed to train us about what virtues to adopt and embrace, Paul went on to instruct us about what we should avoid and eliminate from our lifestyle as fellow citizens of heaven and fellow members of the family of God.

> With the Lord's authority I say this: Live no longer as the Gentiles do, for they are hopelessly confused. Their minds are full of darkness; they wander far from the life God gives because they have closed their minds and hardened their hearts against him. They have no sense of shame. They live for lustful pleasure and eagerly practice every kind of impurity. But that isn't what you learned about Christ. Since you have heard about Jesus and have learned the truth that comes from him, throw off your old sinful nature and your former way of life, which is corrupted by lust and deception. Instead, let the Spirit renew your thoughts and attitudes. Put on your new nature, created to be like God—truly righteous and holy. So stop telling lies. Let us tell our neighbors the truth, for we are all parts of the same body. And "don't sin by letting anger control you." Don't let the sun go down while you are still angry, for anger gives a foothold to the devil. If you are a thief, quit stealing. Instead, use your hands for good hard work, and then give generously to others in need. Don't use foul or abusive language. Let everything you say be good and helpful, so that your words will be an encouragement to those who hear them. And do not bring sorrow to God's Holy Spirit by the way you live. Remember, he has identified you as his own, guaranteeing that you will be saved on the day of redemption. Get rid of all bitterness, rage, anger, harsh words, and slander, as well as all types of evil behavior. Instead, be kind to each

other, tenderhearted, forgiving one another, just as God through Christ has forgiven you.

(Ephesians 4:17-32 NLT)

These instructions from Paul, along with the other teachings from the Scriptures, are designed to provoke us to aspire to live as our family in heaven now lives. It is a clear indication of how God is preparing us for our future lives. After reading these instructions, you may be thinking, *I could never live like this,* You're right. You could never live like this. But God has promised to enter into the heart of every Christian and bring the desire and ability to live according to His will. God's way of preparing us for life in heaven involves instructing us in the ways of heaven and having His Holy Spirit work in us and with us to prepare us for assimilation. The instructions provide us with information and insight, and the Holy Spirit provides us with the desire and power to begin following the instructions. In his letter to the Christians at Philippi, Paul urges them, "Work hard to show the results of your salvation, obeying God with deep reverence and fear. For God is working in you, giving you the desire and the power to do what pleases him" (Philippians 2:12-13 NLT).

Paul commands us to put forth the effort to be obedient to God, with the knowledge that God has committed to helping us to live on earth as the people in heaven live. When anyone sincerely desires to become a follower of Christ, that person only needs to pray and ask God to accept him or her as His child. God answers and places His Holy Spirit within that person. Immediately there emerges a strong desire to please God and live righteously. It is encouraging to know that we are not required to do this in our own strength and power, but we are given the power of God's Holy Spirit to help us. He works inside us, giving us the desire to learn the ways of heaven along with the ability to apply the things we learn to our lives.

Speaking of the grace of God that is in the process of training us for heaven and home, Paul writes to Titus:

> For the grace of God that brings salvation has appeared to all men. It teaches us to say "NO" to ungodliness and worldly passions, and to live self-controlled, upright and godly lives in this present age, while we wait for the blessed hope—the glorious appearing of our great God

and Savior, Jesus Christ, who gave himself for us to redeem us from wickedness and to purify for himself a people that are his very own, eager to do what is good.

(Titus 2:11-14 NIV)

Knowing that we are being prepared for life in heaven with God's personal help should motivate us to seek to practice the heavenly lifestyle. Remember, we are urged to set our sights on the realities of heaven and to think about the things of heaven (Colossians 3:1-2 NLT). If we read the Bible while bearing in mind that its instructions are teaching us how things are done in heaven and preparing us to take our place there, we will be able to see how to put what we learn into practice. Then, the things we learn will be more useful and practical. We may better perceive the value of these instructions for living when we remember their preparatory nature. Christian author Randy Alcorn suggests that God is not only preparing us for assimilation in heaven but also for a very specific role there. He comments, "God is grooming us for leadership. He's watching to see how we demonstrate our faithfulness. He does that through his apprenticeship program, one that prepares us for heaven. Christ is not simply preparing a place for us, he is preparing us for that place."[6]

As we live our lives on this earth, it is important for us to remember that every day is one of training and preparation for our place and position in heaven. It is critical that we keep our eyes on the prize.

Serving One Another Through Humility Out of Love

Two extremely important lessons for the family of God on earth to learn about their brothers and sisters in heaven are those of humility and service. Through the letters of Paul, God discourages self-centered behavior and coaches His children on earth to cultivate humility in their lives. The apostle writes, "Don't be selfish; don't try to impress others. Be humble, thinking of others as better than yourselves" (Philippians 2:3 NLT). Paul recognized that even though self-exaltation and selfish ambition define the most common attitude in this world, it is completely foreign in the kingdom of heaven. Here on earth, pride and selfishness preoccupy us with the desire to gain greater honor, respect, admiration, and personal glory than that of our peers. However, these are not the dynamics that people operate by in heaven.

The heavenly themes of selflessness, love, and service are repeated throughout the New Testament, especially by the apostles Peter, Paul, and John (Galatians 5:13; 1 Peter 1:22; 1 John 4:7). Serving one another out of love is a kingdom concept that the world struggles with. Even most Christians have difficulty embracing this concept. Too often, when we seek to apply this principle of expressing love through service, subconsciously we are thinking about how we can benefit ourselves or climb the ladder of greatness by serving others for a while. Without fully realizing it, our end goal is sometimes to gain honor and status so that others will serve us. In heaven, however, people do not serve with the motivation of later being served. Service to others has no ulterior motive. In heaven serving others out of love is the rule—not the exception.

In heaven the standard is not pride or individuality, but humility. Those who now inhabit heaven are as humble as children (Matthew 18:1-4; 19:13-14). Pride fosters individuality. On earth we want to be celebrated for our individual accomplishments because we believe that everything should be based on individual merit. We want people to admire and praise us for the things we achieve by our own power, cleverness, and ability. But the way of the kingdom is not rugged individualism, but community and unity.

I love the way Harry Blamires expresses this truth. Using sports to contrast the attitude of people on earth to those in heaven, he comments, "The glory of the earthly victor in the games denotes his own uniqueness in relation to those he immediately defeated and those many more who never got past the primary trials for the event. In heaven there is majesty without dominion over anyone. There is glory without superiority to anyone. There is rule without subjection, victory without defeat."[7]

In heaven it would be a shame and humiliation for anyone to seek to exalt self above others. Such a person would be grossly out of step and sorely in need of lessons in the heavenly social graces. Heaven is a place where everyone wins and no one loses. No one has to be defeated for someone else to be victorious. Heaven is a place where everyone shares and no one wants. No one has to look after his own interest because everyone is serving everyone else's interest. The concept of selfless service is repeated over and over throughout the pages of the Scriptures. It is presented in the form of instructions for Christian living and is modeled after the way people are now living in heaven.

To illustrate the importance of service and humility in the family of heaven, Jesus stooped to serve His disciples by washing their feet. John recorded the incident in his Gospel.

> Jesus knowing that the Father had given all things into his hands, and that he was come from God, and went to God; He riseth from supper, and laid aside his garments; and took a towel, and girded himself. After that he poureth water into a basin, and began to wash the disciples' feet, and to wipe them with the towel wherewith he was girded. Then cometh he to Simon Peter: and Peter saith unto him, Lord, dost thou wash my feet? Jesus answered and said unto him, What I do thou knowest not now; but thou shalt know hereafter. Peter saith unto him, Thou shalt never wash my feet. Jesus answered him, If I wash thee not, thou hast no part with me. Simon Peter saith unto him, Lord, not my feet only, but also my hands and my head. Jesus saith to him, He that is washed needeth not save to wash his feet, but is clean every whit: and ye are clean, but not all. For he knew who should betray him; therefore said he, Ye are not all clean. So after he had washed their feet, and had taken his garments, and was set down again, he said unto them, Know ye what I have done to you? Ye call me Master and Lord: and ye say well; for so I am. If I then, your Lord and Master, have washed your feet; ye also ought to wash one another's feet. For I have given you an example, that ye should do as I have done to you. Verily, verily, I say unto you, The servant is not greater than his lord; neither he that is sent greater than he that sent him. If ye know these things, happy are ye if ye do them.

(John 13:3-17 KJV)

This Bible passage emphasizes the fact that even though Jesus was fully aware that He possessed all power, had come from God, and would soon return to God, He girded Himself with a towel and assumed the role of the lowliest servant by washing the disciples' feet. The lesson our Lord was teaching His disciples, along with everyone who would later become a disciple, is that in heaven, greatness is measured by love that is demonstrated through humble service. In heaven the person wishing to demonstrate the greatest love renders the humblest service to others. Washing the disciples' feet was a good way for our Lord to illustrate this.

Peter had a real problem understanding heaven's custom of service. Because he was so accustomed to seeing things according to the norms and customs of this world, he thought Jesus was degrading Himself by stooping to wash His and the other disciples' feet. To his way of thinking, those who are great never stoop to serve those who are beneath them; instead, it is always the great who lord it over the lesser and are served by them. Jesus knew He needed to correct this erroneous mindset.

Another teachable moment presented itself when James and John told their mother to ask Jesus to grant them the chief seats on His left and right when He would reign as king on His throne. All the other disciples were angered and annoyed by the audacity of these two disciples to vie for the highest seat because they all thought they were more deserving. But Jesus corrected their thinking.

> But Jesus called them together and said, "You know that the rulers in this world lord it over their people, and officials flaunt their authority over those under them. But among you it will be different. Whoever wants to be a leader among you must be your servant, and whoever wants to be first among you must become your slave. For even the Son of Man came not to be served but to serve others and to give his life as a ransom for many."

(Matthew 20:25-28 NLT)

Using the very example that the disciples had become accustomed to viewing as the normal way of doing things, Jesus contrasted the ways of heaven with the customs of the Gentile rulers. They were often cruel and oppressive to their subjects and exercised absolute power and authority over them, demanding that they be served by the people but rendering little service to them in return. This corrupt way of leadership is how the disciples expected their rule with Jesus to be. But He showed them that the way things work in His kingdom is just the opposite of how they work in this world.

In heaven rulers serve, so the way to be first involves rendering the humblest service to others. In the kingdom of heaven, people fall all over each other not trying to get to the top to have others serve them, but to get to the top so they can serve others. People in heaven are motivated by such love for each other that they are always seeking some better or greater way to express that love to others and contribute to the joy and happiness in their lives.

Jesus makes it clear that anyone driven by pride and selfish ambition is not fit to lead or rule over others but should rather occupy the lowliest and humblest position. While degrading the ambition to be first and lord it over others, Jesus champions the idea of being ambitious to serve. He places humility over pride and helps His disciples to understand the value of service and humility and the worthlessness of selfishness and pride.

Jesus concluded His lesson by emphasizing the fact that although He is God, the King of heaven and earth, He has not come to earth to be served, but to serve and offer His life as a ransom for many. Although He was their master, he had stooped to serve them. He performed this act to inform them that no matter how high and lofty a position they might be exalted to occupy on this earth or in heaven, they would never be too high to humble themselves and serve others. They would always have His example to remind them of that fact.

Paul also advances this idea and reminds his readers of Jesus' humility and service in his letter to the church at Philippi.

> You must have the same attitude that Christ Jesus had. Though he was God, he did not think of equality with God as something to cling to. Instead, he gave up his divine privileges; he took the humble position of a slave and was born as a human being. When he appeared in human form, he humbled himself in obedience to God and died a criminal's death on a cross.

(Philippians 2:5-8 NLT)

Paul urges us to take on the same attitude of humility and service for one another that Jesus displayed. Although Jesus was God, with all the rights and privileges thereof, He released those rights and lowered Himself to the level of a slave in order to serve humanity. Imagine Jesus becoming a man and being willing to obey His Father's command of giving His life and dying like a common criminal because it served the love of God and the needs of humanity. Jesus displayed the greatest depth of love and service toward humanity that this world has ever known. So we are commanded to follow His example by loving and serving others. Indeed, we are not fit to rule until we are fit to serve. Once we know the value of humility and service, if we are selected to rule, we will do it with a passion to serve the needs of those we lead.

In contrast to the selfish and corrupt ways of this world, through the life and service of Jesus we are provided some very valuable home training to prepare us for the way they do things in heaven. Love that is demonstrated by consideration and service to others is the rule of law written in the hearts and minds of all citizens of heaven, both people and angels. No one is excluded from serving and being served. No one is neglected, and no one neglects others. In heaven there is no such thing as love without service to back it up. Doing good and kind things for each other is one of the greatest producers of joy for both the server and those being served.

The word "symbiosis" is an interesting and relevant term to our discussion about serving one another. A symbiotic relationship is one that is based on cooperation and mutual benefit between people or things in nature. An example of a symbiotic relationship in nature can be seen between a hippopotamus and a certain kind of bird. The bird rests on the hippo's back and eats the parasites all over its body. The bird benefits from resting on the hippo and feasting off the parasites. The hippo benefits by having the parasites removed from its body.

Heaven is the ultimate example of symbiotic relationships because there is a continuum of mutually beneficial activities between heaven's citizens. The server receives the joy that comes from expressing the deepest level of love to someone else, and the one being served receives the joy that comes from having others express their deep love toward him or her, while also deriving joy from rendering service to others. The cycle continues unabated like an ever-flowing stream, with people continually giving and receiving from each other.

Since the culture of heaven is defined by love, humility, and service, those who are great are also accessible to the masses. God the Father, Jesus Christ, the apostles, prophets, patriarchs, and the angels will all be accessible. Imagine being able to walk right up and talk to God, the King of the entire universe, face to face. As family members, we will come to know every resident in heaven by name. Because our mental capacity will be greatly increased and we will not have lapses in memory, we will remember not only the names and faces, but also every minor detail surrounding every family member with whom we come into contact. And with eternity before us, we should eventually have the opportunity to meet everyone in heaven. There will be no foreigners or unknown people from strange, unknown regions in heaven. Everyone we meet will be a family member bound to us by the blood of Christ and the Spirit of God. There will be millions upon millions of family members to meet.

In heaven there is this continuous cycle of love, service, and joy extending throughout eternity with no ill will, negative feelings, or actions to ever think about or deal with. The Scriptures prepare us for this kind of heavenly environment by urging us to begin now, while we are still in this corrupt world, to live like they live in heaven. We are expected by God to begin practicing the ways of heaven even though our acts of kindness will often not be reciprocated in this world. We should do it out of obedience to God as imitators of our heavenly Father, while practicing for that heavenly kingdom and the joy that is derived from obeying our Father and rendering service to others.

As God's people, we should be very intentional and deliberate about the way we live our lives. We should live with a clear sense of purpose. We should understand that life here and now is only preparation for eternity. The life of George Washington Carver was a great example of purposeful and preparatory living. Summarizing the way he lived his life, Carver comments, "It has always been the one ideal of my life to be of the greatest good to the greatest number of 'my people' possible and to this end I have been preparing myself for these many years."[8]

After many years of preparation, Carver arrived at his purpose. He was one of the greatest scientists who ever lived and served as a Christian example to people of all races. Like Carver, we who serve Christ are being prepared for a higher place and purpose. Someday we will arrive at our ultimate destination—heaven. It is extremely important that we keep our eyes upon this life-changing truth as we undergo the training that is designed to prepare us for home.

Chapter 5 | Thought-provoking Questions

1. How does living a life of love and kindness help to prepare us for life in heaven?
2. Christians are ambassadors for Christ. What is the job of Christian ambassadors?
3. How do we demonstrate to the world that we are true children of God?
4. Hatred, evil, and injustice are temporal realities. What is the eternal reality?
5. What did Jesus mean when He said, "My sheep hear My voice . . . and follow Me?"
6. Why did God temporarily separate the Jews from Gentiles?
7. Why is there no justification for the separation of Christians along racial lines?
8. Why did Jesus tell the story of the Good Samaritan?

CHAPTER 6
A World with One Law

Love does no wrong to anyone. That's why it fully satisfies all of God's requirements. It is the only law you need.

(Romans 13:10 TLB)

In the beginning, after God created the heavens and the earth, He gave the first man and woman one law: "But of the tree of the knowledge of good and evil, thou shalt not eat of it: for in the day that thou eatest thereof thou shalt surely die" (Genesis 2:17 KJV). We know that Adam and Eve broke that law, and as a result, the sin and death that infested their bodies was unleashed upon the world. Adam and Eve passed this legacy of sin and death down to all their children and the whole earth.

As the world population increased, sin increased and manifested itself in immoral and violent criminal behavior. The manifestations of sin were increasing so rapidly in the earth that God was grieved by all the violence that corrupted His creation. To save the world from the violence that threatened to destroy it, He sent a great flood upon the earth and destroyed all humanity except the family of one righteous man—Noah. God destroyed all but eight human beings and started over with Noah, his wife, their three sons, and their three wives. All the land animals and birds were also destroyed, except for those Noah took aboard the great ship that God had commanded him to build to survive the flood (Genesis 6).

Shortly after Noah and his family departed the ark, the human population began to increase again upon the earth, and sin began to spread as well. This time God selected a group of people who were the descendants of a man named Jacob, the grandson of Abraham. As we discussed earlier, God separated the Jews from the rest of corrupt humanity by revealing Himself to them through signs and wonders and giving them laws to govern their lives and preserve them as a distinct people from the rest of the world. He put these laws in place until the time He would send His own Son to save humanity from their sins. God chose a descendant of Jacob named Moses to be the one to hand those laws down to the people. Because there were so many ways for God's chosen people to sin, He imposed more than six hundred laws upon them to address those sins, separate them from the corrupt people around them, and create a relatively safe and stable environment.

Because of their sinful nature, people could not be expected to act unselfishly toward others in society and do what was in the interest of others without incentive, so the laws had to have consequences. Without penalties the laws would be completely ignored. Since humanity lacked the love and discipline to restrain their own selfish, sinful appetites and passions, fear of the penalties served as restraints. These laws were necessary to reveal the severity of sin and to stall the downward spiral of humanity until Christ could come and write His laws in the hearts of those who would receive Him.

In heaven there is no need for laws to restrain corrupt and irresponsible behavior. In his letter to Timothy, the apostle Paul explains the purpose behind laws.

> We know that the law is good when used correctly. For the law was not intended for people who do what is right. It is for people who are lawless and rebellious, who are ungodly and sinful, who consider nothing sacred and defile what is holy, who kill their father or mother or commit other murders. The law is for people who are sexually immoral, or who practice homosexuality, or are slave traders, liars, promise breakers, or who do anything else that contradicts the wholesome teaching that comes from the glorious Good News entrusted to me by our blessed God.
>
> (1 Timothy 1:8-11 NLT)

Since there are no lawless people in heaven, there is no need for laws to restrain them. The people in heaven are not governed by external laws, but by love from the heart. Because everyone in heaven overflows with God's love, love is the rule of law. Love is not motivated by fear of punishment. Rather, it is internally driven, completely motivated by genuine care, devotion, and interest and concern for others. In heaven there is not even one law designed to restrain anyone from doing wrong. Not even one forbidden tree exists to test faith and obedience because most of those who now live in heaven have already been tested in these areas by their lives on earth.

After experiencing the ravages of sin and corruption on earth, no one in heaven wants to contaminate a perfect world with sin. Even more importantly, no one in heaven is capable of sinning because every citizen of heaven has the righteousness of Christ. Every person in heaven loves the Lord God with all his heart and his neighbor as himself. Paul Enns expresses it this way: "In this life we are exhorted to 'walk by the Spirit,' to be controlled by the Holy Spirit" (Galatians 5:16). In that future day when we each receive a resurrection body, we will walk according to the Spirit the way God intended for us to walk—it will then be our normal life. The prohibitions of the epistles will be unnecessary. There will be no jealousy, strife, or anger, no unkind word, no drunkenness, or immorality. No one will ever again say, "I wish I hadn't said that."[1] This state of perfect love will be part of the makeup of our new resurrection bodies as Enns suggests, but we do not have to wait until the resurrection. As stated earlier, believers become perfect in love the instant we die (Hebrews 12:23).

Since love does no harm to others, it completely fulfills all of God's requirements (Romans 13:10). But love goes far beyond refusing to do harm; love insists on doing good to others. Love spills out of the heart in every direction with goodness, kindness, and generosity because it cannot be contained. It expresses itself in a myriad of good deeds and earnest service. Citizens of heaven are completely united as one in complete love and are completely empathetic toward each other. They genuinely share in each other's blessings, joys, and successes.

In heaven, expressing love to others is a strong inner compulsion. It is like the basic instinct of self-preservation that we now experience. The selfish ambition that drives much of humanity to do for self has been replaced with an overwhelming drive to do for others. The ambition of people in heaven is turned outward rather than inward. The interest of others has replaced self-interest. The drive for self-promotion and self-recognition has been replaced with the drive to promote others. This serving way of life is the reward in itself. Service itself is extremely gratifying because it is motivated by pure love.

The most beautiful things in heaven are not the gardens, trees, or the beautiful animals. Nor is it the river that is as clear as crystal, the streets and buildings of pure gold, or even the gates of pearl. The most beautiful thing in heaven is love that is free of prejudice, suspicion, stereotyping, fear, apprehension, division, or the need for secrecy.

Better Than Mayberry

One of my favorite television programs is "The Andy Griffith Show," produced in the sixties. The earlier episodes were done in black and white before color became standard. My grandchildren call these old black-and-white reruns, "gray TV." They wonder why my wife and I like to watch them when we have the option of full, living color. I love these old shows for a number of reasons, including their nostalgic value. But what attracts me most is that I am transported to a nearly perfect world when I watch an episode. I imagine the town of Mayberry, the setting of the show, to be the closest thing to heaven on earth. Of course, the town, characters, and story lines are all imaginary, but the values, environment, friendships, and relationships presented are the things that many of us long to experience in our own lives.

When we visit Mayberry, we step into an age of innocence. Although completely fictional, the show does present vestiges of things that were very real in the America of the sixties. We reflect back on these things with fondness, especially those of us who grew up in small-town America. Nevertheless, Mayberry still shields us from most of the harsh realities of our own childhood experiences and the broader realities of this period in American history.

Mayberry was a tiny bit like heaven because it removed us from frightening world events that were going on at the time, such as the Cuban missile crisis, the Vietnam War, racial segregation and oppression, multiple assassinations, and a series of horrible race riots. This escape from reality is one of the reasons I continue to enjoy visiting Mayberry via my television screen. Although I have seen every episode dozens of times, I am still uplifted and encouraged by this staged presentation of ideal life in a bygone era.

The quiet, little town of Mayberry reminds me just a little bit of heaven with its innocence, deep respect for God, honesty, and the portrayal of nearly everyone as a neighbor or friend. Crime is so nearly nonexistent that the sheriff doesn't wear a gun and the deputy carries only one bullet in his pocket. The spirit of goodwill, humor, and genuine hospitality is presented against a backdrop of neighborhood homes, tree-lined streets, sunshine, and chirping birds. There is genuine concern for others, and most of the people are honest citizens who are willing to serve each other. The atmosphere is peaceful, serene, and outdoorsy. I can almost feel the gentle breezes and smell the flowers and newly mowed lawns as I am drawn into each story.

Every story has a happy ending in Mayberry. In the end people tend to always do right by each other. All the positive things we remember about our childhood, or at least how we wished it had been, are portrayed in this nostalgic, imaginary place that millions of people love to visit and wish really exists. If Mayberry were a real place, millions of people would vacation there.

Andy's character, "Andy Taylor," is the star of the show because of the qualities of character he possesses. He is unassuming, kind, forgiving, loyal, humble, devoted to friends and family, honest, compassionate, fair, down-to-earth, and possesses a great sense of humor. Andy is the model of a well-rounded, good man. As I watch some of the heartwarming episodes of "The Andy Griffith Show," I sometimes think how nice it would be to live in a town like Mayberry and have a man like Andy as a close friend.

Mayberry strikes a chord with so many people because its writers, directors, and producers have managed to capture and portray just a tiny bit of what heaven is like. God has placed a longing in each of our hearts for heaven, and since Mayberry conveys in pictures and sound just a pinch of what heaven is like, we connect with it and long for it.

Heaven is full of fun-loving people with good humor, so there is plenty of laughter there. Moreover, heaven is filled with good and caring friends, and the friendships are not severed by death because they last forever. Heaven is a very large place with millions upon millions of people, yet it possesses small-town charm and appeal. There are birds chirping and singing, tree-lined streets, grass, and the best of what earth has to offer, yet it far exceeds earth's best. In heaven there are no harsh realities to gloss over or ignore because they simply do not exist. There are no pressures, no schedules to keep, and no rat race to keep up with. Heaven is a place of rest but also a place of growth and advancement.

The apostle Paul summarizes it this way: "No eye has seen, no ear has heard, and no mind has imagined what God has prepared for those who love him. But it was to us that God revealed these things by his Spirit. For his Spirit searches out everything and shows us even God's deep secrets" (1 Corinthians 2:9-10 NLT). God has prepared things for us that are simply unimaginable. However, as Warren Wiersbe says, "God wants us to know today all the blessings He has planned for us."[2] He has revealed many of these things through His Holy Spirit and the Word. But these many revealed truths that allow us to get a glimpse of heaven are only the tip of the iceberg. There is so much more in store that we cannot even conceive.

Perfect Love

The Bible says that the purpose of biblical instruction is love (1 Timothy 1:5). God is love, so heaven is also love. The aim of the entire Law since its inception has been to introduce earth to heaven. Every commandment is aimed toward getting us to live on earth as they live in heaven. "Thou shalt love the Lord thy God with all thy heart; thou shalt love thy neighbor as thyself; thou shalt not steal, kill, and covet" and so on are all focused on encouraging sinful humanity to move closer to living on earth as they do in heaven.

Of course, part of the process God established in Moses' day was meant to make us understand the futility of trying to keep these laws on our own. In turn, this understanding was designed to lead us to see our desperate need for Christ. But the ultimate end was to bring us into perfect love. All of the laws were ultimately aimed at getting us to someday live on a new earth as people now live in heaven.

The New Testament intensifies the focus on teaching God's people to live on earth as people live in heaven with commandments such as, "Look not every man on his own things, but every man also on the things of others" (Philippians 2:4 KJV); "Love one another with a pure heart fervently" (1 Peter 1:22 KJV); "By love serve one another" (Galatians 5:13 KJV); "Husbands love your wives, even as Christ loved the church" (Ephesians 5:25 KJV); "Love your enemies, do good unto them which hate you" (Luke 6:27 KJV); and "Be not overcome of evil, but overcome evil with good" (Romans 12:21 KJV). These and other commandments compel us to imitate the love and life of heaven despite the strong opposition against us. Like salmon swimming against the current, we are commanded to follow the example of Jesus and press our way through everything that opposes a heavenly lifestyle on earth. We are not supposed to let earth change us but rather use our knowledge of heaven to influence earth. We are charged by God to overcome the evil of earth by living like they do in heaven, even in the face of injustice and mistreatment. In the words of Mahatma Gandhi, "We must become the change we seek." This is how we let our light shine.

When Jesus Christ came to earth, He said, "A new commandment I give to you, that you love one another as I have loved you" (John 13:34 NASB). This commandment was new in the sense that through the selflessness, kindness, and sacrifice of Jesus, we were given the ultimate model of the caliber of love that we should show toward each other.

This model helps to convey to humanity how extremely valuable we all are. We are so valuable that God paid for us with the life of His only begotten Son. We are so valuable that God's Son gave up His life through a brutal, humiliating, and agonizing death as a ransom to purchase us for Himself. If God so loved us then we ought to love one another in the same way (1 John 4:11). If we are this valuable and important to God, we should realize that we are this valuable and important to each other. This lesson has gotten through to the people in heaven, but we on earth are still struggling to grasp it. People in heaven are fully aware of the inestimable value of every other human and angelic being, and they celebrate that value.

Loving thy neighbor as thyself is not just a lofty ideal in heaven; it is common reality. From heaven's perspective, the highest form of human love and affection seen on earth is flawed and inadequate. Earlier I mentioned the fact that Jesus called John the Baptist the greatest man who had ever lived but He added that the person who is the least in heaven is greater than John (Matthew 11:11). He that is least in heaven has a greater quality, intensity, and depth of love than the greatest, godliest person now living on earth. Of course, all that changes when a Christian dies. After death the weakest, most selfish Christian on earth is immediately transformed in nature, enters heaven, and becomes greater than the greatest Christian living on earth.

Love in Marriage

In his book, *The Letter to the Galatians and Ephesians*, William Barclay makes the argument that "marriage is regarded as the perfect union of body, mind and spirit between a man and a woman."[3] Love in marriage is the best example we have on earth of the power of love in heaven. In heaven, however, marriage will be obsolete because the love that is in heaven is far superior even to the love between a woman and man on earth.

Paul commands husbands to love their wives as Christ loved the church (Ephesians 5:25). On earth, men struggle to obey this commandment. While many of us make a good effort at loving our wives on the level that Christ loved the church, we often fail because of selfishness. Our efforts are inconsistent. Some days we may feel that we are coming close to the kind of all-consuming, sacrificial love that Christ demonstrated, but, if we are honest, we will admit that our love on earth can hardly compare to His love for His church.

I love my wife more than anyone else on earth, except myself. I'm working on that, but I have to be honest and confess that I haven't quite arrived. I would risk my life for my wife. I would sacrifice for her, but sometimes I don't want to go to the store for her, especially when I'm in the middle of watching a good movie or documentary.

I have enjoyed such a wonderful relationship with my wife, Joyce, that it is one of the things I most dread to see come to an end. Yet at the same time I realize that the things I most enjoy from our relationship—the comfort she brings, the trust, the good intentions we have for each other, the willingness to serve each other's needs, the joy of each other's company, the close friendship, the transparency, the bond, the faithfulness, and the life presence—are all things that everyone in heaven contributes to everyone else.

I am also assured that my relationship with Joyce will not end but will be perfected. In heaven we will be more than husband and wife; we will be one in the truest sense of the word. We will enjoy a bond and kinship beyond anything achievable on earth. So far, we have had only forty-two years together on earth, and too much of that time has been spent apart during the day when we carry out our separate responsibilities. In heaven we will have an eternity to spend together. We will be able to spend millennia after millennia of waking hours together.

Moreover, on earth our time is punctuated with pain, disappointment, fatigue, struggle, and a bit of contention mixed in with the joy, peace, and contentment. In heaven our time will be spent in perfect love and harmony. We will be able to explore the wonders of heaven together with boundless energy, whereas on earth our energy often wanes before we can complete a sightseeing tour.

In heaven there is only fervent love and total goodwill for every citizen of the kingdom. Love is without hypocrisy. There is no negative talk, thoughts, feelings, or emotions to hide. Instead, there is complete transparency from everyone. Everyone sees everyone else as absolute family or close friends. Even when we meet people we have never seen before, we will automatically perceive and receive them as family because every single person who is so blessed to be in heaven will be a fellow citizen, a member of the family of God who shares a common bond.

We Christians talk a great deal about the family of God, but because of our struggle against sin, we do not really appreciate the magnitude of those words. We say "family," but we really don't mean family—not in the sense that we think of our biological family. In fact, we are often guilty of putting ethnicity above our identity with others who are Christians but happen to be of a different race or national origin. But in heaven we will really see every other intelligent being, both human and angel, as family. As I mentioned earlier, the Bible says that God will bring all things together into one, both in heaven and on earth (Ephesians 1:10). God's whole family in heaven and on earth derives its name from him (Ephesians 3:15).

Paul uses the analogy of the human body in his effort to demonstrate how Christians on earth should relate to one another (1 Corinthians 12:12). He reduces the family of God, which is made up of a variety of people and angelic beings, down to one body, conveying the idea of unity. David Prior makes the following insightful comment on this subject: "The phrase *the body*, introduced in verse 12, perfectly illustrates these two themes of variety and unity. *Many members . . . one body* is Paul's summary of the matter."[4]

While we can easily understand the strength of Paul's analogy of God's family being many members but like one body, the reality tends to break down here on earth because of sin and selfishness. Because we have not yet been made perfect, we strive, exerting great effort to demonstrate selfless devotion to the other members of the body of Christ. We often come up short because of these imperfections, but one day God will perfect us in a moment—"in the twinkling of an eye." We will clearly understand how we fit together like the parts of the human body. The unity we struggle to achieve now will be achieved effortlessly then. We will become God's perfect people in heaven.

In heaven love is active, not passive. Love expresses itself in acts of kindness and thoughtfulness. People use their creative genius to find ways to express their love to those around them. I believe that gift-giving and serving one another is continual. Everyone seeks ways to express the intense feelings of love, kindness, and appreciation that are a natural part of their existence. In his letter to the Corinthians, Paul describes perfect love as it now exists in heaven, and he urges the saints on earth to pursue it.

> Love is patient and kind. Love is not jealous or boastful or proud or rude. It does not demand its own way. It is

not irritable, and it keeps no record of being wronged. It does not rejoice about injustice but rejoices whenever the truth wins out. Love never gives up, never loses faith, is always hopeful, and endures through every circumstance. Prophecy and speaking in unknown languages and special knowledge will become useless. But love will last forever!

(1 Corinthians 13:4-8 NLT)

We will experience love from everyone we encounter in heaven, just as Paul describes it here. In heaven there is no pride, no pretense, no tension, and no embarrassing moments, just complete openness and complete goodwill. In heaven no one has to put his best foot forward or wonder if he will be fully accepted just as he is. In heaven people know each other right down to the core, and everything known is fully accepted and approved. In heaven there is every reason to accept everyone else and no reason to reject anyone, even in private thought. In fact, thoughts in heaven are so pure that there may be very little need for private thoughts. We shudder at that very possibility now, but only because our thoughts are often impure and sometimes downright evil. In heaven, however, they will be completely good and pure and always complimentary.

Naked and Not Ashamed

The Bible says that when Adam and Eve were created, they were naked and not ashamed (Genesis 2:25). Why were they not ashamed? The answer is because they had nothing to hide, nothing to be ashamed of. Their thoughts and attitudes were pure. They were not pretentious. They could speak their thoughts as they thought them without having to filter them through inoffensive language. They had no ill intentions, ill thoughts, or ill will toward each other. They were completely honest and open about everything. Their thoughts and feelings were out in the open, and their intentions toward each other were only good and positive. There was no need to hide them.

After the fall, Adam and Eve covered themselves because they had changed. Their thoughts were now impure, so they could not voice them. They were ashamed because even their thoughts about their bodies were now tainted. Adam turned on Eve and blamed her for the whole mess. This was a sign of selfishness that had previously been foreign to him. Now there were thoughts of blame, resentment, disdain, disrespect, distrust, and suspicion. These thoughts and feelings grew, increased, and intensified with time and hardship. Eve probably hid resentful thoughts about Adam for the pain she suffered in childbirth. Adam probably hid thoughts of blame toward Eve for the life of hard toil he had to endure as a result of her leading them both into rebellion against God.

With each new generation there were more thoughts of resentment and ill will to hide. One generation after Adam and Eve, their son, Cain, became jealous of his brother, Abel, and murdered him. Cain hid his thoughts about the murder from his mother and father. And so, this need for us human beings to conceal much of our thoughts became the norm because of the sinful nature of our hearts.

But when we are made perfect, either by passing through the portal of death or by way of the rapture, our thoughts will become perfectly pure. There will no longer be any reason to hide them from each other because they will all be good thoughts of kindness, compassion, and goodwill. We may again be naked and unashamed, not our bodies but very possibly our minds. Of course, we can only speculate about this. There is no solid Scripture passage upon which I can base this idea, but just as our thoughts are all open before God now, they may well be open to everyone in heaven then.

Concerning how everything is openly exposed to God, the writer of Hebrews says, "Nothing in all creation is hidden from God. Everything is naked and exposed before his eyes" (Hebrews 4:13 NLT). God says through the prophet Isaiah, "I can see what they are doing, and I know what they are thinking" (Isaiah 66:18 NLT). The Bible also says we shall know even as we are known (1 Corinthians 13:12). If we will know as we are known, it is not inconceivable that our thoughts will be exposed to each other in heaven. Since the thoughts and intents of our heart will no longer be offensive but rather generated by the law of love and intentions of service, they will only feed and promote the same kinds of thoughts and feelings in others.

When you find out that someone has been loyal to you and has been saying good things about you in your absence, you tend to warm toward that person. In heaven we will know that everyone is loyal and has good intentions toward us. If we are able to know the good that others think about us, it will only feed our love for them. Again, we can only speculate about the possibility of open thoughts among the people of heaven. The Bible does not emphatically state this, and it should certainly not be taken as a doctrine, but it is something to consider.

Compelling Love

Intense love fills the lives of those in the kingdom of heaven from one end to the other and top to bottom. The instant we pass from this life, God will give us the capacity to actually love as He loves. When we meet new people, they will know that we have this kind of deep, abiding love and appreciation for them, and we will know they have it for us. The sense of familiarity through the family bond will be strongly evident everywhere in God's kingdom. There will be instant bonding, with no need to get to know each other first. Each person meeting someone else for the first time will know that the other is accepted and completely trusted and loved without reservation. Each will know that the other has his or her best interest at heart and will relate to the other as a brother or sister, as the best kind of friend and family. Everyone will have family, God, kingdom citizenship, salvation, love, goodwill, and loyalty to God and every other person in common. There will be every reason to intensely like everyone we meet and no reason for dislike. There will be every reason to love and no reason not to. There will be every reason for trust and no reason for distrust.

This kind of love has very rarely been experienced on this earth, even among family members—and yes, even among Christians. It is a love that Christians have sought but found quite elusive. It is the most important thing God has wanted for His people, but it has been difficult to capture and possess. It is the second greatest commandment, but it is probably one of the most often broken and neglected.

While here on earth, Jesus demonstrated the fact that love requires sacrifice and service. He said, "This is my commandment: Love each other in the same way I have loved you. There is no greater love than to lay down one's life for one's friends" (John 15:12-13 NLT).

Christians have claimed to possess this kind of love, but our profession often has not borne the weight of close scrutiny. To love each other the way Jesus commands is very challenging, even for redeemed humanity. But one day God will change us so completely that this kind of love will be as common as the air we now breathe. Loving God with all our heart and others as we love ourselves will be what we do naturally. The joy and peace that exudes from such a completely loving attitude from every inhabitant of heaven will be beyond measure. The phrase the angels spoke to the shepherds on the night of Jesus' birth, "peace on earth, goodwill to men will be more than a promise and a dream. It will be the way of life for every inhabitant of the new heaven and the new earth.

Parents have a special love for their own children, the kind of love that compels them to labor and sacrifice time, energy, and money. Parental love embraces patience and pain to do what is in the interest of the child. A sacrifice often doesn't feel much like a sacrifice because of the deep love that motivates parental actions. Parents spend hours working to provide a decent home, clothing, food, and the other necessities for their children, and they do it with joy. At Christmas time parents shop and spend their money buying gifts for their children. It gives them the greatest joy to do so because they are doing something they believe will bring joy to their little ones.

Grandparents have a special kind of love for their grandchildren. They are even more doting on the children than the parents. They spoil them with gifts and bend rules that they never would have bent for their own children. They put up with noise, mess, and other things that they would not have tolerated with their own children because they have so much joy and delight just being in the presence of the grandchildren.

This is the kind of love that everyone has for everyone else in heaven. The new heaven and new earth will be a place of unimaginable loving and caring, joy and pleasure. Every day will be immeasurably more exciting and pleasurable than Christmas with the family. The citizens of heaven will serve each other as willingly and as effortlessly as the cells of the human body. Each member of God's family does its part for the good of the whole body. We will have the complete realization that we are indeed one body, one family, and one kingdom governed by the love that naturally resides in the heart of every person. We will be completely regenerated to fit perfectly into an environment of love and righteousness. When we enter the presence of God, we will be one with the family of God.

Empathy

Empathy is an interesting word. It means the ability to feel what others feel, to be able to see from the perspective of other people, and to be able to identify with others and understand their struggles and pain. God allows us to experience certain hardships and difficulties in this world so we can better understand the difficulties that other people experience and be better equipped to minister to them. Although there is no pain there, people in heaven are completely empathetic with each other. They are one, joined together by their feelings, just as much as the parts of the human body are joined. The human body is so united that if the eyes are complimented, the whole body shares the compliment. If the finger receives a beautiful ring to adorn it, the whole body is appreciative and shares in the joy and excitement of it. This is exactly the way people in heaven feel each other's joy and pleasure.

In the effort to get His people on earth to act like the people in heaven, God says through the apostle Paul, "Bear ye one another's burdens and so fulfill the law of Christ" (Galatians 6:2 KJV). William Barclay comments on this passage, "There is a kind of burden which comes to people from the chances and changes of life; it is fulfilling the law of Christ to help everyone who has such a burden to carry."[5] John Phillips referred to this law of Christ as "the all-encompassing law of love."[6]

The apostle Paul says, "Rejoice with those who rejoice and weep with those who weep" (Romans 12:15 NASB). Here on earth, it is sometimes more difficult to rejoice over the joys and successes of others than it is to be jealous and inflict pain upon them. The propensity to hurt others rather than rejoice with them results from the fact that sin has robbed us of a sense of empathy. When we truly love, empathy is activated. Because I love my wife, when she hurts, I hurt. Because I love her and feel her pain, I will not inflict pain upon her because it hurts me to hurt her. When my children hurt, I hurt.

Teach Me About Heaven and Eternal Life

Parents used to say to their children before administering a spanking for misconduct, "This is going to hurt me more than it does you." Although it is difficult for a child to understand, this is a statement of empathy. Because we love our children, we want to avoid hurting them or making them feel bad, even when we know it is in their best interest to do so. When our children hurt, we hurt. Some parents allow their empathy to get in the way of good judgment, which causes them to neglect this aspect of their parental responsibility. Grandparents are especially guilty of allowing their love and empathy to cloud their good judgment. We spoil them and send them home. However, the empathy we feel here on earth, even for those we love, falls far short of the pure form of empathy that those in heaven feel for each other.

Because we are deficient in this ability to feel the pain and pleasure that others experience, we are able to do terrible things to each other—sometimes without even feeling a twinge of guilt or remorse. We experience jealousy because we lack empathy. We act selfishly because we lack empathy. But Jesus urges us to practice being empathetic, even to our enemies, because this will certainly put us in harmony with the rest of the family in heaven.

Our Lord commands us to feed our enemy if he hungers and be good to those who mistreat us. In this way we will demonstrate that we are the children of our Father in heaven. We will be imitators of God, who is good to evil people as well as good people (Matthew 5:44-45). Paul also exhorts us to be imitators of God as dearly loved children (Ephesians 5:1 NIV). We are not supposed to conform to this world, where the rule is to treat others the way they treat us. Rather, we should be transformed by renewing our mind and learning the ways, customs, and culture of heaven and transferring it to earth in the here and now. We must not allow this fallen world to shape our values and conduct.

There is power in exposing earth to the ways of heaven. Paul's command for us not to be overcome by evil but to overcome evil with good is effective spiritual warfare (Romans 12:21). It is God's plan and strategy for how we are to engage the enemy, the Devil, and defeat him. Exposing earth to heaven can have a leavening effect. Jesus said the kingdom of heaven is like leaven (yeast) that is mixed into a measure of flour until it fills the whole batch of dough (Matthew 13:33).

Of course, this does not mean that the whole world will be perfected because of the influence of God's family on earth. What it does mean is that if we live on earth like they do in heaven, it will influence more and more people to join the family of God. Then there will be a steady increase of kingdom people, until they can be found in every part of the world. Finally, God will create an entirely new earth where only righteous people live (Isaiah 65:17; 2 Peter 3:13; Revelation 21:1). This is exactly what Jesus meant when He said, "Let your light so shine before men, that they may see your good works, and glorify your Father which is in heaven" (Matthew 5:16 KJV). When we practice living a heavenly lifestyle, people are attracted to the light that may draw them to us but ultimately direct them to our Father.

The greatest example of empathy was demonstrated by Jesus when He descended from His royal and lofty position as the king of the universe to become a servant (Philippians 2:7). He took on a human body that was exactly like ours, but without sin. He experienced the total human experience, even torture and death, just to rescue us and become our great high priest. Even though Jesus is God, He knew exactly what it meant to be human. He was touched with the feelings of our infirmities. The Bible says, "This High Priest of ours understands our weaknesses, for he faced all of the same testings we do, yet he did not sin" (Hebrews 4:15 NLT).

Jesus has firsthand knowledge about how it feels to have strong desires for what you must deny yourself. He knows what it is like to experience disappointment, fear, rejection, excruciating pain, hunger, thirst, loneliness, unfulfilled sexual desires, grief over the death of loved ones, and every other human experience. He faced them all, yet without sin. Jesus became a human being in order to be able to fully empathize with humanity and represent us before God as our great high priest and advocate.

After experiencing what it is like to be a human being in a world of sin, He offered His own body on the cross to pay for our sins and bring forgiveness of those sins. He also brought freedom from slavery to sin and the death that results from sin. The writer of Hebrews explains,

"Because God's children are human beings—made of

flesh and blood—the Son also became flesh and blood. For only as a human being could he die, and only by dying could he break the power of the devil, who had the power of death."

(Hebrews 2:14 NLT)

Just as God came to earth and experienced human nature, He has made it possible for us to experience His divine nature (2 Peter 1:4). Just as Christ came to earth and lived like humans, He has extended us the privilege of going to heaven and living like God. God walked among men, so we will walk with God. Because of His human experience, God is fully capable of empathizing with humanity. When we pass into heaven, we will share in God's divine love and empathy with every other person in heaven. God's divine nature of love will govern our lives and behavior for all eternity. It will indeed be the only law we need.

Chapter 6 | Thought-provoking Questions

1. What is the purpose of laws?
2. What is the law of heaven?
3. Why is there only one law in heaven?
4. Are the people in heaven capable of sinning?
5. Why does love completely fulfill all of God's requirements?
6. How does love express itself in heaven?
7. How does God help us to empathize with others?
8. How is lack of empathy revealed in the lives of people on earth?
9. Who demonstrated the greatest example of empathy, and how?

CHAPTER 7
Absolute Peace

> *For unto you is born this day in the city of David a Saviour, which is Christ the Lord. And this shall be a sign unto you; Ye shall find the babe wrapped in swaddling clothes, lying in a manger. And suddenly there was with the angel a multitude of the heavenly host praising God, and saying, Glory to God in the highest, and on earth peace, good will toward men.*
>
> (Luke 2:11-14 KJV)

Peace is the absence of war, conflict, and anxiety and the presence of tranquility and serenity. There are a number of promises of peace on earth in the Bible that we will examine, but the one most often cited during the Christmas season is the preceding passage from the Gospel of Luke. This scene of the Christmas story has been depicted for centuries in everything from spectacular pageants to children's Christmas plays. It is, of course, the story of the announcement of the birth of Christ. One angel announces to the shepherds who are in the field with their sheep at night that Christ the Savior has been born. Then the one angel is joined by a host of other angels, who inform the shepherds that the birth of this child would have a wonderful result: "Glory to God in the highest, and on earth peace, good will toward men." This is great news, because Christ is the Savior of the world and the Prince of Peace (Isaiah 9:6). This newly born child will indeed be the one who will bring peace and goodwill to earth.

Eighteen hundred years after the angels made their announcement of peace on earth through the newborn Prince of Peace, Henry Wadsworth Longfellow wrote a famous poem that was later arranged into a Christmas carol entitled "I Heard the Bells on Christmas Day." The words of that poem are worthy of reflection.

> I heard the bells on Christmas day
> Their old, familiar carols play,
> And wild and sweet the words repeat
> Of peace on earth, good will to men!
>
> And I thought how, as the day had come,
> The belfries of all Christendom
> Had rolled along
> The unbroken song
> Of peace on earth, good-will to men!
>
> Till, ringing singing, on its way,
> The world revolved from night to day,
> A voice, a chime, a chant sublime,
> Of peace on earth, good will to men!
>
> Then from each black, accursed mouth
> The cannon thundered in the South,
> And with the sound
> The carols drowned
> Of peace on earth, good-will to men!
>
> It was as if an earthquake rent
> The hearth-stones of a continent,
> And made forlorn
> The households born
> Of peace on earth, good-will to men!
>
> And in despair I bowed my head;
> "There is no peace on earth," I said;
> "For hate is strong,
> And mocks the song
> Of peace on earth, good–will to men!"

Then pealed the bells more loud and deep:
"God is not dead, nor doth he sleep!
The wrong shall fail
The right prevail,
With peace on earth, good-will to men!"[1]

Longfellow's poem conveys the fact that on each Christmas Day bells ring out, and Christmas carols herald the promise of peace on earth and goodwill to men. After listening year after year about this promise of peace, Longfellow confessed that he had become hopeless and cynical about it all. He looked at the world around him and saw hatred and hostility instead of peace and goodwill. At the time he wrote this poem, America was engaged in the Civil War, during which hundreds of thousands of lives were being sacrificed. America was being split apart over the issue of whether Americans should have the right to continue to enslave their own brothers and sisters. Longfellow came to believe that the promise of peace was only mocked by the prevailing hateful attitude among the people of earth. But in the face of his despair, the bells of Christmas continued to ring even louder, and in his heart he heard them say, "God is not dead, nor does He sleep. The wrong shall fail, the right prevail with peace on earth goodwill to men."

Longfellow suddenly realized that there would indeed come a day when things would change. His faith in God's promise of peace was restored and renewed. He knew in his heart that the earth would someday revolve from the night of hatred and hostility to the day of peace and goodwill to men, just as God promised through the angels. From childhood many of us have enjoyed listening to Longfellow's song of peace. It is still one of my favorite Christmas carols. Like Longfellow, we have the faith to believe that the day will come when God's promise of peace will be fulfilled.

This prophecy of peace on earth through the Prince of Peace did not originate with the angels in the Christmas story, as presented by Luke. It reaches back over seven hundred years before the birth of Christ. The prophet Isaiah foretold a day when the Christ child would be born into the world and grow up to rule in peace.

> For unto us a child is born, unto us a son is given: and the government shall be upon his shoulder: and his name shall

> be called Wonderful, Counsellor, The mighty God, The everlasting Father, The Prince of Peace. Of the increase of his government and peace there shall be no end, upon the throne of David, and upon his kingdom, to order it, and to establish it with judgment and with justice from henceforth even forever. The zeal of the LORD of hosts will perform this.
>
> (Isaiah 9:6-7 KJV)

In this prophecy Isaiah predicted that at some point in history, God would be born into the world in the body of a human child, and this child would govern the world with peace. His just and righteous kingdom would be ruled with fairness and its peace would continue to expand forever.

This announcement from Isaiah and the one from the angels in the Book of Luke encompass both the first and second comings of Christ to earth. He came the first time as the God-man to sacrifice His life for the purpose of saving humanity from their sins. He will come again as the resurrected Savior to establish new heavens, a new earth, and His rule of peace and righteousness over all.

It is understandable that those of us expecting this promised new world of peace might become a little weary after waiting for more than two thousand years now. But like Longfellow, we must ask God to restore our faith and renew our hope so that we can continue to wait for the promise. We are cautioned in the Scriptures not to abandon our faith by becoming slothful but to follow the examples of those in the Bible who through faith and patience obtained the promises they hoped for (Hebrews 6:12). It is also important to remember that no individual has waited for more than one lifetime for this time of absolute peace. Each Christian enters into God's rest and peace at the end of his or her short lifetime on earth (Revelation 14:13). But because the fulfillment of God's promise to bring peace to earth has been so long in coming, some people have become cynical. These people do not believe Christ will ever return. The apostle Peter predicted that as the day of the return of Christ draws near (in the last days), people will laugh and scoff at the idea.

> Most importantly, I want to remind you that in the last days scoffers will come, mocking the truth and following their own desires. They will say, "What happened to the promise that Jesus is coming again? From before

the times of our ancestors, everything has remained the same since the world was first created." They deliberately forget that God made the heavens long ago by the word of his command, and he brought the earth out from the water and surrounded it with water. Then he used the water to destroy the ancient world with a mighty flood…The Lord isn't really being slow about his promise, as some people think. No, he is being patient for your sake. He does not want anyone to be destroyed, but wants everyone to repent. But the day of the Lord will come as unexpectedly as a thief. Then the heavens will pass away with a terrible noise, and the very elements themselves will disappear in fire, and the earth and everything on it will be found to deserve judgment. Since everything around us is going to be destroyed like this, what holy and godly lives you should live, looking forward to the day of God and hurrying it along. On that day, he will set the heavens on fire, and the elements will melt away in the flames. But we are looking forward to the new heavens and new earth he has promised, a world filled with God's righteousness. And so, dear friends, while you are waiting for these things to happen, make every effort to be found living peaceful lives that are pure and blameless in his sight.

(2 Peter 3:3-6, 9-14 NLT)

Peter's prophecy is being fulfilled in these last days in which we now live. Scoffers now look at the long passage of time since the first coming of Christ and cite it as evidence that He will never return. But what they fail to take into account is the fact that human beings are finite, with a lifespan of only seventy or eighty years on average. We measure time from this finite existence and perspective. On the other hand, God is infinite. He has always existed and always will exist. He has an unlimited number of years from which He measures time. So to God, one day is like a thousand years and a thousand years is like a day (2 Peter 3:8). Days or thousands of years do not diminish Him, while every minute diminishes the amount of time we have left on earth.

What we have in verses 3 and 4 may be a prediction from Peter of the rise of naturalists, evolutionists, and atheists in the last days. What Peter did not include in his prophecy is the fact that in the last days these scoffers would even abandon belief in a creator. Instead, they would conclude that everything we see around us did not come into existence through a creator, but simply evolved.

Peter did predict that these skeptics would argue that everything has continued to naturally occur, as it has from the beginning of time and no supernatural God has ever intervened in the affairs of history. But he also points out that they would willingly ignore how God, by His Word, called the earth out of water when He created it and later interrupted human history with a great flood. Noah's flood is a fact skeptics want to regard as a myth, ignore, or localize.

Michael Green put it this way: "They willfully neglected the flood, when God did intervene in judgment. The lesson taught by the flood was that this is a moral universe, that sin will not forever go unpunished; and Jesus himself used the flood to point this moral (Matthew 24:37-39)."[2] By ignoring or rejecting the flood, they don't have to be reminded of God's past intervention in human affairs, and they can more easily reject His promise of returning in the future. These skeptics mock God by sneering, "This God that the Christians believe in is slow regarding His promise to return and bring peace or judgment."

Peter responds that the Lord is not slow in His promise to return, but He is patient. His purpose for waiting is to give time for more people to repent and turn to Him so that more souls will be added to the family of God. God doesn't want anyone to perish, but He wants everyone to have ample time to repent. With each generation, millions more people join His family. Heaven will be populated by billions of people (Revelation 7:9).

But Peter makes it clear that God will not wait forever. The day of the Lord will surely come like an unexpected thief in the night. Without going into very much detail, Peter tells us that Christ will destroy the old earth and the heavenly bodies, not with nuclear weapons as some suggest, but through His own mighty power. The very elements will melt. But then He will bring forth completely new heavens and a completely new earth, fulfilling His promise. Peter's prophecy of the destruction and re-creation of the old heavens and earth is in harmony with the biblical theme of death and resurrection. Anthony DeStefano describes it in just such terms. He comments, "In the New Testament, there is much talk of a 'new heaven and a new earth.' What this simply means is that in the same way human beings are destined to experience death, bodily resurrection, and transformation, so too will our own planet."[3]

This new earth will be the home of God's family. We are encouraged by Peter to anxiously look forward to the fulfillment of this promise of the return of the Prince of Peace. But as we wait, we should determine to live pure and blameless lives and practice being at peace with God.

Peter was not the first to prophesy that God would create new heavens and a new earth. Isaiah clearly predicted it in his day: "For, behold, I create new heavens and a new earth: and the former shall not be remembered, nor come into mind" (Isaiah 65:17 KJV). The new heavens and the new earth that God creates will be a world where sin and its negative effects will not be known. Scholars differ in their position about exactly how God will go about doing this work of re-creation. Some argue that God will completely destroy the old heavens and earth and create completely new ones from scratch. Others argue that God will not completely destroy them but will simply renovate them by fire and use what is left of them to re-create new heavens and a new earth. Whatever the case, when God is finished the heavens and earth will be completely new.

Prior to destroying this earth and creating a new one, the Bible predicts that Christ will return to this present earth, destroy the wicked, and lock Satan away in a bottomless pit (Revelation 20:3). He will clean up the earth and the environment and establish a kingdom of righteousness for a thousand years. This is referred to as the millennial reign of Christ or the peaceful kingdom. The millennial reign of our Lord on this old earth will be a prelude to the new heavens and the new earth that He will create at the end of His thousand-year reign.

Christ's return will spell the end of all trouble for His people. It will usher in a time of rest, defined by peace and freedom from worry and stress. The rest we enjoy will be rest from turmoil and struggle. There will be no more storms in our lives to rob us of peace. There will be no one or nothing to cause uneasiness in us. The prophet Job described this rest in one sentence: "There the wicked cease from troubling, and there the weary be at rest" (Job 3:17 KJV).

Every minute of every day, we will enjoy a calm, carefree serenity that will never be broken by thoughts, concerns, or worries about some trouble we must face later in the day or the next day, week, or year. There will be no shortage of funds to have to deal with or the IRS to negotiate with. There will be no strange lumps or persistent pain to spark fears of cancer or some other malady. We will not wonder if there is more bad news when the phone rings. Our minds will be completely at peace and at ease.

Peace from Fear

> There is no fear in love; but perfect love casteth out fear: because fear hath torment.

(1 John 4:18 KJV)

Fear is the great robber of peace. Imagine a world with absolutely no thoughts of anything to fear ever again. The apostle John informs us that love is completely free of fear. In fact, love casts out fear. Fear is the great tormentor. Most of our fears are about things that will never happen. But although many of the things we fear are only illusionary, the fear itself is very real. In heaven and the new earth, we will enjoy inner peace like nothing we are able to imagine. According to John, when we have been made perfect in love, we will have no fear. John is speaking specifically about fear of judgment from God in this passage. But when we pass from this life and enter heaven, all of our fears will be left behind us. Additionally, when God creates the new heavens and the new earth, nothing will be included that will cause His people to fear.

The prophecy of Isaiah about this time of absolute peace gives us hope and expectation.

> The Lord will mediate between nations and will settle international disputes. They will hammer their swords into plowshares and their spears into pruning hooks. Nation will no longer fight against nation, nor train for war anymore.

(Isaiah 2:4 NLT)

Probably the greatest and most common fear we experience, and thus the greatest threat to our inner peace, is the fear of other people. Being violated, injured, or killed by another human being is one of the things that people are most concerned about. We are afraid of each other. We fear for our own safety and that of our children. We worry, if only a little, when our children leave home for a simple bike ride around the neighborhood. Worry turns to near panic if they are late returning home. We are probably more afraid of people than any other possible cause of harm in the world.

Gun violence is one of the leading causes of fear. Acts of terrorism and mass murder are quickly becoming a common occurrence in schools, on college campuses, in places of worship, and in other public places. We eye each other with suspicion and look for the nearest exit before we settle ourselves in our seats. We lock our doors at night. We make sure our car doors are locked when we pass through high-crime areas, or we try to avoid them altogether. We invest in alarm systems to alert us of possible home invasion. We take every precaution to ensure our safety, and in our present world these precautionary measures are wise and reasonable.

Globally, crime and violence take the form of war, which threatens the whole world. The violent behavior of early human beings was the main reason God had to send the flood upon the earth in Noah's day. Genesis 6:13 (NIV) says, "So God said to Noah, 'I am going to put an end to all people, for the earth is filled with violence because of them. I am surely going to destroy both them and the earth.' "

While teaching His disciples a few days before His death, Jesus predicted that just before His return, conditions will once again be violent and dangerous like they were in Noah's day (Luke 17:26). Paul also warns us that "in the last days perilous times shall come"(2 Timothy 3:1 KJV). Today the world is filling up with violence, yet in the midst of it all people continue with their lives. But the prophet Isaiah foretells a day when God would bring an end to all of the violence in the earth. He predicts that Christ will settle disputes between all nations and end all wars forever. The resources and effort that are now being used to produce weapons will someday be used to produce technology that advances the good of all humanity for only peaceful and pleasurable pursuits. All violence and hostility between people will come to an end.

Isaiah predicts that God will not only end violence between people, but He will also tame the animal world so that animals that are now ferocious will become completely docile. Animals will no longer be carnivorous, feeding on the flesh and blood of other animals. Instead, God will restore everything to its original state, when all animals were herbivores that fed only on grass and plants.

> In that day the wolf and the lamb will live together; the leopard will lie down with the baby goat. The calf and the yearling will be safe with the lion, and a little child will lead them all. The cow will graze near the bear. The cub and the calf will lie down together. The lion will eat hay like a cow. The baby will play safely near the hole of a cobra. Yes, a little child will put its hand in a nest of deadly snakes without harm. Nothing will hurt or destroy in all my holy mountain, for as the waters fill the sea, so the earth will be filled with people who know the Lord.
>
> (Isaiah 11:6-9 NLT)

In the original creation, God designed a world of absolute peace and safety, free of danger. In his prophecy, Isaiah describes a future world that will be remade into the one that was originally intended. In this new world, there will be animals just like the ones in the original creation. Animals we have come to fear because of their ferocity will no longer be feared. Wolves, leopards, and lions will live peacefully with lambs, calves, and baby goats. None of these animals will be a threat to the others. In fact, Isaiah says that the once fierce and ferocious animals will be so tame that a little child will be able to lead them around with no concern for injury.

Isaiah then points out that bears and cattle will graze together. Bear cubs and calves will lie down in the meadow together. Lions and bears will eat grass like grazing animals do now. This prophecy says that even poisonous snakes will be so harmless that a baby will be able to crawl among them and even play with them without being harmed. There will be absolutely nothing that will bring harm or destruction in all of God's kingdom. Most importantly, every human being will know God. Every human being will be full of the knowledge, will, and ways of God. No one will be ignorant about God.

Isaiah's prophecy is about the earth during the thousand-year reign of Christ. During this time the earth we now live on will be brought to a nearly perfect state. But the new earth that will be created at the end of the thousand-year rule of Christ will be absolutely perfect. This new creation will be the perfect paradise with animals, mountains, trees, grasses, flowers, bees, butterflies, and all the things that make up the earth's ecosystem—only there will be no curse of death. There will be no violence and no killing, not by people or animals.

Other prophets in the Bible have also foretold of a time of peace upon the earth. The prophet Ezekiel writes, "And I will make with them a covenant of peace, and will cause the evil beasts to cease out of the land: and they shall dwell safely in the wilderness, and sleep in the woods" (Ezekiel 34:25 KJV). There is indeed a future of absolute peace for the people of God. We will enjoy peace from burdens of responsibilities and schedules, the fear of embarrassment, the fear of failure, the fear of harm or danger, the fear of lack, and the fear of loss of employment.

One of my most often recurring bad dreams is one in which I find myself out of a job and experiencing the uncertainty and anxiety of not knowing how I will provide for my wife and myself. In some countries there is the fear of starvation. In heaven and in the new earth, however, we will be completely free of all such fears.

We will also be free from the fear of some great, unknown catastrophe. We will be free from the fear of flying, public speaking, and illness. We will be free from the fear of storms, exposure, or loneliness. We will be free from the fear of the dark, ghosts or spirits, or noises at night. We will be free from the fear of death and the end of the world. God will wipe away all tears from our eyes, and there will be no more death nor sorrow or tears (Revelation 21:4). Everything that plagues us today by robbing us of peace and causing fear or anxiety will be completely done away with. Then we will rejoice in the God of our salvation, who is also our protector.

The Dream

It was only a dream. I don't claim to have seen a vision. I don't claim to have any gift of interpreting dreams, visions, or any such thing. I don't claim to have visited heaven. I share my experience reluctantly because what I have presented thus far has been based on information taken from the Bible. I do not claim that my experience is any true representation of heaven. I only share this dream as a point of illustration.

One night when I was in my early thirties, I went to bed and had a dream. In this dream, I found myself in a long procession of other Christians lined up outside the city of heaven, waiting to proceed, but the line wasn't moving. We were all waiting for something. The thing that was most memorable to me and had the greatest impact on my mind was the absolute peace I felt. In the dream I had evidently died and was with a number of other saints preparing to enter heaven. I was filled to overflowing with joy and happiness and very deeply relieved to be there. There was absolutely no concern about the fact that my body had died. I did not feel in any way diminished. In fact, I felt great! I kept saying, "I made it! I can't believe I made it! I'm here! I'm actually here! It's all over and I made it!"

This may sound callous, but I didn't think about my wife, my three small children, or anyone else left behind on earth. There were no worries or concerns about their welfare. They were in God's hands, and I was totally free from care. I overflowed with peace and joy. The thought that all my struggles and troubles were over gave me so much release that it was indescribable.

In addition to the great peace I experienced, I found that I was able to defy gravity. I ascended about six feet into the air to look down the line to see what was happening ahead. I saw Jesus and Peter standing near a well and looking at a set of what appeared to be plans or blueprints.

Then Jesus turned to me and said, "You have to go back." I begged and pleaded with Him not to send me back. I said, "Lord, please! Please! Please don't send me back down there!" But He didn't argue with me. My pleading did no good. Without changing the tone in His voice, He simply repeated, "You have to go back."

I suddenly awakened from the dream, totally disoriented. For an instant, I didn't know what day it was or which direction I was facing. As I became reoriented, I awakened my wife and told her about the beautiful dream I had just had. I could still feel the deep disappointment.

Even though my experience was only a dream, there are certain aspects of it that harmonize with the Scriptures. One of the most appealing things about heaven in my dream is the absolute peace that I experienced. This kind of peace that is beyond human comprehension is promised in the Bible (Philippians 4:7). The freedom and release from the cares and responsibilities of life that I experienced in my dream are also promised in the Word.

The Scriptures also inform us that once we enter heaven, there is a deep desire to stay there rather than return here. Remember that Paul said he would rather be absent from the body and present with the Lord (2 Corinthians 5:8). Everything in the Bible suggests that no one who enters heaven will want to leave and return to earth.

The feelings of absolute joy and happiness are also validated in the Scriptures, as well as the feeling that nothing about me was incomplete or missing. The fact that I was able to defy gravity in my dream is at least suggested in the Bible by the promise that when Christ returns we will rise to meet Him in the air (1 Thessalonians 4:17). There is also the promise that we will be like Him (1 John 3:2).

When we enter heaven, we will be completely unburdened, just as I experienced it in my dream. Depression, pain, hopelessness, boredom, failed relationships, job loss, bereavement, health issues, lack of self-worth, lack of fulfillment, chemical imbalance, mental illness, financial challenges, disappointment, obesity, betrayal, and broken dreams are just some of the things we struggle with in this world. They are mixed in with the good times so that our experience on earth is a bittersweet burden that becomes weightier for some of us as the years disappear behind us.

God promises that heaven will be such an awesome place and experience that we will live there eternally, never to die again, yet always wanting to continue the experience. There will be overwhelming peace, but absolutely no anxiety. There will always be excitement, but never boredom. We will never become weary of living and want to end it all. As we enter our new eternal home, we will suddenly be faced with the stark realization that there is absolutely nothing to be concerned or worried about. The peace and finality of the end of our struggle on earth will be like tons of weight lifted off our shoulders, and we will be with the Lord for all eternity. Heaven is indeed worth the wait.

Pursue Peace

While we wait for this great time of peace to overtake us, God's people are urged to practice living in peace and do what we can to promote a climate of peace, right now during this present life. Peace must become our primary pursuit (1 Peter 3:11). Wayne Grudem aptly remarks, "To seek peace and pursue it recalls Jesus' statement, 'Blessed are the peacemakers' (Matthew 5:9). To work for reconciliation and harmony among people (rather than returning evil for evil) is pleasing to God."[4]

William Barclay discusses four virtues that are necessary in this pursuit of peace: "These four great virtues of Christian life—humility, gentleness, patience, love—lead to the fifth, peace. Peace may be defined as right relationships one with another. This oneness, this peace and these right relationships can be preserved only in one way. Every one of the four great Christian virtues depends on the obliteration of self. As long as self is at the centre of things, this oneness can never fully exist."[5]

Howard Marshall adds, "It is important to understand that we cannot hope to succeed in the pursuit of any spiritual virtue and certainly not the o*bliteration of self* without hard work and the help of God. *Pursue expresses vigorous effort to attain something.*"[6]

The attainment of peace must become a serious goal. We have to realize how important this virtue is in the Christian life and work to attain it. It helps to reflect on the words of the apostle Paul: "That's why I work and struggle so hard, depending on Christ's mighty power that works within me" (Colossians 1:29 NLT). We are partners together with God in the pursuit of peace. Without God's help our best effort will surely fail. We are admonished in the Scriptures to work hard, using the power that God gives us to pursue peace as we wait for the time when living in peace will no longer be fleeting and elusive. The day is coming when obtaining peace will no longer be the struggle that it is today. When that day comes, living in peace and harmony will be as natural as breathing.

Chapter 7 | Thought-provoking Questions

1. When will God's promise of peace on earth be realized?
2. Peter predicted that scoffers would come in the last days. What did Peter predict that they would say?
3. What did Peter say is the reason the Lord is waiting before returning to earth?
4. What did Jesus predict that the earth would be like before He returned?
5. What will conditions be like in the animal kingdom during Christ's thousand-year reign on earth?
6. What are we urged to do as we wait for this time of world peace?

CHAPTER 8
Joy and Pleasure Forever

Thou wilt shew me the path of life: in thy presence is fullness of joy; at thy right hand there are pleasures for evermore.

(Psalm 16:11 KJV)

Joy can be described with words like pleasure, delight, rapture, ecstasy, satisfaction, and happiness. God is a God of joy and pleasure. He intentionally created human beings with the capacity to experience these wonderful emotions from the very beginning. Pleasure or the anticipation of pleasure has the capacity of triggering joy in our lives. Without realizing it, we experience an almost continual flow of pleasurable experiences throughout our entire lives. God created us in such a way that we are able to experience pleasure through our physical senses and emotions. One or more of these senses is being fed pleasurable experiences on a continual basis. It is up to us to choose to give our attention to them and enjoy them.

We experience the pleasure of taste through our taste buds. A juicy steak, a chocolate sundae, or a good cup of coffee are just a few examples of the thousands of pleasurable experiences we enjoy through our sense of taste. The downside is that these experiences are so pleasurable that they sometimes entice us to eat too much of the wrong things.

The fragrance of flowers, cologne, or perfume gives us pleasure through our sense of smell. The appetizing smell of bacon cooking or coffee percolating are both pleasurable aromas. The fresh smell of a baby after a bath or the natural smell of a newly mowed lawn are simple pleasures that excite the joy of living within us.

We also enjoy the pleasures we experience through the sense of feeling or touch. Examples of this would be holding the hand of the person we love, experiencing a gentle caress, or holding one of our children or grandchildren. We derive pleasure from the soothing feeling of a warm bath or hot shower, or a cool breeze on a hot day. We enjoy the pleasure of the comforting feeling of a warm bed at the end of a hard day, and of course, there is the pleasure of sexual intimacy between a husband and his wife.

Our sense of sight feeds us the pleasure derived from beholding beautiful things such as the sight of winter snow, snow-capped mountains, a garden of flowers, a clear blue sky, the moon and stars at night, or the human figure. We enjoy the pleasure of watching a movie or observing butterflies flitting from flower to flower.

In a similar way, we receive pleasure through the exercise of our sense of hearing. We enjoy the sound of birds singing, bees buzzing, music playing, or children laughing. We enjoy the pleasures of a movie soundtrack, the distant sound of barking dogs, the howl of the wind, the rumble of a late-night train, or the honking of wild geese flying overhead. Even the absence of sound is pleasurable when we seek an escape from the noise of too many discordant sounds.

Exposure to one or a number of these pleasurable experiences through our senses and emotions is almost constant. Every one of these experiences has the capacity to trigger inner feelings of joy. When we fall in love, it is triggered by the pleasure we receive from the person to whom we are attracted. All of our senses or certain combinations of them excite something inside our center of emotions and create pleasurable feelings of joy and the desire to be near the person we have come to love.

The great lift and intoxicating feelings we experience when we fall in love and the warm and comforting pleasure we experience when we look at our children and grandchildren are of God's making and design. God has gifted us with the pleasure of love, laughter, excitement, adventure, and thrills. There are also the emotional pleasures that are tied to accomplishing some great or small task, as well as those extended to us by being in the company of friends and family. These are just a few examples of the pleasurable experiences God has designed for us to enjoy.

Additionally, God has given us the ability to recall and imagine. With our minds, we can call up pleasurable experiences from the past, relive them, and receive even more pleasure from them. When we see someone staring into space with a big smile, we know from experience that he or she is reliving a pleasurable moment. We can also receive pleasure by looking forward with anticipation to coming events such as a vacation, wedding, or graduation.

Of course, we can become oblivious to this steady stream of pleasures that are designed to give us joy. We can take them for granted, tune them out, ignore them, and choose instead to focus on the cares and concerns that create anxiety and fear rather than joy. Unfortunately, this is exactly what too many of us choose to do. We take little time to stop and enjoy the many pleasures that stream in through our senses because along with this steady stream of pleasures is also a steady stream of distractions and demands.

The world that we now inhabit is an environment that challenges the enjoyment of pleasures. The struggles to survive and get ahead often drown out the pleasures that are all around us. The troubles and challenges of this world keep us distracted from enjoying the good things that God has given to us for our pleasure. But if we stop, pay attention, and begin to notice and relish the continual stream of pleasures that God is giving us, our lives will be so much more enjoyable. That's why God, through the letters of Paul, instructs us exactly on what to focus our minds. He urges us to "fix [our] thoughts on what is true and honorable and right. Think about things that are pure and lovely and admirable. Think about things that are excellent and worthy of praise" (Philippians 4:8 NLT).

In heaven the troubles and distractions are removed and the pleasures dramatically heightened and enhanced. There are no worries or cares to compete with the enjoyment of these pleasures or distract us from drinking in every moment. Our new bodies will be designed to take it all in and revel in the good pleasures and joys God has for us. We will enjoy the memories of past pleasures in heaven while living out present ones and looking forward to the pleasures of the future.

To understand the joy that heaven promises, we need to resort to some frame of reference. By drawing from past and present experiences of joy, we can reflect on these good feelings and remind ourselves that this is what heaven is like, only far better.

Think of the happiest, most exciting, and joyful day of your life. Was it graduation day? Was it your wedding day or the day you had your first child? Perhaps it was the day you retired.

Without a doubt, the happiest day of my life was my wedding day. The thing I wanted most in life was to marry the girl of my dreams and raise a family. I awakened with the sense that the day I had long awaited had finally come and my dreams were about to come true. I was full of joy and happiness. Everything went as planned, and by four o'clock on the evening of May 13, 1972, I was a married man. But even though all seemed right with the world during those memorable days, there were little nagging concerns, fears, and worries that nipped at my mind. Then, the four-day honeymoon was over, and I had to come back down to earth, where the cares and concerns of everyday living were waiting for me. However, being married to my dream girl made life much better from that day forward. The struggles of life are much more bearable with someone helping to share the load, but there are struggles nonetheless.

Heaven is like the happiest, most joyful day of your life multiplied many times over but with absolutely nothing to mar it. Imagine such a joy-filled experience with no little nagging fears or dread in the back of your mind. Imagine that the joy and excitement you derive from that experience will never end but only increase— that there is no let-down but continuation and intensification of joy as the months and years pass. Now imagine that you have the energy and capacity to enjoy it all without ever growing weary or breaking down. Finally, imagine growing right along with that ever-increasing joy. That's what heaven promises, joy that only increases and never ends. In heaven we will forever be in God's presence, and in His presence is fullness of joy and pleasures that will never cease—only increase.

There are many things that bring me joy, but as a parent and now a grandparent, one of the most joyful times of the year for me is the Christmas season. From the time our children were born, we have enjoyed celebrating Christmas. When our first child was a toddler, we received great joy and delight in going to the stores and shopping for little dolls, stuffed animals, and pull toys to give to her on Christmas Day. We experienced great joy when she grew old enough to desire and appreciate certain toys. She would watch the toy commercials on television and express a desire for the things that appealed to her. We delighted in telling her to wait until Christmas to see what she would get. We derived more joy than she did as we watched her open each gift and squeal with satisfaction and delight. As our family grew from one child to three, the joy of the Christmas season increased threefold. The pleasure we received from giving to the ones we loved was our gift, and that gift of joy far exceeded the gratification we derived from the other gifts we received. We felt joy because we had brought joy to the objects of our love and affection, our three children.

The joy of the Christmas season that I sought to pass on to my children was rooted in my own childhood experiences. When I was a child, Christmas Day was a day of great joy and peace in the Sullivan household. It may not have been a time of peace on earth, but it was a time of peace and goodwill in our modest little home. Even my sister and I buried the hatchet and got along, at least through the morning hours of the day. Somehow, without even being told, we knew that this was a time to demonstrate kindness and patience with each other. We would have plenty of time to resume sibling hostilities after this special time of peace and goodwill.

Although we were not lavished with gifts, we all got at least one, and we also received a great deal of love and affirmation. We were so excited about the day that we had awaited for so long, it was difficult to sleep. The radio stations began playing Christmas music just before Thanksgiving Day. The television commercials heralded the coming event on our 21-inch black-and-white screen. As the great day of our dreams and anticipation approached, our joy and excitement grew. The excitement of the holiday season was heightened by the Christmas decorations that adorned our little town of Humboldt, Tennessee. Although belief in Santa Claus was never a tradition in our home, friendly adults asking what we wanted Santa to bring us contributed to our mounting excitement and piqued our anticipation.

About a week before Christmas, my parents would make the traditional Christmas trip to the store and return with a large grocery box filled with fruit, candy, and nuts. The arsenal, where my dad worked in nearby Milan, would also provide all the employees with a Christmas basket that contained a ham or turkey, a box of peanut and coconut brittle, a box of delicious assorted chocolates, an assortment of nuts, and a huge peppermint stick. When Christmas Eve finally arrived, we were so filled with joy and excitement that we felt as if we would explode. My mother would begin her annual Christmas Eve ritual of baking cakes and cooking Christmas dinner. I can still hear the whirl of the mixer as she mixed the cake batter from scratch. She used a cake pan to trace wax paper as she lined each pan to prevent the cake from sticking. Then, she poured the batter into each pan. There was no other aroma like that of cakes baking in the oven on Christmas Eve.

In an attempt to hasten the arrival of Christmas morning, we would voluntarily go to bed early and try to sleep away the remaining hours—but to absolutely no avail. Instead of falling asleep early, we would lie awake late into the night, waiting for sleep to take us. Christmas Eve would usually be one of the longest nights of the year. We would lie there with our eyes closed, trying to find sleep, but our minds were wide open, racing with thoughts of the expected festivities of the coming day. I would always be the last to finally fall asleep, usually sometime past midnight, but my eyes would pop open long before daylight on Christmas morning. We would awaken our parents and ask permission to open our present. Sometimes they would order us back to bed, but sometimes they would rise and allow us to open the gift they had bought for each of us. Christmas Day never disappointed us. We relished every minute of the day, which was spent playing, feasting, and spending time with family and friends.

The two most difficult things about my Christmas experiences as a child were the long wait for the day to arrive and the short time it all lasted. Although the wait for Christ's return for His entire church has been very long, the good news is that our wait to go and be with Him is only one short lifespan, and once we get there the experience will never end. It is worth repeating that the instant we close our eyes for the last time on this earth, we open them in heaven. Then, the joy and pleasure of being in God's presence and with His people instantly begins. Pleasure is defined as "a source of happiness, joy, or satisfaction. Pleasure can also be defined as recreation, relaxation or amusement, especially as distinct from work or everyday routine."[1]

We experience samples of that joy and pleasure here on earth. But what we experience here is only a tiny foretaste of what we can expect to experience there. That's another reason the apostle Paul said that he would rather be absent from the body and present with the Lord (2 Corinthians 5:8). That's why he said to depart and be with Christ is far better than remaining on earth (Philippians 1:23). Christians should stop thinking in terms of death and begin the practice of thinking in terms of departure and the continuation of life. We simply depart this life for the far better life that awaits us.

In his book, *Heaven*, Randy Alcorn talks about the number of people who depart this life every day. He comments, "Worldwide, three people die every second, 180 every minute, and nearly 11,000 every hour. If the Bible is right about what happens to us after death, it means that more than 250,000 people every day go either to Heaven or Hell."[2]

If only one out of ten or 10 percent of these people are true Christians, then at least twenty-five thousand people leave this earth and enter heaven every day, and 9,125,000 enter heaven each year. This means that there is a continual procession of angels escorting those who transition from this earth to heaven.

We are led to believe that death is a journey we must make alone. But true Christians are really never alone, not in life nor in death. Christ is with us every second of our lives, and He doesn't leave us at the time of our death. His presence only becomes more real to us as we move from this stage of life on earth to life eternal. Angels, or watchers (as they are called in the Old Testament), are also with us (Daniel 4:17). They watch over God's people and minister to us. Although we cannot see them during life on earth, they reveal themselves and escort us to heaven the instant we die (Hebrews 1:14; Luke 16:22). It is also important to understand that death is not a journey, but more like a door with a sign above it marked "Exit" and "Entrance." As we exit this life, we enter the next. Jean Syswerda puts it this way, "Death is only a doorway, a split second leap from this reality to the next."[3] We make this leap through the door, and we're instantly able to see and know things we cannot see and know here on earth.

Habermas and Moreland uses the same metaphor to describe the passageway from this life to the next: "God through Christ has turned death into the door that opens to the fullest possible joy—heavenly bliss (Psalm 16:11)."[4]

On this side of life we see death as a fearsome intruder, a grim reaper. But on the other side of life we see death as the exit from struggle to freedom, toil to rest, and sorrow to joy. It is comforting to know that we will not pass through this portal alone. Immediately after death our eyes will be opened, and we will see all that we cannot see now. We will see Jesus, multitudes of angels, and countless numbers of fellow Christians surrounding us, welcoming us, and sharing in the joy and delight that is in God's presence.

An example of this ability to see the unseen is presented in the second book of Kings. The prophet Elisha and his servant awoke one morning to find themselves surrounded by thousands of menacing Syrian enemy soldiers. The servant was deeply distressed when he saw the terrifying host with horses and chariots filling the hillsides around them. He cried out in panic, but Elisha calmed him by telling him that those who were with them far outnumbered their enemies. The servant was bewildered because all he saw were the enemy soldiers. Then Elisha prayed and asked God to open his servant's eyes and allow him to see. God did so, and suddenly he saw what previously had been concealed from human eyes and revealed only to Elisha. There, surrounding the enemy was a host of angels with fiery horses and chariots (2 Kings 6:15-23). They were there all the time, but cloaked. That is exactly the way it is with the angels that minister to us. They are there, but concealed. They care about us and are assigned to help us. When our life is over on this earth, they will appear to us and escort us to heaven.

As the royal children of the King of the universe, we will leave this part of our lives behind and enter into the joy of the Lord, and

God Himself will welcome us in (Matthew 25:23). In comparison to the part of our life that is ahead of us, this life is like a night of weeping, even for those of us who lead rich and rewarding lives. The life that awaits us is like the sunrise of a brand-new day and the end of night (Psalm 30:5). The contrast between this portion of our lives and that part beyond the portal of death is, indeed, as stark as the contrast between night and day.

Jesus comforted His disciples who were grieving over the news that He would have to suffer and leave them for a while. He pointed their attention to the great joy that was ahead of them.

> I tell you the truth, you will weep and mourn over what is going to happen to me, but the world will rejoice. You will grieve, but your grief will suddenly turn to wonderful joy. It will be like a woman suffering the pains of labor. When her child is born, her anguish gives way to joy because she has brought a new baby into the world. So you have sorrow now, but I will see you again; then you will rejoice, and no one can rob you of that joy.

(John 16:20-22 NLT)

The joy that is to come is preceded by periods of weeping and mourning. Jesus attempted to help His disciples deal with the time of sorrow that stood between them and their upcoming joy by urging them to fixate on that future joy rather than the immediate suffering. He emphasized the fact that their grief would suddenly be turned to joy. He wanted them, and us, to understand that the joy that is to come will be as sudden as death or as sudden as His return.

To illustrate the transition from sorrow to joy, Jesus uses the analogy of a woman in the throes of childbirth. The pains of labor rack the body of the delivering mother. It is a terrible time of suffering. But when the baby finally comes, the pain of delivery is replaced by the joy of knowing that the pain is past and a new baby has been born. The pain is forgotten and the joy remembered.

When our first child was born, my wife was in labor for forty-eight hours. I felt so helpless that I wanted to escape the scene and wait in the waiting room. I ached for her but couldn't do much to relieve her pain. When our little baby girl was finally delivered, however, the suffering disappeared into the past. It was swallowed up by the great joy of being able to hold our very own child, the product of our own bodies and the love we shared. The anticipated joy to come, as the result of the actual birth of a child, was what helped to endure the suffering that preceded it.

God's love for us is like the love of a mother who is willing to endure the pains of childbirth to hold her child in her arms. Jesus uses this metaphor of labor and childbirth to describe how God's people will transition from sorrow to joy at the sight of seeing Him again. But the writer of Hebrews uses the same metaphor to convey the deep love of God and His willingness to give up the Son He loves to bring many children into His family.

> God, for whom and through whom everything was made, chose to bring many children into glory. And it was only right that he should make Jesus, through his suffering, a perfect leader, fit to bring them into their salvation.

(Hebrews 2:10 NLT)

God used the suffering of Christ to deliver millions upon millions of baby Christians into the glory of being born into His family and then living with Him both now and in heaven.

After encouraging His disciples to focus on the joy that would follow their sorrow, Jesus followed His own counsel by fixing His mind upon the joy beyond the torture and abuse he chose to experience for us. He added pleasure to the excruciating pain He suffered while hanging for six hours on the cross. He meditated on the joy that awaited Him beyond the suffering, as well as His return to His place in heaven. He occupied His mind before and during the suffering by thinking of all of us who would be in heaven with Him because of the very suffering He endured. He set His mind on the joys ahead instead of the momentary suffering He had to endure. The author of Hebrews puts it this way, "He was willing to die a shameful death on the cross because of the joy he knew would be his afterward" (Hebrews 12:2 NLT).

When I was growing up in Tennessee, my cousin "Nick" would come from Indiana each year for a visit. Nick was the kind of fun-loving, life-of-the-party guy people loved to be around. He brought excitement into a room. There was never a dull moment when he was around. He was mischievous yet good-natured and loads of fun. The summer of the year I turned twelve and he turned thirteen, Nick's mother arranged to make the trip through Humboldt by catching a ride with some friends. They dropped him off at our house and continued on to Memphis for a church convention. The plan was to pick him up in about a week on their return trip. He was instructed to be ready to go when they returned because the driver was on a tight schedule and had to be back in Indianapolis by a certain time.

    Nick and I became so attached to each other and were having so much fun rambling in the woods, climbing trees, flirting with girls, and swimming in the ponds that the week went by much too fast. As the time for his departure approached, we decided we weren't ready to part company. As the week wound down to the last day, we were both very sad at the prospect of his leaving so soon, so we hatched a plan. On the morning he was scheduled to leave, we decided to hide back in the woods until they had to go ahead and leave him behind with my family. We made the calculation that his mother would finally be forced to leave him because she knew he would be safe with us. After all, his mother and mine were sisters, so most summers he would spend several weeks with us anyway. We felt short-changed with this one-week arrangement. We knew that the people she was carpooling with could only wait a few hours before having to leave, so we waited it out.

    I knew from the beginning that my daddy wouldn't be happy about this little rebellion of ours. I was about 100 percent sure I'd get a good whipping with his belt for my part in all this, but I was willing to pay the price. I knew the whipping would hurt, but I also realized that it wouldn't hurt long. I also knew that after the pain was over, all would be forgiven, and my buddy would be able to stay for at least another week, if not more. I had counted up the cost and was willing to pay the price. I thought it was worth the pain to have him to hang out with for a while longer. Nick's father had passed away years earlier, and because he had no father in his life, I doubt if he knew the price we would both have to pay for our little rebellion. But there was no question in mind that we would pay for this because I was my father's son. I didn't tell Nick in any great detail what we had coming for fear it might scare him into abandoning the plan.

    So we carried out our little plan. Early on the morning of Nick's scheduled departure, he and I were nowhere to be found.

Teach Me About Heaven and Eternal Life

We found a place far enough back in the woods that we knew they would never find us. My oldest brother was the look-out man. His assignment was to covertly come tell us when they had finally left town. Everything worked just as we planned it. They waited and waited until they couldn't wait any longer and finally left without Nick. My brother came to give us the "all clear." He told us they were gone but that everybody, including my daddy, was very angry with both of us. I felt a mixture of joy over the fact that Nick was going to stay and be with us for a while longer, but my heart began to pound at the thought of the ordeal of facing daddy.

We came out of hiding, slowly walked up the dusty road to the house, and faced the music. Dad put his belt to both our backsides—Nick first, then me. He was harder on me because I was his son and knew better. I have to admit that for a few minutes, during the worst part of that whipping, I wondered if Nick was worth all this, *Maybe I should have just let him go back home.* But a few minutes after the pain was over, there was only joy as we, figuratively, licked our wounds and anticipated all the fun we would have in the next few days. Nick ended up staying nearly another whole month before taking the Greyhound bus back home. That ended up being the best summer we ever had.

Shared Experiences

The example of what I was willing to suffer to have my cousin with me for a few days may not be the best possible illustration, but hopefully it helps to convey in some small way what Jesus felt for us when He faced the cross. The greatest joy that Jesus envisioned was the joy of having us with Him and His Father in heaven and sharing the fun and excitement of heaven with us. His passionate prayer to His Father concerning the longing in His heart to have us with Him in heaven is very revealing. He prayed, "Father, I want these whom you have given me to be with me where I am. Then they can see all the glory you gave me" (John 17:24 NLT).

The glory of Christ will be seen in the beauty and splendor of His own person and in his new creation. It will be seen and experienced in every mountain, animal, rock, tree, angel, planet, star, redeemed person, and the holy city, "New Jerusalem." Everything we will see and experience will be part of the glory of Christ that He wants to share with us. Jesus' love for us, and His desire to have us with Him, is very clear and powerful in the preceding verse of Scripture. When you love someone, you want that person to be with you wherever you are. You want to share everything you have with the one you love. You want what is yours to become theirs.

My wife and I like to travel. We especially like to go on road trips in the car or travel by train because it allows us to see so much more of the countryside. As we traverse the beautiful American countryside, every time we see some spectacular sight she points it out to me or I to her, and we take it all in together. Whenever I travel alone and see some beautiful spot, I think to myself, *I wish Joyce was here to see this.* Sometimes I take pictures to show her, but no picture can convey the experience of actually being there. Shared experiences are the most rewarding experiences. It is double the fun and joy to share experiences with the people you love.

Joyce and I founded and operated a Christian school in urban Indianapolis for a number of years. Most of the children we served had never been out of the city. So it was our joy and delight to take them on trips and share with them the beauty and splendor of this great country. Each year we raised money and planned these sightseeing trips for our fourth- through sixth-grade students. We took them to Florida one year and allowed them to indulge all their senses as they experienced for themselves the wonders of this southernmost state. We wanted them to swim in the ocean, taste the seawater, see the palm trees and the wildlife, and experience 80-degree weather in the dead of winter. We took them to Washington, D. C., one year and they saw the White House, the monuments, the Smithsonian, and other great historical sites. Another year we took them to New York to tour the Empire State Building, Ground Zero, the Statue of Liberty, the Chrysler Building, Times Square at night, as well as to see a Broadway play, among other things.

We took them to many places and allowed them to see many things. I am absolutely sure that our joy in exposing them to these glorious things far exceeded their joy in seeing these things for the first time. Being with them during their first experience of all these things was, for us, like experiencing them for the first time all over again. We were giddy with joy over their joy. We were excited over

Teach Me About Heaven and Eternal Life

their excitement. We were gloriously happy over their happiness.

This is how Jesus feels about us. We have never been out of this world, but He has. He has seen and done an infinite number of joyful and wonderfully exciting things, and He wants to share them with us. He wants us to experience His glory and the glory of heaven. He wants us to be where He is and to lead us in discovering the glory of the new creation as it unfolds before us. Jesus loves us so much that He wants us to enjoy the things He enjoys and know the wonderful things He knows. He wants us to experience what He experiences. He wants to share all of the joys of heaven with us. When we finally get to heaven, we will be like little children from the country visiting the big city for the first time. We will gaze with wide-eyed amazement at the towering architecture and all the wondrous sights of our new country, and Jesus will be just as excited as we are.

Each year, before we took our students on these field trips, we had to make arrangements for them in advance. We contracted with a tour bus company to arrange the transportation for them. We made arrangements for their meals. Reservations were made at restaurants, tickets were reserved for the tours and shows, a tour guide was secured, and reservations were made at the hotels we would be staying in. We took care of all of our students' needs because we loved them, cared about them, and wanted this to be a very rewarding, educational, and joyful experience for them, with no loose ends to spoil the experience.

What we did for our students is a rather pale illustration of what Jesus has done for His children. He has made all the arrangements for us to make the trip to heaven to be with Him. He has made sure that everything we will need has been taken care of, and He has taken every precaution to be sure that nothing will spoil the joy of our experience when we go to live with Him. The apostle John recorded Jesus' words that clearly reveal His care for us and the arrangements He has made for our trip and residency.

> In my Father's house are many rooms; if it were not so, I would have told you. I am going there to prepare a place for you. And if I go and prepare a place for you, I will come back and take you to be with me that you also may be where I am.
>
> (John 14:2-3 NIV)

There is nothing that generates more joy than knowing that someone loves you and is delighted to have you with them. It is a fact that God has focused His love upon us. God loves us so much that the thing He wants most is for us to be with Him. Randy Alcorn makes a very relevant statement: "All heaven will be our special home. But Christ says, "In my Father's house are many rooms . . . . I am going there to prepare a place for you" (John 14:2). 'Place' is singular, but 'rooms' are plural. This suggests that Jesus has in mind an individual dwelling for each of us, which is a smaller part of the larger place and is home to us in the most unique sense. ('Room' is a cozy and intimate term)."[5]

Randy focuses our attention upon the fact that although Jesus has made plans for us as a group, he has not lost sight of our individuality. He will relate to us as a family but also as individual children with individual needs that will be addressed personally and intimately. The fact that He mentions the word "rooms" suggests that He has made plans for each one of us, person by person and name by name.

God has attempted to convey the depths of His love to us through His Word and deeds. We have been told throughout the Scriptures how much God loves us and what He has done to show it. When we enter His presence, the reality of His love and how very much He wants us will suddenly become crystal clear. But even then, there will be more for us to learn about His great love. Our understanding of His love and desire for us will continue to unfold throughout eternity. Our joy will increase exponentially as we go deeper and deeper into the knowledge of the depths of God's love for us.

These tender words from the psalmist convey the deep love that God has for us. They also help us understand why having us with Him in heaven is so important to Him and will bring Him so much joy.

> You made all the delicate, inner parts of my body and knit me together in my mother's womb. Thank you for making me so wonderfully complex! Your workmanship is marvelous—how well I know it. You watched me as I was being formed in utter seclusion, as I was woven together in the dark of the womb. You saw me before I was born. Every day of my life was recorded in your book. Every moment was laid out before a single day had passed. How

precious are your thoughts about me, O God. They cannot be numbered! I can't even count them; they outnumber the grains of sand! And when I wake up, you are still with me!

(Psalm 139:13-18 NLT)

    This passage reveals how intimately involved our God is with the details of our lives and existence. God knew us before we were conceived, and He carefully orchestrated our development from the very moment of conception. Especially revealing about the nature of God's love is the amount of time He spends thinking about us. His thoughts about us are precious and numberless, outnumbering the very grains of sand on the seashore. God's attitude toward us is not casual. He is intensely interested in our lives. Indeed, He is deeply involved in the lives of His children from the beginning of life on this planet and will be throughout eternity. He has been working and planning the restoration of all things even before creation (Ephesians 1:4).

    God anticipated humanity's sin even before the foundation of the world. He knew before creating human beings that they would rebel against Him and plunge the world into darkness. Jesus, the Son of God and creator and sustainer of all things, was fully aware that He would have to suffer and die a terrible death to rescue humanity from their choice to corrupt themselves and the world. Even though He fully understood the harm, pain, and damage we would do to the world, ourselves, and God Himself, He said, "Let us make man in our image, after our likeness" (Genesis 1:26 KJV). That's love!

    As human beings, we know before we have children that there will be certain sacrifices we will have to make for them. We cannot anticipate many of the things our children will do that will cost us in pain, anguish, and money. However, despite the sacrifices we do anticipate, as well as those we know we can't, we still want children so badly that we have them anyway. But imagine knowing every destructive thing every one of your children will do to hurt you, your other children, and the world you so lovingly created. Imagine knowing every murder, robbery, and rape each one of your children will commit against your other children. Imagine knowing everyone who will suffer and die in every war from the beginning of history until the end. Imagine knowing everyone who will suffer and die as the result of disease, famine, and starvation. Imagine having to watch and endure the suffering and deaths of millions upon millions of your children and knowing all the violence they will bring upon the earth.

Why would God go ahead and have children in spite of the fact that He knows all these terrible things about their future? He did it because He loves us that much. His love is beyond our ability to understand. God loves every one of His children infinitely more than the most loving, caring parent on earth.

God has billions of children in this world who are all descendants of Adam. The fact that there are so many of us causes us to think that this diminishes God's love and care for so many children. The sheer vastness of all these numbers of people seems to render them impersonal to God, but this is not the case. God knows every person on this planet intimately. Earlier we noted how personally involved God is in the life and existence of each one of His children from conception, development, and adult life here on earth and beyond (Psalm 139:13-18). But the Bible also says that God knows every one of His children so well that the very hairs of our heads are all numbered (Luke 12:7). No parent has that kind of intimate knowledge of his or her children.

God wanted us to understand that although we will be a united community of people in heaven, we will each have personal time and attention from Him. Each one of us will be intimately and personally known by God. The apostle John writes, "Whoever has ears, let them hear what the Spirit says to the churches. To him who overcomes, I will give some of the hidden manna. I will also give him a white stone with a new name written on it, known only to him who receives it" (Revelation 2:17 NIV).

God will give each person who overcomes the world by faith and enters heaven, a secret name that is known only to Him and the person to whom it is given. That means we will have at least two names—the one that everyone uses to address us by and a secret name that only God uses. God will speak to us in total privacy using this secret name that no one else is privy to. What is the significance of this secret name? Intimacy. In heaven we will not be just one face in a sea of people in God's sight. Instead, there will be personal intimacy between God and us.

In my family, as with most families, I tagged my children with pet names that expressed my affection for them. They had formal names everyone used to address them by, but their pet names were intimate terms of endearment. These names spoke of a close and personal relationship between my children and me. Most people outside the family didn't know them by these names. On the occasions that their friends happened to be visiting and heard me inadvertently address one of them by a pet name, they were surprised or even amused by the secret name.

God will give each of us a name that is a secret between Him and us. For all eternity we will share something secret and special with God that no one else shares. God wants us to know that we are special to Him as individuals and we will never be lost in the crowd. He will give each of His children individual attention.

God also said that He will write His name and the name of His city, "The New Jerusalem," on each one of His children (Revelation 3:12). To wear the name of God and our new home, which is also our Father's address, will be one of the highest honors imaginable. We will be like our God and wear His name and the name of His new home and ours for all eternity. We will belong to Him and Him to us, forever and ever. This is one of many ways our God will demonstrate His love to us.

God's capacity to know us and love us is difficult for us to understand. His love is so broad, high, and deep that we have to take time to ponder and study it to even begin to understand it. Concerning God's great love, the apostle Paul writes,

> And I pray that Christ will be more and more at home in your hearts, living within you as you trust in him. May your roots go down deep into the soil of God's marvelous love; and may you be able to feel and understand, as all God's children should, how long, how wide, how deep, and how high his love really is; and to experience this love for yourselves, though it is so great that you will never see the end of it or fully know or understand it. And so at last you will be filled up with God himself.

(Ephesians 3:17-19 TLB)

We will never understand God's love until we pass from this life into heaven or are transformed, body and soul, when Christ returns for us. At that time a light will suddenly come on, and we will really begin to know something of the height, width, and depth of God's love. I am convinced that even then we will not fully know it. Our understanding of the greatness of God's love will be something that continually unfolds before us throughout all eternity. Throughout the eons of time, we will learn and grow in our knowledge of God's unfathomable love for us. With each new level of discovery of who God really is and of the things He has done for us, our knowledge of His love for us will increase, and our love for Him will also increase more and more. As our love and knowledge grows, so too will our joy from height to height and from glory to glory.

When we finally unite with Christ in heaven, there will be a great explosion of joy in our hearts and the heart of our Savior. Our joy will merge with His joy and fill heaven itself, and this will only be the beginning of the joys that we will experience there. There will be laughter, singing, and celebrations all over heaven. There will be everything to celebrate and nothing to dread or regret. Our Lord Jesus will experience even greater joy in receiving us into His presence than the joy we will experience in being there because of His great love for His children.

Perfected To Live Eternally

Looking forward to this great reunion in heaven with excitement and anticipation, the apostle Jude says, "Now all glory to God, who is able to keep you from falling away and will bring you with great joy into his glorious presence without a single fault (Jude 1:24 NLT). The King James Version says that God will present us before Himself *faultless with exceeding joy.* The New International Version says that God will present us before Himself *without fault and with great joy.* Each of these translations conveys the same idea but with slightly different words. When the time comes for us to depart this world, either by way of death or the return of Christ, we will be brought before God completely sinless and filled with overflowing, intense, and abounding joy. This is the kind of joy that will make us leap, dance, and shout. We will be sinless, faultless, completely unburdened of the cares and concerns of this life, and completely free to enjoy all the pleasures of heaven forever and ever.

Imagine living forever on earth as it is today without the joy that God provides those who love and follow Him. After Adam and

Eve fell into sin, God put an angel with a flaming sword to guard the tree of life to prevent them from eating its fruit and receiving eternal life in their miserable fallen state. Eternal life would be a curse, not a blessing, if we had to live forever in our present corrupt condition and environment in which we live.

In order to be able to enjoy eternal life the way God really wants us to, we need to be perfect in our bodies, minds, and spirits, and we have to live in a perfect environment. That's why God sent His Son to prepare the way for us to be perfected. Our spirits or souls are unburdened from sin and enter perfection at the instant of death, but our resurrection bodies are reunited with our spirits at the time of the resurrection and rapture. We will live eternally in our glorified resurrected bodies.

In order to be able to live eternally and enjoy it, we will be filled with joy. Every burden and care will be removed. We have absolutely no frame of reference to compare with a life that never ends. Imagine the misery that a person sentenced to live eternally would suffer if he or she were burdened with the cares of this life. Even one small burden might become increasingly more burdensome as time stretches into eternity. But heaven will not be a burden, it will be a celebration for eternity with continual new discoveries, new pleasures, new joys, and new things to enjoy perpetually. The joy will be progressive, increasing as we grow.

Because we cannot imagine life without struggle, the thought of life without end can be distressing. It is extremely difficult to divorce the struggles, pain, and disappointments of this present existence from the thought of eternal life. So, when we think of eternal life, we think of it as something that will eventually become boring, and tiresome. The thought of this kind of an eternal existence can be frightening. But God promises that the eternal life He provides for us is completely different from the present struggle that we now call life. Life as we now know it, in comparison to the life we shall know, is like life in a prison. It is life fraught with trouble. Job 5:7 (KJV) says, "Man is born unto trouble, as the sparks fly upward," and Ecclesiastes 1:2 says, "All is vanity." Paul tells us that the things we suffer in this present world are not worthy of comparison to the glory God will give us (Romans 8:18).

Our best life is indeed ahead of us. Our destiny is to be loosed from this prison life here on earth to enjoy the freedom and joys of eternal life with Christ. Despite the burdens and troubles of this life, with its mixture of joy and pleasure, we struggle to stay here rather than go there. But if we could really see heaven, our struggle would reverse itself. Our minds would be filled with thoughts of escaping this life and getting on with the next. In his book, *What the Bible Reveals About Heaven*, Daniel Brown comments on the life that lies ahead of us: "Each moment in Heaven will be so vivid, so new, so full of wonder and life that we will live in constant amazement and awe."[6]

The prophet Malachi describes this overwhelming joy of heaven in a way that reflects his exposure to farming and livestock. Speaking by the Spirit of God, he remarks, "But for you who fear my name, the Sun of Righteousness will rise with healing in his wings. And you will go free, leaping with joy like calves let out to pasture" (Malachi 4:2 NLT). Malachi gives us a picture of energetic little calves that had been locked into close quarters, hemmed in on every side and unable to move about freely as they desired. But suddenly the stall swings open, and they are let loose to romp in a huge meadow full of beautiful, lush, green grass with plenty of room to leap, play, graze, roll around, and lie down in. Being released from this life is literally like these little calves being freed from their prisons. They are freed to live life to its fullest measure.

The life that is ahead of us will be a continual party and a daily celebration—a veritable explosion of life with sights, sounds, colors, smells, feelings, and experiences that we cannot imagine. There is already a celebration going on in heaven every day, as God's saints depart this life and enter there. But the grand celebration is set for the day when Christ returns to earth with those saints, including our friends and loved ones who have gone ahead of us. He will then gather all of us who remain alive on earth, and then the party will begin.

Chapter 8 | Thought-provoking Questions

1. What are some of the pleasures that trigger feelings of joy in us?
2. How often are we being exposed to pleasurable things?
3. Why is the steady stream of pleasurable experiences often unnoticed by people?
4. What is God's advice on how to enjoy life's pleasures that He gives us?
5. To get a feel for the joy of heaven, what are we urged to do?
6. Why are Christians never alone in life or in death?
7. What are angels assigned to do for Christians?
8. Death is not a journey; it is more like _____.
9. What happens to our level of knowledge and awareness after death?
10. On this side of life, we see death as a fearsome intruder. How will we see it on the other side?

CHAPTER 9
Paradise Heaven

> *Then he said, "Jesus, remember me when you come into your Kingdom. And Jesus replied, "I assure you, today you will be with me in paradise."*
>
> (Luke 23:42-43 NLT)

As mentioned in chapter 2, these are the words of the dying thief who turned to Jesus in his last hours of life and acknowledged Him as the King. In so doing, the thief confessed his faith in Christ. Our Lord responded by promising that they would be together in paradise that very day.

So far, we have examined what it will be like to pass from this life to the next. We have examined what it will be like to have new, glorified bodies like Jesus' body. We have examined our glorified intellectual capacity. We have looked at the kinds of relationships we will have in heaven and the kind of society that will exist there. We have looked at the freedom, perfection, peace, pleasure, and joy we will experience there. But very relevant questions remain: What is the environment of this paradise that we call heaven like? What kind of ecosystem exists there? What is heaven's terrain like? What will the new heaven and the new earth be like in their make-up?

A careful examination of the original creation reveals God's plan and intent for earth and its inhabitants, thus showing us a bit of what heaven is like and what the future re-created earth and the new heaven will be like. The original earth was modeled after what is in heaven. So as we examine details from the account of the original creation recorded in Genesis, a picture of heaven unfolds, as well as one of the new earth of the future. Of course, there are many things that now exist in heaven and will exist in the new earth that were not included in the creation of this present earth. There are many things that God has chosen to keep secret, but by examining the books of Genesis and Revelation, we can glean more information about the environment of the new heavens and the new earth. Genesis is important because it records the beginning of things, and Revelation is important because it records the end of the old order of things and the beginning of the new.

Genesis 1:11-12 records the creation of trees and plants.

> Then God said, "Let the land sprout with vegetation—every sort of seed-bearing plant, and trees that grow seed-bearing fruit. These seeds will then produce the kinds of plants and trees from which they came." And that is what happened. The land produced vegetation—all sorts of seed-bearing plants, and trees with seed-bearing fruit. Their seeds produced plants and trees of the same kind. And God saw that it was good.

(Genesis 1:11-12 NLT)

God is master of the arts and sciences. He is the great lover of beauty. The greatest sculptor or painter can only capture forms that are crudely representative of what God has created. Yet God is the originator of beautiful sights, sounds, smells, forms, and textures. He does not work with lifeless materials such as paint and clay. He is the creator and sustainer of the beauties of life. He created beautiful sunrises and morning light shows with sun rays penetrating morning mists and falling on forest floors. He created the early stirring of birds just ahead of the morning light. God created towering trees, wildflowers, and the endless number of colorful designs that adorn nature.

Human artists, artisans, and designers have been inspired by nature since the beginning of creation. God is the master creator, and we behold, admire, and try to capture on canvas and other materials gestures of what He has done. When God creates a masterpiece, however, He is not limited to copying life. He creates things using the very elements of life and motion. Randy Alcorn expresses this concept well: "To study creation is to study the Creator. Science should be worshipful discovery because the heavens and all creation declare God's glory. God reveals his character in flowers, waterfalls, animals, and planets. God's name is written large in nature, in his beauty, organization, skill, precision, and attention to detail. He's the Master Artist."[1]

Yes, there is much of heaven to be seen in this earth and the universe around us. The Bible declares, "From the time the world was created, people have seen the earth and sky and all that God made. They can clearly see his invisible qualities—his eternal power and divine nature. So they have no excuse whatsoever for not knowing God" (Romans 1:20 NLT). Indeed, the whole earth is filled with His glory. The way a worm becomes a butterfly, the way a seed becomes a tree, and the sweetness and juiciness of a fresh piece of fruit are all products of His creative genius. His glory and majesty can be seen through the beauty of a sun-drenched summer morning or the radiant beauty of a sunset. The many pleasures that abound in earth and sky reflect something of the nature of God, our creator, and the new heavens and the new earth. A passionate botanist and Christian, George Washington Carver once exclaimed in wonderment, "You must learn to read the great and loving God out of all forms of the existence He has created. Converse with God. Oh, what a joy will come to you. Oh yes, God is so lavish in the display of his handiwork!"[2]

As the maker and master of all things, God is required to be more than creative. He has to understand the minutest details of the science and mechanics of life. More than creating a form to admire, God has to create atoms and molecules and fit them together to make up cells that are capable of functioning together with other cells to sustain and reproduce the life He infuses into things.

God plans and executes the ways each living organism interacts with other organisms to create a viable ecosystem that is sustainable. Birds and insects that have the capacity to move around in their environment are designed to pollinate flowers and budding plants that are immobile so they can reproduce after their own kind. One plant cannot uproot itself and walk over to another plant and pollinate it. Birds, insects, and the wind had to be programmed to do it for them. God designed plants with colorful blossoms, strong fragrances, and sweet nectar to attract birds and insects. He also designed the birds and insects with feathers, hairs, and a sweet tooth.

When the birds and insects feed on the nectar in the blossoms, they unintentionally pick up the pollen from one plant and then move to another plant for more nectar. When the pollen brushes off onto a plant of the same kind, pollination occurs. The plant can then produce fruit, or pods with fertilized seeds in them. When the fruit or pod ripens, the seeds are expelled, fall to the ground, and germinate. Some seeds are specifically designed to be carried away by the wind, while others are carried by water. Sometimes animals eat the fruit, and the seeds pass out of their bodies onto the soil in their feces. Some of these seeds germinate, new trees and plants are born, and they grow up to repeat the cycle. This is one of the ways God planned for vegetation to reproduce itself.

The Genesis account of creation does not tell us all that went into creation. God in His wisdom only recorded the simple facts of creation without delving into the science of creation. These simple facts, without the science behind them, cause some people to doubt the Genesis account. But from this portion of the account, we know that God made trees, grasses, plants, and flowers in the original creation and everything He designed had both form and function.

From this information in Genesis and Jesus' promise of paradise to the thief on the cross in the Gospel of Luke, we are able to deduce that heaven is a beautiful garden paradise adorned by a variety of trees, grasses, and beautiful flowering plants. Trees grow out of soil, so we can deduce that heaven as it exists today, along with the new earth, will have soil and beautiful vegetation.

The creation account also includes a mention of seas, rivers, and streams that are filled with fish and a variety of marine life, as well as birds that fill the skies.

> Then God said, "Let the waters swarm with fish and other life. Let the skies be filled with birds of every kind." So God created great sea creatures and every living thing that scurries and swarms in the water, and every sort of bird—each producing offspring of the same kind. And God saw that it was good. Then God blessed them, saying, "Be fruitful and multiply. Let the fish fill the seas, and let the birds multiply on the earth."
> (Genesis 1:20-22 NLT)

Since the original earth had lakes, streams, rivers, and seas that were full of fish and marine life and varieties of birds filled the skies above, it is reasonable to believe that we will see these things in heaven. However, although there will certainly be rivers and very likely large lakes and streams, there will be no seas in the new earth (Revelation 21:1). Perhaps God's plan is to use the space that the seas would have occupied to include more inhabitable land for people and animals. We can only speculate as to why God has decided not to include seas in the new world. Nevertheless, we can be sure that whatever He does in place of oceans will be spectacular and will not disappoint us in any way. Are there seas in heaven now? There is no information provided in the Scriptures to answer this question. So, any attempt to answer would be absolute speculation.

God freely expressed His masterful creativity when He made birds and marine life. When we look at the many different designs in color, texture, and form that decorate fish and birds, we are able to clearly discern that our creator is a lover of beauty and diversity in nature. He is not the God of the mundane or the drab. The explosive designs that He uses in the natural world are highly suggestive of His joyful and celebratory nature. Our God is a God of joy and delight, a God of laughter and celebration. God is a lover of fun, excitement, and pleasure.

Yet, He is also a God of order and complexity. No one who designs with the flair and generosity exhibited in the many natural wonders we enjoy on this planet could possess a morose or melancholy nature. When we look at the things He has created, we are convinced of His unfathomable intellect and His gloriously loving, tender, caring personality. After beholding and reflecting on creation, the psalmist was awestruck and remarked, "The heavens proclaim the glory of God. The skies display his craftsmanship. Day after day they continue to speak; night after night they make him known" (Psalm 19:1-2 NLT).

Our world is not the work of an aloof, uncaring, angry creator. In its original form there was only love and beauty, until it became marred by the curse of sin and the influence of the Evil One (Genesis 3). Heaven is not some completely foreign place where we have absolutely no frame of reference. We do have a frame of reference to go by—the original earth as it was created, perfect in form and function. Chuck Smith insightfully declares, "God has designed earthly things to be similar to heavenly things."³

Randy Alcorn details some of the similarities between heaven and the original earth:

> Scripture gives us images full of hints and implications about heaven. Put them together, and these jigsaw pieces form a beautiful picture. For example, we're told that heaven is a city (Hebrews 11:10; 13:14) . . . . Cities have buildings, culture, art, music, athletics, goods and services, events of all kinds. And, of course, cities have people engaged in activities, gatherings, conversations, and work. Heaven is also described as a country (Hebrews 11:16). We know about countries. They have territories, rulers, national interests, pride in their identity and citizens who are both diverse and unified. If we can't imagine our present earth without rivers, mountains, trees, and flowers, then why would we try to imagine the New Earth without these features?⁴

Daniel Brown agrees with Randy Alcorn. He adds, "Though constituted of dissimilar stuff, just as our glorified bodies will be composed of different substance than our earthly frames, the new cosmos will be as material and substantial and sensory as the old cosmos. Sky and soil and streets and banquet tables and crowns and music and light-all tangible and perceptible items—will exist in Heaven . . . . In Heaven there are trees and rivers, gates that never close and celebrations."⁵

I agree wholeheartedly with these pastors and authors and their conclusion that heaven will be much like the original earth. However, the original earth is only a beginning reference point for what heaven is like. It bears repeating that there will be many things in heaven that will be new to us. We will have bodies that are capable of doing things and fully enjoying these things that we have never known.

There will be things that will excite all our senses and would overwhelm us if we were not prepared for them by God. That's why we are told that "flesh and blood cannot inherit the kingdom of God" (1 Corinthians 15:50 KJV). What we will see and experience in heaven will be too much for these mortal bodies to handle. For example, the Bible says that God "lives in light so brilliant that no human can approach him" (1 Timothy 6:16 NLT). The sheer brilliance of God's glory and the light emanating from the saints and angels, along with the brightness of the light of heaven, would be too much for a mortal body to view and still survive.

On one occasion Moses asked God to allow him to see His glory. God informed Moses that no mortal could look at Him in His glory and survive the experience. So, God told Moses to hide in the cleft of a rock to shield him from the brilliance and consuming power of His glory. In this way, He allowed Moses to see just the trail of His glory. Even then, Moses' face absorbed some of the brilliance of God's glory, and his face began to shine like a light bulb (Exodus 33:18-23; 34:35).

Heaven is also filled with the light and glory of God and that of the saints and angels. But heaven and the new earth will someday merge, and God will live among His redeemed people (Revelation 21:3). While there will be many new things resulting from this heaven and new earth merger, much of it will be based and founded upon things that we know and are familiar with. Much of what we see and know now will be seen there. However, everything we see now has been tainted by the curse, while everything there will be absolute perfection.

The original creation included a large variety of land animals, such as livestock and wild life.

> Then God said, "Let the earth produce every sort of animal, each producing offspring of the same kind—livestock, small animals that scurry along the ground, and wild animals." And that is what happened. God made all sorts of wild animals, livestock, and small animals, each able to produce offspring of the same kind. And God saw that it was good.

(Genesis 1:24-25 NLT)

God created large and small land animals including elephants, cattle, insects, lizards, worms, snakes, and every conceivable kind of animal life—even dinosaurs. Although many of these animals have now become extinct, it is conceivable that we will see them in heaven and the new earth. We can expect to see dodo birds and other oddities. It is reasonable to expect that there will be dinosaurs, woolly mammoths, and mastodons roaming beside elephants, cattle, and bison grazing on beautiful grassy meadows.

We should look for mountain goats, rams, and sheep navigating great mountains. We can also expect to see pristine lakes, rivers, and streams teeming with beautiful fish and marine life. These fish will be for observing, not for catching and eating. Furthermore, we can expect great forests with beautiful flowering gardens and unspoiled wilderness areas.

On the sixth and final day of creation, God made Adam, and from this one man came all other human beings. It is not necessary for us to make a case for the presence of people in heaven, but the fact that heaven is now inhabited with millions of people suggests to us that every other thing God created on earth can now be seen in heaven and will likely be included in the new world. Genesis records,

> Then God said, "Let us make human beings in our image, to be like us. They will reign over the fish in the sea, the birds in the sky, the livestock, all the wild animals on the earth, and the small animals that scurry along the ground." So God created human beings in his own image. In the image of God he created them; male and female he created them. Then God blessed them and said, "Be fruitful and multiply. Fill the earth and govern it. Reign over the fish in the sea, the birds in the sky, and all the animals that scurry along the ground."

(Genesis 1:26-28 NLT)

It is evident from these three verses that God's original intent was for human beings to possess His image and likeness, populate the earth, and rule over it in righteousness. When Adam and Eve committed sin, they lost the likeness of God and failed to righteously rule over the planet. Instead, the sin that they were infested with was passed on to everyone until the whole world became sinful. Human beings began to exercise unjust and corrupt rule over the earth. Today we see the end result of that corrupt rule. We live in a world of wars, mass murders, terrorism, exploitation of the poor by the rich, and a preoccupation with violence.

God's plan of redemption through Jesus Christ includes restoring His likeness in us. The apostle John emphatically declares that when Jesus returns to earth, we will instantly become like Him (1 John 3:2). It is important to remember that this likeness of God occurs in all of us believers when we pass from this life to the next. Those of us who remain alive will be transformed into His likeness when Christ returns.

Moreover, whether we are dead or alive at Jesus' coming, God's plan to restore His righteous nature in us will allow us to regain our righteous rule over the earth, under Christ. Paul made this point unequivocally clear in his first letter to the saints at Corinth. Not realizing their lofty status as children of God and the wisdom God had given them to settle their own disputes, some of these Christians were taking each other to court before ungodly judges to settle their grievances. Paul rebuked them for this and then informed them of their future destiny as world rulers.

> Don't you realize that someday we believers will judge the world? And since you are going to judge the world, can't you decide even these little things among yourselves? Don't you realize that we will judge angels? So you should surely be able to resolve ordinary disputes in this life.

(1 Corinthians 6:2-3 NLT)

John also adds his testimony attesting to the fact that God's people will rule over the new world.

> And they sung a new song, saying, Thou art worthy to take the book, and to open the seals thereof: for thou wast slain, and hast redeemed us to God by thy blood out of every kindred, and tongue, and people, and nation; And hast made us unto our God kings and priests: and we shall reign on the earth.

(Revelation 5:9-10 KJV)

John prophesies of a day when true Christians would be given a new song to sing. In this song they would declare Jesus' worthiness to bring judgment upon the world for its rebellion and wickedness. The song also declares that Jesus was slain to redeem people of every nation on earth and had made them into kings and priests to rule on the earth.

The Prophet Daniel also prophesies of the day when God will return, subdue the earth, and turn rule and domination over to Christians.

> But in the end, the holy people of the Most High will be given the kingdom, and they will rule forever and ever." Then the sovereignty, power, and greatness of all the kingdoms under heaven will be given to the holy people of the Most High. His kingdom will last forever, and all rulers will serve and obey him."

(Daniel 7:18, 27 NLT)

God's original plan was for human beings to live in a world

of righteousness and peace that was governed by mankind. This human rule included a peaceful animal kingdom. An examination of Genesis 1:29-30 informs us that God's original intent was for people and animals to be vegetarians. They were created to eat fruits and vegetables, not each other.

> Then God said, "Look! I have given you every seed-bearing plant throughout the earth and all the fruit trees for your food. And I have given every green plant as food for all the wild animals, the birds in the sky, and the small animals that scurry along the ground—everything that has life." And that is what happened.

(Genesis 1:29-30 NLT)

God's original people and animals did not kill and eat flesh. Since the creation account declares that there was no death prior to Adam's sin, it directly contradicts the theory of evolution and natural selection, which declares that death has existed from the very beginning and is the means by which nature sorts out the weak and selects the strong to survive, flourish, and reproduce. The theory of evolution and the biblical account of creation are irreconcilable. They cannot both be true. One is true; the other is false.

The whole foundation of Christianity rests upon the literal interpretation of the Genesis account of creation and of when and how death entered the world. If it was not the result of Adam's sin being passed on to the world, then Christ could not have died to redeem us from sin. The foundation of the Christian faith falls apart if death is not the result of sin. If Genesis is not credible, then neither are these words from the Book of Romans: "When Adam sinned, sin entered the world. Adam's sin brought death, so death spread to everyone, for everyone sinned . . . For the sin of this one man, Adam, brought death to many. But even greater is God's wonderful grace and his gift of forgiveness to many through this other man, Jesus Christ" (Romans 5:12, 15 NLT). If Romans and Genesis are not credible, then neither are the words of Jesus, who emphatically declared that He came to give His life as a ransom for many (Matthew 20:28).

Survival of the fittest was not part of God's creation. The idea of natural selection was not then and is not now part of God's plan for the survival of species. Natural selection requires weakness and strength. In God's original creation there were no weak creatures. Natural selection requires the strong to kill and eat the weak; consequently, it requires the death of one species so that another might survive and thrive. But in God's original creation, every animal, fish, and bird ate only grass, vegetation, fruits, and grains. It was not until sin entered the world that death entered as the consequence of sin (Genesis 2:17; 3:19). After sin entered the world, animals began to kill and eat each other, and they became a food source for people as well. God did not sanction the eating of meat for human beings until after the flood (Genesis 9:3).

The animals in heaven are not carnivores, but herbivores. And as we discovered in chapter 7, all the animals in the new world will again become docile herbivores (Isaiah 11:6-9). Everything God originally created was excellent in every way. And the time is coming when He will restore all things to its original state of excellence and perfection, just as it is in heaven. Heaven is a paradise with many unfamiliar things, but there are also many things that are wonderfully familiar.

Through the words of the prophet Ezekiel, we are given some sketchy details of the topography of heaven, as well as a description of the kind of royal attire worn by those who live there. Ezekiel is pronouncing an indictment against Satan, referring to him as the "king of Tyre," possibly because he was the spirit that seduced the people of Tyre to carry out their wicked deeds. Also included in this condemnation of Satan is information surrounding his adornment, position, and workmanship—as well as some details of heaven's terrain.

> "Son of man, sing this funeral song for the king of Tyre. Give him this message from the Sovereign Lord: "You were the model of perfection, full of wisdom and exquisite in beauty. You were in Eden, the garden of God. Your clothing was adorned with every precious stone—red carnelian, pale-green peridot, white moonstone, blue-green beryl, onyx, green jasper, blue lapis lazuli, turquoise, and emerald—all beautifully crafted for you and set in the finest gold. They were given to you on the day you were created. I ordained and anointed you as the mighty angelic guardian. You had access to the holy mountain of God and walked among the stones of fire. "You were blameless in all you did from the day you were created until the day evil was found in you. Your rich commerce led you to violence, and you sinned. So I banished you in disgrace from the mountain of God. I

expelled you, O mighty guardian, from your place among the stones of fire.

(Ezekiel 28:12-16 NLT)

This passage strongly implies that the original garden of Eden was in heaven. This confirms that the Eden on earth was a replica of the one in heaven. We can also see that high fashion is a standard in heaven as it is on earth. Satan was a high angelic official, so he wore clothing that was beautifully adorned with very precious jewelry. His royal attire was specially tailored for him and set in the finest gold. We also see that Satan was issued his attire on the day God created him. Indeed, opulence and finery are not reserved for the royal courts and palaces of this earth. God values the finest of things, and He lavishes the most luxurious clothing and jewelry on those who are His. Heaven is a very fine place. We can be sure that the courts and palaces of heaven are highly stylistic architecture ornately decorated with the finest fabrics and gemstones imaginable.

This passage also mentions the mountain of God, which clearly indicates that heaven has beautiful and majestic mountains. If heaven has mountains, it would seem that there would also be valleys. Indeed, the beautiful mountains we enjoy on earth from the Grand Tetons in the American Northwest, to the Alps of southern Europe, to Mount Everest of the Himalayas are all mere replicas of the beautiful mountain peaks we will see in heaven. Will we climb them? Possibly. Will we ski down their slopes? Who can say? But I am convinced that the things we do on earth for excitement and an adrenalin rush will not even begin to compare with the excitement and pleasures that heaven and the new world holds for us.

Note that Satan wore fine clothing. This indicates that although he was a spirit being, he had a body that clothing adorned. The fact that God decked Satan out in fine apparel, jewelry, and precious stones reveals that He and the inhabitants of heaven approve and place value on these things. In fact, the value we place upon beauty, craftsmanship, and finery are values that have been imported from heaven.

Another example of the value that God places upon quality and craftsmanship can be found in the Book of Exodus. A whole chapter was dedicated to how the garments worn by Aaron and his sons should be designed and tailored (Exodus 28). These garments were designed to give them dignity and honor. The priests who served God wore stunningly beautiful and ornate garments made from the finest, skillfully woven fabric. God gave the tailors and craftsmen special wisdom to weave and craft each part of these priestly garments.

The finest earthly courts, palaces, art, architecture, and landscaping are pale reflections of their heavenly counterparts, which will be included in the new earth. Buckingham Palace would be considered cheap and gaudy in comparison to the palaces, parks, and courtyards of heaven. Further evidence that the things on earth are only replicas of those in heaven is provided by the author of Hebrews. Speaking about the tabernacle that Moses was instructed by God to make, he says,

> That is why the Tabernacle and everything in it, which were copies of things in heaven, had to be purified by the blood of animals. But the real things in heaven had to be purified with far better sacrifices than the blood of animals. For Christ did not enter into a holy place made with human hands, which was only a copy of the true one in heaven. He entered into heaven itself to appear now before God on our behalf.

(Hebrews 9:23-24 NLT)

The tabernacle was only a tent, designed to be used as the place of worship for the Israelites during their travels through the wilderness. Later, after they settled in Canaan, they were instructed to build a temple that more closely represented the one in heaven. Even the tent had posts and other parts that were fashioned or overlaid with gold. It included furnishings and vessels that are also replicas of the things that are in heaven. Note that Hebrews twice mentions the fact that the tabernacle, the temple, and everything in them were only copies of the things that are in heaven.

The apostle John was actually allowed to see the temple in heaven and look inside: "Then, in heaven, the Temple of God was opened and the Ark of his covenant could be seen inside the Temple" (Revelation 11:19 NLT). But as we will see, there will be no need for a temple in the new heaven when heaven and the new earth merge and God lives with His people.

In the account of the original creation, it is recorded that everything God made was "excellent in every way" (Genesis 1:31 TLB). Excellence was God's original intent for this planet, so excellence that far exceeds the original creation is what we can expect to see in heaven and in the new earth. God is a God of excellence, and His love for His people compels Him to lavish excellent things upon us.

One of the most familiar verses in the Bible expresses God's love for the people He created and the world He gave us to live in: "For God so loved the world, that he gave his only begotten Son, that whosoever believeth in him should not perish, but have everlasting life" (John 3:16 KJV). This verse conveys God's love for the world and humanity thousands of years after Adam and Eve sinned and plunged the world into corruption. God loved the world so much that He gave up His only Son as a ransom to rescue us from our sins, bring forgiveness, restore all things and give eternal life to all who would believe (Mark 10:45, Acts 3:21).

This great love of God was also tenderly expressed in the beginning in the Genesis account of creation. The way God created the world and made special preparations for everything to be perfectly suited for the people He had in mind conveys His deep love and care for us. God did not create Adam until the last day of creation because everything had to be ready and perfect for him when he arrived. Yet an excellent world was not enough for Adam and Eve. By planting a special garden for His first children, God went far beyond excellence and perfection in expressing His love for them.

> Then the Lord God planted a garden in Eden in the east, and there he placed the man he had made. The Lord God made all sorts of trees grow up from the ground—trees that were beautiful and that produced delicious fruit. In the middle of the garden he placed the tree of life and the tree of the knowledge of good and evil. A river flowed from the land of Eden, watering the garden and then dividing into four branches.

(Genesis 2:8-10 NLT)

Note that God personally planted the garden of Eden Himself. He did not speak it into existence. Instead, He personally landscaped Eden and made it into a garden paradise. The whole garden was a labor of love. It is important to note that Eden was not a small garden. Referred to as the land of Eden, it was the starting point of a river that divided into four other rivers. This might suggest that it was a place of considerable size, possibly covering hundreds of square miles. We can only speculate about the size of Eden.

When God created Eden, He gave the earth some of the very best that heaven has. He lavished riches and beauty upon Adam and Eve that extended way beyond the splendor of the rest of the earth. Eden was the most beautiful and most luxurious spot on the planet, and God placed Adam there (Genesis 2:8). If the Eden on earth was a replica of the Eden in heaven, then we can expect to see in heaven at least some of what was described on earth. But as suggested by the author of Hebrews, the things in heaven are far superior to the things on earth.

Genesis 2:25 records that Adam and Eve were both naked and felt no shame. Of course, this suggests that they were innocent, pure, without sin, and had no knowledge of sin. But it also tells us something about the climate of the original earth. The fact that they wore no clothing suggests that earth's weather was warm and perfectly comfortable; there was nothing to bite or stick their naked flesh. In heaven the climate and living conditions are also perfectly comfortable (Revelation 7:15-17).

The Bible also suggests that there is a continuum of time in heaven. Those who are there are waiting for the culmination of all things—the time when Christ will return to earth and judge the wicked. While they may not be fully aware of the day-to-day activities of earth, these saints are fully aware of what they experienced while on earth (Revelation 6:9-11). These saints have to know that God had not yet avenged them at that time. This implies that they are at least informed about some of the major dealings that God has with the people of planet earth. The Bible says that there is joy among the angels when a sinner repents (Luke 15:10). If angels know when a salvation occurs, it is possible that the saints are also informed about major news from earth such as this.

So what can we conclude so far about heaven and life for the people who live there? Drawing upon a compilation of verses from various books of the Bible, we can conclude that heaven is not some mythical, dreamlike wonderland without form or substance.

Heaven is not some fable that originated from human imagination. Heaven is not some huge cathedral where we dress up and try to look and act pious.

Moreover, it is not just the place we go to as the alternative to hell. Heaven is a very real physical paradise that is well documented in the Scriptures. Heaven is a place of rest, comfort, and beauty. It has buildings, streets to walk on, and beautiful landscapes. There are varieties of trees, grasses, and beautiful flowering plants that grow out of soil, as well as peaceful animal and marine life. Heaven has rivers, lakes, streams, mountains, and valleys. Heaven is not some sad, melancholy place, but a delightful place filled with laughter.

Heaven is a place that appreciates high fashion. God and those who live there have a healthy value of precious things. The courts and palaces of heaven are highly stylistic architecture ornately decorated with the finest fabrics and gemstones imaginable.

Heaven is populated with people who have been made perfect. The people in heaven are like Christ, so they enjoy perfect relationships with each other. In other words, they have a compelling desire to express their love for each other through service.

Yet we are constrained to admit that even with all the information that God has revealed to us about heaven through His Word, there are many, many things that remain unseen and unknown about this wonderful place. We cannot fully imagine all the good things that now await us in heaven—nor in the new heavens and the new earth that will be unveiled and opened up for God's children to enter one day. But the things we know about heaven excite a deep longing in our hearts for home.

Chapter 9 | Thought-provoking Questions

1. How can we determine what heaven is like?
2. What was the original earth modeled after?
3. What two books reveal to us the beginning of creation and the end of old things and the beginning of the new?
4. How do we know that heaven has trees, vegetation, animals, and much of what is seen on earth?
5. Will there be seas in the new earth?
6. How do we know that God is a lover of beauty and diversity?
7. How can we deduce that God is a God of joy, laughter, fun, and pleasure?
8. How can we deduce that God is also a God of order?
9. How do we know that God possesses unfathomable intellect and a loving, caring personality?
10. What was the earth like before sin entered it?
11. How does the Genesis account of creation contradict the theory of evolution?
12. How does evolution contradict Christianity?

CHAPTER 10
New Heavens and a New Earth

> *"Look! I am creating new heavens and a new earth, and no one will even think about the old ones anymore.*
>
> (Isaiah 65:17 NLT)
>
> *As surely as my new heavens and earth will remain, so will you always be my people, with a name that will never disappear," says the LORD.*
>
> (Isaiah 66:22 NLT)
>
> *But we are looking forward to the new heavens and new earth he has promised, a world filled with God's righteousness.*
>
> (2 Peter 3:13 NLT)
>
> *Then I saw a new heaven and a new earth, for the old heaven and the old earth had disappeared. And the sea was also gone.*
>
> (Revelation 21:1 NLT)

From the time of the Old Testament prophets, God has promised to create new heavens and a new earth to replace the present ones that have fallen under the curse of sin. The final two chapters of the Book of Revelation provide more details about heaven and the new earth than any other book in the Bible. We have already examined a portion of this great book to reveal some of the wonders of life in heaven. But the last two chapters are particularly relevant to our study of our future home. From these final two chapters, we will examine those parts of John's vision that provide us with further information about heaven, the new earth, and our existence there. John begins his description of the new heaven and the new earth in chapter 21 and continues relating details of what he saw into chapter 22.

> Then I saw a new heaven and a new earth, for the old heaven and the old earth had disappeared. And the sea was also gone. And I saw the holy city, the new Jerusalem, coming down from God out of heaven like a bride beautifully dressed for her husband. I heard a loud shout from the throne, saying, "Look, God's home is now among his people! He will live with them, and they will be his people. God himself will be with them. He will wipe every tear from their eyes, and there will be no more death or sorrow or crying or pain. All these things are gone forever." And the one sitting on the throne said, "Look, I am making everything new!" And then he said to me, "Write this down, for what I tell you is trustworthy and true." And he also said, "It is finished! I am the Alpha and the Omega—the Beginning and the End. To all who are thirsty I will give freely from the springs of the water of life. All who are victorious will inherit all these blessings, and I will be their God, and they will be my children.
>
> (Revelation 21:1-7 NLT)

John saw the long-awaited promise of a new heaven and a new earth finally fulfilled. He mentions the fact that the old ones had passed away, just as Peter and others had predicted. He must have been thrilled as he saw, with his own eyes, the place where he would spend eternity. Imprisoned in a penal colony on a desolate island, dressed in filthy rags, suffering from the elements and plagued by vermin, John was greatly encouraged and inspired by what he was now allowed to behold. Any sorrow and discouragement he felt quickly evaporated as he was given a look into the home he was destined for.

    Before he could comment on what the new earth was like, John was completely captivated by an amazing sight. He saw a huge and massive golden city, dazzling bright and designed like a giant golden jewel set with huge precious gemstones. It was emanating an assorted array of colored light and descending upon the new earth. The city was breathtakingly beautiful, and John was enraptured by its splendor. He compared the beauty of the city with the most beautiful thing he could imagine on earth—a beautiful bride adorned for her husband. Indeed, this picture represents the highest and purest form of love that earth can produce among human beings. The picture of a bride and groom in love and about to be married is earth's best representation of God's love for His people. The prophet Isaiah expresses his God-inspired thoughts about this marriage between the Son of God and His redeemed people in explicit terms: "For your Maker is your husband — the LORD Almighty is his name — the Holy One of Israel is your Redeemer; he is called the God of all the earth" (Isaiah 54:5 NIV).

Marriage unites two people into one. Before a couple is married, they live in separate homes and lead separate lives. But after the marriage they move in together and begin to live one life in one home. They unite in heart, body, and possessions. What they once owned separately, they own jointly after they are married. This is why the Bible says that we are joint heirs with Christ (Romans 8:17). Through the public address system in heaven, John heard a loud voice shouting from the throne and announcing, "Look, the home of God is now among His people! He will live with them, and they will be His people. God Himself will be with them." John goes on to emphasize the details of God's tender care for His new bride. He makes it clear that He will take away all of our sorrows and we will no longer be bothered with death, tears, or pain because the old earth, where these evils now exist, will be gone forever. Like a doting husband, Jesus will use all His power, wealth, and resources to protect His bride from harm, grant her the desires of her heart, and make her happy. In his book, *Heaven Revealed*, Paul Enns makes the following pointed comment:

> Jesus Himself described the kingdom as 'compared to a king who gave a wedding feast for his son' " (Matthew 22:2). What would a wedding feast arranged by a king for his son be like? Lavish! Imagine heaven's rule on earth in Christ's kingdom, pictured as a king's wedding banquet for his son—and that is precisely what the kingdom will be. The church is the bride of Christ. The kingdom will be the eternal celebration of the wedding of Christ and the church. We will enjoy rapturous celebration as the bride of Christ in the eternal kingdom.[1]

God will indeed make everything new for the ones He loves and eternity for believers will be more joyful than a wedding celebration.

The apostle John continues describing the incredible things he saw:

> Then one of the seven angels who held the seven bowls

> containing the seven last plagues came and said to me, "Come with me! I will show you the bride, the wife of the Lamb." So he took me in the Spirit to a great, high mountain, and he showed me the holy city, Jerusalem, descending out of heaven from God. It shone with the glory of God and sparkled like a precious stone—like jasper as clear as crystal. The city wall was broad and high, with twelve gates guarded by twelve angels. And the names of the twelve tribes of Israel were written on the gates. There were three gates on each side—east, north, south, and west.

(Revelation 21:9-13 NLT)

John's analogy that compares the prepared city with a bride adorned for her husband was right on target because the bride, the wife of the Lamb, is exactly what the angel called it. Standing on a high mountain on the new earth and completely mesmerized by what he saw, John immediately began to describe this golden city of pure light in vivid detail. According to him the city was completely lit up—not by an artificial light source, but by the light of the glory of God.

I recently walked past a jewelry store in a local mall. I noticed how the jewels sparkled and glistened under the light cast upon them from somewhere above in the display case and thought about John's description of the New Jerusalem. John says, "It sparkled like a precious gem, crystal clear like jasper." Jasper is probably what we refer to as a diamond. Transparent gold and diamonds are prominent in the make-up of the city. The city is a giant piece of priceless jewelry lit from within and so transparent that the light of God shining through the gold and jewels captures and transmits each one of the colors of the stones. The city is made of transparent gold inset with gemstones that allow light to pass through.

John gives a general description of the gates and walls in these verses, but he will give more details as we proceed further down into the chapter. He mentions that the walls are *broad and high* and the city has *twelve gates*, three in each wall. Each gate is guarded by an angel and engraved with the name of one of the twelve tribes of Israel. It is likely that these gates will be identified by those names. For example, one might say: "Meet me at the Judah gate," or "Meet me at the Zebulun gate." These details are meant to help us visualize what living on the new earth—and particularly in the New Jerusalem—will be like.

John then continues his description of the city, adding more meticulous detail.

> The wall of the city had twelve foundation stones, and on them were written the names of the twelve apostles of the Lamb. The angel who talked to me held in his hand a gold measuring stick to measure the city, its gates, and its wall. When he measured it, he found it was a square, as wide as it was long. In fact, its length and width and height were each 1,400 miles. Then he measured the walls and found them to be 216 feet thick (according to the human standard used by the angel).
>
> (Revelation 21:14-17 NLT)

The wall of the city is 216 feet thick, which is equal to about half the length of a city block. The city itself is shaped like a cube, extending fourteen hundred miles in every direction and out into space. This means that the city runs approximately half the length of the entire United States, from coast to coast, and about three-fourths its width, from the Canadian border to the gulf. The city is so tall that it reaches beyond the earth's present atmosphere. Jet airliners normally fly at an altitude of six miles up but the city reaches 1400 miles up. If it is divided into floors, jet altitude would be near the bottom floors. Most people living in the city would look down on jet altitude. Imagine what an observatory the top floor of New Jerusalem would make.

Dr. Erwin Lutzer presents an interesting thought regarding the living space in the New Jerusalem. He comments, "Remember, Jesus said: 'In my Father's house are many rooms' (John 14:2 NIV). If we take that literally, heaven will be composed of 396,000 stories (at twenty feet per story) each having an area as big as one half the size of the United States! Divide that into separate condominiums, and you have plenty of room for all who have been redeemed by God since the beginning of time."[2] Although we are given little information about the way the city will be compartmentalized, Dr. Lutzer's scenario does offer food for thought. Of course, the New Jerusalem is not all there is of heaven. It is only the capital city of the kingdom of heaven.

It appears that the city will descend to the new earth and rest upon a huge mountain that will be the highest peak in the new world. It is possible that the top of the mountain will be level, either created or excavated to receive this magnificent fourteen hundred mile, cubed-shaped city. If so, New Jerusalem will shine like a giant lighthouse from atop the tallest mountain in the world. The city will sit like a crown upon the new earth, lighting the whole earth and shining out into the new heavens. This seems to be what the prophet Micah is alluding to when he prophesies, "And it will come about in the last days that the mountain of the house of the Lord will be established as the chief of the mountains. It will be raised above the hills, and the peoples will stream to it. And many nations will come and say, 'Come let us go up to the mountain of the Lord and to the house of the God of Jacob, that He may teach us about His ways and that we may walk in His paths' " (Micah 4:1-2 NASB).

Although Micah's prophecy is likely a reference to the millennial kingdom of Christ upon the earth before the creation of the new earth, it is a possible indicator of how God will situate the New Jerusalem upon the new earth. Pastor and scholar John MacArthur agrees that this great, high mountain will be on the new earth. He comments, "An angel took John in his vision to a mountain on the new earth from which he could watch God's masterpiece, the capital city of the infinite heaven, descend from God, out of the third heaven, and become the crown jewel of the new heavens and new earth."[3]

Some pastors and teachers have suggested that the city will not actually sit upon the earth but descend out of heaven and either orbit the earth or remain suspended like a satellite. However, this idea is debatable. There is no Scripture reference that actually suggests the city will stop its descent somewhere above the earth. The Bible says the city came down out of heaven, which indicates that it came down to earth. Revelation 21:3 also says that God's dwelling will be with men, meaning that He will live among us. I believe this signifies that God will live with us in the New Jerusalem upon the new earth.

This golden city will sit upon the new earth like a golden jeweled capstone. It is the crown of the new earth. Perhaps the city itself, with its cubed shape, is representative of Jesus, who is referred to in the Scriptures as the cornerstone. Prophesying of the coming of Christ, Isaiah declares, "Therefore, this is what the Sovereign LORD says: Look! I am placing a foundation stone in

Jerusalem. It is firm, a tested and precious cornerstone that is safe to build on. Whoever believes need never run away again" (Isaiah 28:16 NLT). Nearly seven hundred years after Isaiah's death, Peter refers to Christ as the fulfillment of this prophecy when he quotes it in one of his letters: "As the Scriptures say, 'I am placing a cornerstone in Jerusalem, chosen for great honor, and anyone who trusts in him will never be disgraced'" (1 Peter 2:6 NLT).

The Jewish religious leaders rejected Jesus, but God chose Him to be the Savior of the world. On the Day of Pentecost, Peter emphatically declared Jesus to be the fulfillment of this prophecy about the stone that was rejected by men but chosen by God. Speaking directly in the faces of some of those who were responsible for having Jesus crucified, he declared, "For Jesus is the one referred to in the Scriptures, where it says, 'The stone that you builders rejected has now become the cornerstone.'" (Acts 4:11 NLT).

By designing the city in the shape of a perfectly formed cornerstone, God could be communicating for all time the message that Jesus is that stone the human builders rejected but God chose. The city itself could be an eternal symbol of Jesus, who said, "Upon this rock I will build my church; and the gates of hell shall not prevail against it." (Matthew 16:18 KJV).

The walls of the city were built upon twelve foundation stones, each with the name of one of the apostles, just as the twelve gates were engraved with the name of each of the twelve tribes of Israel. Thus, twenty-four Jewish leaders were prominently represented in the architecture of the New Jerusalem. The twelve foundation stones were probably layered one atop another, so they were meant to be seen. Foundations of earthly buildings are usually buried, but in New Jerusalem, even the foundation stones are exposed, highly decorative, and designed to add to the beauty and splendor of this magnificent city.

John continues his description of the city:
> The wall was made of jasper, and the city was pure gold, as clear as glass.
>
> (Revelation 21:18 NLT)

Concerning this wall, Daniel Brown makes the following observation: "The wall consists of jasper, probably meaning diamond. We cannot even begin to calculate the worth of such a diamond; the earthly measure of karats is meaningless on such a grand scale."[4] Remember that God used all transparent materials to allow the light of His glory to freely pass through. Even the gold was transparently clear as glass. The city was obviously designed to serve as a source of light for new earth.

As previously mentioned, the city was constructed of pure gold. We often hear people talk about streets of gold when they refer to this celestial city, but it is important to note that the entire city was constructed of pure, transparent gold. Speaking of the transparent quality of this gold, John MacArthur writes, "Unlike earth's gold, this gold will be transparent so the overpowering radiance of God's glory can refract and glisten through the entire city."[5]

In other words, the gold was so transparent that light passed through it as uninterrupted as the light that passes through colored light bulbs. The light passing through the gold and gemstones would be exceedingly more brilliant than Christmas lights. The colors of the transparent gold and gems would be reflected in the light as it passes through and out of the city. The New Jerusalem will be so brilliantly and colorfully lit that it will illuminate the earth and the sky with dazzling, celebrative multicolored light.

John moves on to describe the wall that surrounded the city:

> The wall of the city was built on foundation stones inlaid with twelve precious stones: the first was jasper, the second sapphire, the third agate, the fourth emerald, the fifth onyx, the sixth carnelian, the seventh chrysolite, the eighth beryl, the ninth topaz, the tenth chrysoprase, the eleventh jacinth, the twelfth amethyst.
>
> (Revelation 21:19-20 NLT)

These are the same kinds of stones that God commanded to be inlaid in the breast- piece worn by the priests of Israel and used to ask the Lord specific questions, make decisions, and determine God's will. Each of these stones represented one of the twelve tribes of Israel (Exodus 28:15-21). The twelve tribes of Israel and the twelve apostles are represented throughout the architecture of the New Jerusalem. They are symbolized by the twelve gates, the twelve foundations, the twelve engravings, and the twelve stones in the foundation.

Describing the twelve gates, John writes,

> The twelve gates were made of pearls—each gate from a single pearl! And the main street was pure gold, as clear as glass.

(Revelation 21:21 NLT)

Imagine a pearl that was large enough to construct an entire gate. These gates were set in the wall of the city, and it is not clear just how large they were. The wall was 216 feet thick. It is not clear from John's description whether or not the wall was as high as the city itself. If so, proportionally it would be a very thin wall—216 feet thick by fourteen hundred miles tall and fourteen hundred miles long. It is possible that the gates of pearl were at least as thick as the wall and several stories high if they did not run the entire height of the wall. These were huge and massive gates.

John continues to share what he was shown:

> I saw no temple in the city, for the Lord God Almighty and the Lamb are its temple. And the city has no need of sun or moon, for the glory of God illuminates the city, and the Lamb is its light.

(Revelation 21:22-23 NLT)

Temples are formal buildings that represent the presence of God. Yet there is no need for a temple when God Himself lives among His people. We will bask in the light and beauty of God's presence. The very atmosphere of the heavenly city will be charged with love, adoration, and joy.

Heaven will not be one long church service. Our time with God will be more like Thanksgiving Day or Christmas Day with the family or a wedding day and honeymoon than a church service. As nice as church services are, we sometimes want them to end so we can get out and have lunch with the family, go fishing, play golf, or just relax with friends. Although church attendance is extremely important, church services are sorely lacking in demonstrating to us what it will be like to be in God's presence.

Life in the presence of God will be intellectually stimulating, jubilant, fun, and exciting. We will worship and adore the God of the universe who knows every one of us, not just by name, but intimately. God, who created everything and knows everything about everything, will smile at us with complete approval and interact with us on a close and personal level. Our relationship with God will be the pure and perfect relationship of family. Although He is the King of the universe, He is also our Father.

In verse 23, John says there is no need for the sun or moon in this city because God's glory illumines it "and the Lamb is its light." Imagine an entire city designed like a precious, transparent jewel. It is worth repeating that every part of the city is designed to allow the bright light of God and His Son to pass through it. The foundation is inlaid or decorated with giant gemstones of the finest quality. These stones are so massive that they are possibly miles in height and length and probably as thick as the wall itself.

The New Jerusalem is one of the highest expressions of God's love. It is a demonstration of the fact that He will withhold no good thing from those who belong to him (Psalm 84:11). Nothing God has is too good for those who are the objects of His love and affection. When reading John's description of the city, it is easy to see that New Jerusalem is the work of a God in love.

When a man is about to marry the woman of his dreams, he is willing to lavish all that he possesses upon that woman. His soon-to-be bride is the center of his whole world. He is willing to give up comfort and make the ultimate sacrifice to obtain her love and affection, and once that love is his, then all that he has becomes hers. Dr. J. Vernon McGee makes the following observation about marriage: "The marriage relationship is a mystery that is now being opened to us. The marriage relationship is the most beautiful and wonderful relationship. It is the oldest ceremony that God has instituted for man. It goes right back into the Garden of Eden, the very beginning, and it is all-important."[6]

To demonstrate his deep abiding love for his bride, the man in love does two things, if he is able. He goes out and buys the finest wedding ring he can afford, and then he builds or buys the finest house he can afford and presents them both, along with himself and all he has, to his bride. The man in love is overjoyed to have his bride share in ownership of everything he holds dear. Because he loves her as himself, he wants her to enjoy everything he enjoys. He withholds nothing from her. He loves her and trusts her with everything he is and everything he has. The New Jerusalem is the wedding ring and the dream home all in one. God has limitless wealth, and the New Jerusalem is the finest demonstration of God lavishing His unlimited wealth upon His bride.

Note that in verse 9 of Revelation 21, the angel refers to the city as the bride, the Lamb's wife. This is because the city becomes synonymous with the church that will inhabit it. Just as God's throne room was designed to express who He is, the New Jerusalem was designed to extend the church and express who she is. It appears that when John sees the city, it is uninhabited by the saints. When the saints move into the city, it will be complete and actually become the bride of Christ. This will not happen until Christ returns. The New Jerusalem is reserved for the time when God will create the new heavens and the new earth. This will be the city of God, which will be the crowning capital of His new creation.

John further describes the city and those who will populate it:

> The nations will walk in its light, and the kings of the world will enter the city in all their glory. Its gates will never be closed at the end of day because there is no night there. And all the nations will bring their glory and honor into the city. Nothing evil will be allowed to enter, nor anyone who practices shameful idolatry and dishonesty—but only those whose names are written in the Lamb's Book of Life.

(Revelation 21:24-27 NLT)

Several times John lets us know that the city takes the place of the sun and moon. It will become the source of light for the whole world, lighting up the entire earth. The city will be so bright that it can be seen from space. This may be one reason Paul refers to God's kingdom as the kingdom of light (Colossians 1:12). Of course, light is also a metaphor for knowledge, enlightenment, and righteousness. In the New Jerusalem there will be no night because the light of God and Christ will create a perpetual state of daylight.

Isaiah prophesies that the old earth would be seven times brighter during what some scholars believe to be the millennial reign of Christ. He says of the old earth, after its reconstruction period and after surviving the great tribulation, "The moon will be as bright as the sun, and the sun will be seven times brighter—like the light of seven days in one! So it will be when the LORD begins to heal his people and cure the wounds he gave them" (Isaiah 30:26 NLT). If this is the case with the old earth during the millennial reign of Christ, it is reasonable to assume that the new earth will be at least as bright as the old one.

Since there will be no night there, it is highly possible that we will not need sleep to regenerate ourselves. It is possible that, like plants, we will draw our energy from the glory of God as well as from the vegetation we eat. It is also possible that our bodies will be 100 percent efficient, using every bit of what we eat as energy and passing nothing as human waste. Perhaps this is part of what Paul means when he says Christ will "change our vile body, that it may be fashioned like unto his glorious body" (Philippians 3:21 KJV). Of course, this is somewhat speculative, but it is something to consider.

Notice that the kings or rulers of the earth will add the light of their glory and splendor to brighten the city. The people of all the nations will come into the city from all over the new earth and bring the splendor and honor of their presence into it.

John mentions that the gates would never be closed. In ancient times the gates of a city were open during the daylight hours and closed at night for reasons of security. But since there will be no nighttime there, the custom of closing the gate will not be observed. Of course, neither the gates nor the walls of the New Jerusalem are designed for security purposes. Instead, they connect with old earth history, serve as symbols of safety and security, and are designed for their beauty and aesthetic value. We are assured that there will be no threat to the security of those who inhabit the city or the new earth.

John moves on to talk about the waterworks of the city:

> Then the angel showed me a river with the water of life, clear as crystal, flowing from the throne of God and of the Lamb. It flowed down the center of the main street. On each side of the river grew a tree of life, bearing twelve crops of fruit, with a fresh crop each month. The leaves were used for medicine to heal the nations.

(Revelation 22:1-2 NLT)

As John continued on his tour of the golden city and the new earth, the angel showed him another wonderful sight. Flowing directly from the thrones of God and the Lamb (Jesus Christ) was a crystal-clear river. The waters were so pure and clear that it was like looking through glass.

Teach Me About Heaven and Eternal Life

John refers to the water that filled this river as "the water of life." Like the tree of life in the midst of the Garden of Eden, this water is believed to imbue those who drink from it with life. Jesus and the prophets spoke about the waters of life and referred to God as the fountain of living water and invited their listeners to come to Him and drink freely (John 4:14; John 7:37; Jeremiah 2:13; 17:13). Jesus is speaking both figuratively and literally. Figuratively, He means that those who place their faith in Him will be given the gift of eternal life. Literally, He means that those who place their faith in Him will be allowed to enter this New Jerusalem, drink from this river of life, and be filled with the life that it gives.

Notice that the throne of God and the Lamb are the fountainhead from which this water originates and flows. It is described as a great river that flows down the middle of the main golden street, right down the center of the city. Rivers are usually not pure because the swift-moving waters tend to stir up silt from the bottom and muddy the water. Where the water travels over rocks, it is often clearer but not as clear as crystal as these waters are. God gives this water of life freely to everyone in the new heaven and the new earth to drink from. This beautiful crystal-clear river divides the main golden street.

One can imagine the miles and miles of banks along this beautiful river as a likely gathering place for us citizens of the new earth to lounge around and bask in the light and glory of God as we picnic and enjoy the people and pleasures there. It is hard to imagine a scene like this without including grass, flowers, park animals, and beautiful birds. John does not mention these things in his description of the river of life so we can only speculate about them. But it is reasonable to believe that the God of beauty and variety of natural life would include these things along the banks of the crystal river of life. One day we will see for ourselves.

It is interesting that in the new creation there are several resources of life, but they all originate with God Himself. God is the source of life, and the waters that flow from God are a resource of life. John also describes fruit trees that grow on both sides of the river of life as resources of life. On each side of the river these trees of life grow, "bearing twelve crops of fruit, with a fresh crop each month." Imagine one tree bearing twelve different crops of fruit, and with each month there is a new harvest season.

John was told that the leaves of these trees were for the healing of the nations. We can only theorize as to what this means since the Bible says that there will be no sin in heaven, and thus there will be no sickness there. Perhaps God has chosen to use these leaves as one of His means of preserving health. Perhaps rather than healing illnesses, these leaves are used to maintain and enhance health. Maybe these leaves are like super vitamins for the immortal.

John MacArthur suggests that these leaves actually enhance life rather than heal diseases. He comments, "The English word 'therapeutic' comes from the Greek word translated 'healing.' The leaves somehow enrich heavenly life, making it full and satisfying."[7]

The fact that these trees bear fruit all year round suggests that there will be no winter months. The climate of the new earth will probably be warm and comfortable all year round with no winter blizzards to contend with and no hot summer droughts to endure. The Bible does not suggest that there will be the dramatic change of seasons that most of the world experiences now. However, there still may be some degree of change in the seasons. If so, these changes will likely be subtle and not as dramatic as they are now. They will certainly not be dramatic enough to interrupt the twelve harvest seasons of the trees of life. It is possible that other trees will also bear fruit throughout the year, if not twelve times, then possibly several times each year.

Since there were no rain or storms in the original creation, they will probably not exist in the new earth. When the earth was originally created, a mist came up from the ground and watered the whole earth (Genesis 2:5-6). It is possible that rather than using dark clouds and rain, God will water everything the way He originally designed it. Dark clouds, thunder, lightning, and heavy rains are reminders of Noah's flood. It seems unlikely that these kinds of weather patterns will be part of the new creation. However, the Bible does speak of rain during the millennial kingdom that will precede the eternal kingdom (Isaiah 30:23). But will there be rain in the new earth? Perhaps, but if there is rain, we can be sure it will be a gentle, peaceful, and refreshing rain.

Isaiah also mentions an abundance of crops and livestock. Of course, since there will be no death in heaven, the purpose for livestock would be limited to harvesting wool for fabric and milk for processing into butter, cheese, and other foodstuffs. Paul Enns suggests that God is able to provide meat to eat in the eternal kingdom without the slaughter of animals.[8] It is likely that the food heaven provides for us will be so deliciously satisfying that we will have no desire for anything remotely resembling meat.

Although John does not mention days and weeks as measures of time in heaven, he does mention months when he cites the monthly harvest of varying fruit produced by the trees of life (Revelation 22:2). This suggests the passage of time that may be measured in months rather than hours, days, and weeks. Of course, it will be possible to measure time as we do now with clocks and calendars, but time will not govern our lives as it does now. Since John said there would be twelve months, we can assume that these twelve months will make one-year cycles of time, as they do now. Thus, the changing of the kind of fruit on the trees of life each month may act as a kind of calendar in the new earth.

The light of the glory of God will replace the light of the sun, so daylight will be continuous. There will be no day and night cycles that delineate twenty-four hour days and seven-day weeks in the New Jerusalem. This adds weight to the theory that the cycle of time may only be measured in the passage of months. There may be other natural ways to determine the passage of time such as the periods when different kinds of flowers blossom and bloom, or the times when other trees and bushes bear fruits, nuts, and berries. However, since we will have all eternity before us, time will be a limitless commodity, so we will not be compelled to hurry or rush.

John gives us more insight into life and conditions in heaven:
> No longer will there be a curse upon anything. For the throne of God and of the Lamb will be there, and his servants will worship him. And they will see his face, and his name will be written on their foreheads.

(Revelation 22:3-4 NLT)

As earlier stated, every hardship and difficulty that exists in the world today is the result of the curse of sin. John says that sin and its subsequent curse will pass away with the old heavens and the old earth. The fact that the throne of God and the Lamb will be on the new earth in the New Jerusalem is added assurance that there will be no curse there. The new earth will be a literal paradise, without a trace of the curse that our present world is now under.

In verse 4, John mentions the fact that we will see God's face. The fact that God will allow us to look upon His face is symbolic of complete and total acceptance. Jesus informs us that those who see God are pure in heart (Matthew 5:8). Seeing the face of God in peace is one of the most anticipated privileges that a Christian can look forward to. Of all the things that heaven has in store, beholding the face of God in love and peace will be most rewarding.

Not only will we see God's face, but His name will be permanently written on our foreheads. Having the name of God written on our foreheads will be an eternal badge of honor. We will be visibly identified as God's redeemed. We were once sinners living on a sin-cursed earth under the burden of trials and temptations, but we were chosen and rescued by God. This redemption experience will distinguish us for all eternity from every angelic being. As great and wonderful as the angels are, they have not been redeemed by the blood of Christ.

The name of God on our foreheads will be honorably displayed everywhere we go. God's name will adorn us in a fashion that is similar to the way a wedding ring distinguishes a married person from someone who is single. God's name denotes the honor of ownership and belonging. God will be extremely pleased to have us wear His name, and we will be extremely pleased to wear it. Paul alludes to this in his letter to the church at Ephesus. He talks about how God would be able to present us as symbols of his goodness and grace.

> For he raised us from the dead along with Christ and seated us with him in the heavenly realms because we are united with Christ Jesus. So God can point to us in all future ages as examples of the incredible wealth of his grace and kindness toward us, as shown in all he has done for us who are united with Christ Jesus.

(Ephesians 2:6-7 NLT)

Throughout the millions and millions of years of our eternal existence, God will always be able to point to us as examples of His grace. We will be living reminders of just how good God is and

His great kindness toward us. Like the wounds in Jesus' hands, our very existence in the new world with His name written prominently on our foreheads will present a picture of how much God loves us.

A Very Real World

After examining the words that John and the apostles and prophets use to describe the new earth and its capital city, it appears that the new earth will be as physical as the present earth. It will not be some completely unfamiliar, nebulous, dreamlike, never-never land, but a place with form and substance. It will be a tangible place that can be touched, felt and handled, just like the resurrected body of our Lord Jesus Christ (Luke 24:39). Tim Sheets provides the following words of insight into heaven's reality: "The real thing is in Heaven! It is not heaven that is figurative; it is earth. The sad truth is that most of us believe the exact opposite. The devil has been quite successful in making us picture reality backwards. We're usually convinced that the earth we see is all there is and that heaven is figurative."[9]

To gain an idea of what God intends for the new earth to be, we have looked at the original creation before it was cursed and the new creation after the curse has been removed. It is very likely that many, if not all, of the things mentioned in the original creation will be in the new one and probably much more. Although the new creation will likely be based on the old one, it will be much more wonderful. We can easily see this in the opulence of the New Jerusalem that will serve as the capital city and by the fact that God the Father and the Lord Jesus Christ will live there with us.

We can assume that since there will be flowing rivers and animals and people moving about over the surface of the new earth, it will have some form of gravity to hold everything in place, just as the present earth does. There will be food to eat and water to drink. There will be rivers and lakes to swim and play in, if we so choose. It also appears that there will be mountains to climb and valleys to wander. There will be homes and buildings. There will be animals. There will be trees that have fruit and leaves on them. Although there will be no sun or moon there, it appears that we will experience the passage of time. There will be a comfortable climate, grass, flowers, bushes, and birds.

Since there will be no death, we can naturally assume that nothing or no one will eat meat. However, we can be sure that there will be so many other delicacies and dainties that no one will want to eat meat. There will be beautiful parks with endless daylight and no night. We will appreciate, value, and enjoy gold, jewels, and fine clothing as we do now, but there will be no avarice, jealousy, or greed. It is likely that we will enjoy works of art, music, poetry, fine craftwork, high architecture, and technology that will possibly advance as time passes and as we are led by Christ in discovering new things about the universe.

God the Father, the Lord Jesus Christ, people, and angels will live together in peace and harmony. There will be perfect relationships, perfect love, unfathomable joy, peace, and pleasure with no pain, sorrow, crying, or regrets. We will enjoy all eternity in the prime of life without burden, worry, or care in an absolutely perfect world with the God we adore, people we love, and things we enjoy.

A Final Note

It is possible that after reading this entire book, you have not yet taken the necessary steps to ensure your future in heaven by becoming a disciple of Jesus Christ. Becoming a Christian is as simple as confessing Jesus as Lord and believing that God raised Him from the dead. Paul explains, "If you confess with your mouth that Jesus is Lord and believe in your heart that God raised him from the dead, you will be saved. For it is by believing in your heart that you are made right with God, and it is by confessing with your mouth that you are saved. As the Scriptures tell us, 'Anyone who trusts in him will never be disgraced.' " (Romans 10:9-11 NLT).

By confessing Jesus as Lord, you communicate the fact that you believe in your heart that He is indeed the only begotten Son of God and Lord of all creation. Your confession is more than mental or verbal assent; it is a statement of your willingness to submit to Jesus as your leader and the head of your life. Following is a simple prayer designed for the specific purpose of helping you to become a Christian by leading you in confessing your faith in Christ. If you pray the following prayer with a sincere heart, God will forgive your sins, save you, accept you into His family and secure your place in heaven:

Father God, I confess that I am a sinner. I'm sorry for my sins. Please forgive my sins and cleanse me from all unrighteousness. I believe that Jesus Christ is the Son of God. I believe Jesus died for my sins and rose again from the dead. I ask you to come into my life, save me, and adopt me into your family. I now confess Jesus Christ as my Lord and Savior. Father, send Your Holy Spirit to fill me, work in me, and give me the desire and the ability to do Your good will. I thank You for saving me today. In the name of Your Son Jesus Christ, Amen.

If you prayed with a sincere heart, I congratulate you and welcome you into the family of God. You are now a child of God and a new Christian disciple. The next important step is for you to find a good church. Pray and ask God to lead you to a church where the pastor believes and teaches from the Bible. Ask the pastor to baptize you, and then join the church, get involved in the life of the church, and begin to follow the teachings of Christ. We pray that God will bless you to grow and develop into a strong and productive member of His church and kingdom and that He will use your life to bring many other people into His family.

Today (Date)_____ I accepted Christ as my Lord and Savior.

Name _____

If reading this book has led you to become a Christian or strengthened your walk with Christ, like us on Facebook and add a brief comment at *https://www.facebook.com/teachheavenbook*

To help in your walk with Christ, Dr. Sullivan has written a special book entitled *Stand: A Handbook for Building Strong Disciples*. You can order a copy through our website www.emergecurriculum.com.

Chapter 10 | Thought-provoking Questions

1. How many gates did John see in the New Jerusalem?
2. What will be the shape of the New Jerusalem?
3. What will be the length, width, and height of the city?
4. How will the city and the new earth be lit?
5. How many foundation stones will the walls of the city be built upon?
6. What will be the predominant material the city will be built of?
7. Why will all the construction materials of the city be transparent?
8. What kind of material will the gates be made of?
9. Where will the crystal-clear river that courses down the main street originate?
10. The trees along the river will bear fruit each month. What does this suggest about time in the new heaven and earth?
11. People in heaven and the new earth will probably not eat meat. Why?

NOTES & CITATIONS

Chapter 1—After Death, Life Goes On

1. Paul Enns, *Heaven Revealed* (Chicago: Moody Publishers, 2011), p. 33.
2. William F. Graham Jr., *The Heaven Answer Book* (Nashville: Thomas Nelson, 2012), p. 72.
3. Gary R. Habermas and J. P. Moreland, *Beyond Death* (Wheaton, IL: Crossway Books, 1998), p. 231.
4. Ron Rhodes, *Heaven: The Undiscovered Country* (Eugene, Oregon: Wipf and Stock Publishers, 1996), p. 38.
5. Randy Alcorn, *Heaven* (Carol Stream, IL: Tyndale House, 2004), p. 57.
6. Enns, p. 74.
7. Ron Rhodes, *The Wonder of Heaven: A Biblical Tour of Our Eternal Home* (Eugene OR: Harvest House, 2009), Kindle edition.
8. Erwin Lutzer, *One Minute After You Die* (Chicago: Moody Publishers, 1997), Kindle edition.
9. Paul Lee Tan, *Encyclopedia of 7,700 Illustrations* (Rockville, MD: Assurance Publishers, 1992), p. 139.

Chapter 2—Your Best Life After Death

1. C. S. Lewis, *The Problem of Pain* (New York: Macmillan, 1962), p. 148.
2. Gary R. Habermas and J. P. Moreland, *Beyond Death* (Wheaton, IL: Crossway Books, 1998), p. 347.
3. John MacArthur, *The Glory of Heaven* (Wheaton, IL: Crossway, 1996), p. 85.
4. Randy Alcorn, *Life Promises for Eternity* (Carol Stream, IL: Tyndale House, 2012), p. 35.
5. Billy Graham, *Angels: God's Secret Agents* (Garden City, NY: Doubleday, 1975), p. 152.

Chapter 3—Comforting Facts About the Resurrection

1. Nicholas Wade, *Your Body is Younger Than You Think* (*The New York Times*: August 2, 2005).
2. Warren Wiersbe, *Be Wise: A New Testament Study (1 Corinthians)* (Colorado Springs: David C. Cook, 1982), pp. 156-157.
3. Sally M. Walker, *Fireflies* (Minneapolis: Learner Publications, 2001), p. 22.
4. Bruce B. Barton, et al., *Life Application Bible Commentary: 1&2 Corinthians* (Wheaton, IL: Tyndale House, 1999), p. 235.
5. Joni Eareckson Tada, *Heaven: Your Real Home* (Grand Rapids: Zondervan, 1995), Kindle edition.
6. J. Vernon McGee, *Revelation* (Nashville: Thomas Nelson, 1991), p. 161.
7. Erwin W. Lutzer, *One Minute After You Die* (Chicago: Moody Publishing, 1997), Kindle edition.

Chapter 4—A Brand New Body and a Brand New Mind

1. Bobbie Kalman, *The Life Cycle of a Butterfly* (New York: Crabtree Publishing, 2002), pp. 18-19.
2. Hank Hanegraaff, *AfterLife: What You Want To Know About Heaven* (Brentwood, TN: Worthy Publishers, 2013), Kindle edition.
3. John MacArthur, *The Glory of Heaven* (Wheaton, IL: Crossway Books, 1996), p. 137.
4. Daniel A. Brown, *What The Bible Reveals About Heaven* (Ventura, California: Regal Books, 1999), p. 182.
5. Anthony DeStefano, *A Travel Guide To Heaven* (New York: Doubleday, 2003), pp. 33-34.
6. MacArthur, p. 144.
7. Hanegraaff, Kindle edition.
8. Joni Eareckson Tada, *Heaven: Your Real Home* (Grand Rapids: Zondervan Publishers, 1995), Kindle edition.
9. Mark Wilson, *Wonders of Creation: Human Life, Crown of Creation*. Vol. 6. DVD. (Chicago: Questar Inc, 2005).
10. Gary R. Habermas and J. P. Moreland, *Beyond Death* (Wheaton, IL: Crossway Books, 1998), p. 279.

11. DeStefano, pp. 106-107.
12. DeStefano, p. 117.
13. David Prior, *The Message of 1 Corinthians* (Downers Grove, IL: InterVarsity Press, 1985), p. 272.

Chapter 5—Home Training: On Earth As It Is In Heaven

1. Martin Luther King Jr., *Stride Toward Freedom: The Montgomery Story* (New York: Harper Collins, 1958), p. 207.
2. Linda Washington, *Everything the Bible Says About Heaven* (Minneapolis: Bethany House, 2011), p. 44.
3. Harry Blamires, *Knowing the Truth About Heaven and Hell* (Ann Arbor, MI: Servant Books, 1988), pp. 122-123.
4. Peter J. Kreeft, *Heaven: The Heart's Deepest Longing* (San Francisco: Harper and Row, 1980), p. 110.
5. Anthony T. Evans, *Are Blacks Spiritually Inferior to Whites? The Dispelling of an American Myth* (Wenonah, NJ: Renaissance Productions, 1992), p. 140.
6. Randy Alcorn, *Heaven* (Carol Stream, IL: Tyndale House, 2004), p. 215.
7. Blamires, p. 120.
8. Rackham Holt, *George Washington Carver: An American Biography* (New York: Doubleday, 1943), p. 149.

Chapter 6—A World with One Law

1. Paul Enns, *Heaven Revealed* (Chicago: Moody Publishers, 2011), p. 81.
2. Warren Wiersbe, *Be Wise: A New Testament Study (1 Corinthians)* (Colorado Springs: David C. Cook, 1982), p. 35.
3. William Barclay, *The Letter to the Galatians and Ephesians* (Louisville, KY: Westminster John Knox Press, 2002), p. 194.
4. David Prior, *The Message of 1 Corinthians* (Downers Grove IL: InterVarsity Press, 1985), p. 210.
5. Barclay, p. 64.

6. John Phillips, *Exploring Galatians: An Expository Commentary* (Grand Rapids: Kregel Publications, 2005), p. 203.

Chapter 7—Absolute Peace

1. Horace E. Scudder, *The Complete Poetical Works of Henry Wadsworth Longfellow* (Mattituck, NY: Amereon House, 1920), pp. 289-290.
2. Michael Green, *Tyndale New Testament Commentaries: 2 Peter & Jude,* revised edition (Grand Rapids: William B. Eerdmans, 1999), p. 140.
3. Anthony DeStefano, *A Travel Guide to Heaven* (New York: Doubleday, 2003), p. 37.
4. Wayne Grudem, *Tyndale New Testament Commentaries: 1 Peter* (Grand Rapids: William B. Eerdmans, 2002), p. 151.
5. William Barclay, *The Letter to the Galatians and Ephesians* (Louisville, KY: Westminster John Knox Press, 2002), p. 161.
6. Howard Marshall, *The IVP New Testament Series: 1 Peter* (Downers Grove, IL: InterVarsity Press, 1991), p. 111.

Chapter 8—Joy and Pleasure Forever

1. *Funk and Wagnalls Standard College Dictionary,* text ed., s.v. "pleasure."
2. Randy Alcorn, *Heaven* (Carol Stream, IL: Tyndale House, 2004), p. xxi.
3. Jean E. Syswerda, *Is Heaven Real? Meditations on Scriptures About the Afterlife* (Grand Rapids: Zondervan, 2011), p. 7.
4. Gary R. Habermas and J. P. Moreland, *Beyond Death* (Wheaton, IL: Crossway Books, 1998), p. 350.
5. Randy Alcorn, *In Light of Eternity* (Colorado Springs: Waterbrook Press, 1999), p. 58.
6. Daniel A. Brown, *What the Bible Reveals About Heaven* (Ventura, CA: Regal Books, 1999), pp. 213-14.

Chapter 9—Paradise Heaven

1. Randy Alcorn, *Heaven* (Carol Stream, IL: Tyndale House, 2004), p. 309.
2. Sam Wellman, *George Washington Carver: Inventor and Educator* (Uhrichsville, OH: Barbour Publishing, 1998), pp. 166-167.
3. Chuck Smith, *What the World is Coming To: A Commentary on the Book of Revelation* (Costa Mesa, CA: The Word for Today, 2001), Kindle edition.
4. Randy Alcorn, *Life Promises for Eternity* (Carol Stream, IL: Tyndale House, 2012), p. 47.
5. Daniel A. Brown, *What the Bible Reveals About Heaven* (Ventura, CA: Regal Books, 1999), p. 189.

Chapter 10—New Heavens and a New Earth

1. Paul Enns, *Heaven Revealed* (Chicago: Moody Publishers, 2011), p. 71.
2. Erwin W. Lutzer, *One Minute After You Die* (Chicago: Moody Publishing, 1997), Kindle edition.
3. John MacArthur, *The Glory of Heaven* (Wheaton, IL: Crossway Books, 1996), pp. 116-117.
4. Daniel A. Brown, *What the Bible Reveals About Heaven* (Ventura, CA: Regal Books, 1999), p. 202.
5. John MacArthur, *Revelation: The Christian's Ultimate Victory* (Nashville: Word Publishing, 2001), Kindle edition.
6. J. Vernon McGee, *Revelation* (Nashville: Thomas Nelson, 1991), p. 166.
7. MacArthur, Kindle edition.
8. Enns, p. 127.
9. Tim Sheets, *Heaven Made Real: The Best Is Yet to Come* (Shippensburg, PA: Destiny Image, 1996), p. 28.

Answer Key

Chapter 1

1. Paul compares the human body to a tent because it is temporary and houses the human spirit.
2. No, the soul does not sleep when a person dies.
3. When a Christian dies, the body begins to decay, but the spirit goes to heaven, fully conscious and alert.
4. The first position is that the spirit remains without a body until the resurrection. The second position is that the spirit receives an interim body immediately while in heaven, awaiting the resurrection and the resurrection body.
5. The body of a dead person is called the remains because it is what remains when the spirit leaves the body.
6. Paul says he would rather be away from his body because he knows that death for the Christian means going home to the Lord and heaven.

Chapter 2

1. Paul says he would rather die than live on because for a Christian, life after death is much sweeter, more pleasurable, and more rewarding than life before death.
2. Suicide is never an option because it is a terrible sin against God.
3. The knowledge of heaven relieves Christians from the fear of death because knowing that death cannot harm us releases us to the joy and pleasure of life, removing any reason for fear.
4. Death entered the world through Adam's sin.
5. When the wicked die, they enter into hell.
6. From John's report of the saints in heaven, we learn that they have form, they are very much alive and conscious, they have hands, they can speak, they wear clothing, they have desires, and they are fully aware.
7. John's report about the population in heaven reveals the fact that heaven is made up of people of all nationalities all mixed in together.

Teach Me About Heaven and Eternal Life

8. The Bible says that those who died in the Lord are blessed because Christians who have died have entered into rest, great joy, pleasure, happiness, and peace.
9. Christians are made perfect the instant they die.

Chapter 3

1. As Christians, we are assured that we will be raised from the dead because Jesus was raised.
2. The order of the rapture and resurrection is this: Jesus Christ was the first to rise; then the departed saints will rise, and finally, the living saints will be changed and caught up.
3. The spirits of the saints will return with Christ from heaven and enter their bodies that will be raised from their graves.
4. When Paul says the departed saints sleep, he was speaking about the dead bodies of the saints that appear to be asleep.
5. A planted seed is similar to the resurrection because the seed is planted in one form and then dies and comes forth in a much different, much more glorious form.
6. Our glorified new bodies will be like Jesus' body. We will be immortal, strong, and powerful with much greater mental and physical capabilities.
7. Some examples of things that go through radical transformation without losing their identity include a human infant that changes into an adult, a tadpole that changes into a frog, a caterpillar that changes into a butterfly, and a seed that changes into a plant.
8. Just as we are now like Adam, we will one day be like Christ.
9. Just as there is a natural body, there is also a spiritual body.
10. We are encouraged to meditate on heaven to encourage us, give us joy and comfort, and help us keep a right perspective on life and this world.

Chapter 4

1. Attributes of our new bodies include strength, as well as beauty and splendor.
2. Christians will know each other in heaven.

3. Some things Christ did after His resurrection include eating, suddenly appearing and disappearing, and ascending.
4. Some things angels are able to do include the exercise of great power, the ability to fly, and the ability to enter fire without harm.
5. Job declared that after his body had decayed, yet in his body he would see God.
6. Job's words suggest that he believed he would be resurrected from the dead.

Chapter 5

1. Living a life of love and kindness helps to prepare us for life in heaven by acclimating us to the culture of heaven.
2. The job of Christian ambassadors is to represent Christ and heaven in this world.
3. We demonstrate to the world that we are true children of God by treating everyone, even our enemies, with love and kindness.
4. The eternal reality is love.
5. When He said, "My sheep hear My voice ... and follow Me, Jesus meant that His disciples should follow His ways and teaching and seek to imitate His lifestyle.
6. God temporarily separated the Jews from Gentiles to prevent them from engaging in pagan practices and to preserve the knowledge of the one true God.
7. There is no justification for the separation of Christians along racial lines because Christians of all races are members of one great family, with no reason for division. There is no division of the races in heaven.
8. Jesus told the Parable of the Good Samaritan to help the Jews and everyone else to begin to rid themselves of racial prejudice and to realize that there is no racial prejudice in heaven.

Chapter 6

1. The purpose of laws is to restrain people from committing crimes and stall the downward spiral of corruption and violence.
2. The law in heaven is love.
3. There is only one law in heaven because laws are for lawless people

and there are no lawless people in heaven.
4. No, people in heaven are not capable of sinning.
5. Love completely fulfills all of God's requirements because love does no harm to anyone.
6. Love expresses itself in heaven through acts of kindness and thoughtfulness.
7. God helps us to empathize with others by allowing us to experience certain hardships and difficulties.
8. Lack of empathy is revealed in the lives of people on earth through the terrible things people do to each other.
9. Jesus demonstrated the greatest example of empathy by becoming a man and experiencing what human beings experience.

Chapter 7

1. God's promise of peace will be realized when Christ returns to earth.
2. Peter predicted that they would say, "Where is the sign of His coming? Nothing has changed since the beginning."
3. Peter said the Lord is waiting to give more people time to repent because He doesn't want anyone to perish.
4. Jesus predicted that the earth would be as it was in Noah's day — full of evil and violence.
5. The animal kingdom will be completely peaceful during Christ's thousand-year reign on earth.
6. We are urged to practice living in peace with each other as we wait for peace.

Chapter 8

1. Some of the pleasures that trigger feelings of joy in us include pleasurable tastes, smells, feelings, sights, sounds, experiences, and thoughts about pleasurable people and things.
2. We are almost constantly being exposed to pleasurable things.
3. The steady stream of pleasurable experiences are often unnoticed by people because they are distracted by troubles and problems that are also present.

4. God's advice on how to enjoy life's pleasures is to meditate on things that promote joy and pleasure, as well as things that are pure, lovely, and admirable.
5. To get a feel for the joy of heaven, we are urged to reflect on the most joyful feelings of our lives and know that heaven is like that, only far better.
6. Christians are never alone, in life or in death. Christ and the angels are always with us.
7. Angels are assigned to watch over and minister to Christians.
8. Death is not a journey; it is more like a door.
9. Our level of knowledge and awareness after death will be greatly increased. We will see and know things we cannot see and know now.
10. On the other side, we will see death as the exit from struggle to freedom, from sorrow to joy, and from toil to rest.

Chapter 9

1. We can determine what heaven is like by examining the original earth.
2. The original earth was modeled after things in heaven.
3. The two books that reveal to us the beginning of creation, the end of old things, and the beginning of new things, are Genesis and Revelation.
4. We know that heaven has trees, vegetation, animals, and much of what is seen on earth because the earth is modeled after things in heaven.
5. There will be no seas in the new earth.
6. We know that God is a lover of beauty and diversity because of the great variety of beautiful designs in color, textures, and forms in nature that He created.
7. We can deduce that God is a God of joy, laughter, fun, and pleasure because of the explosion of colorful and pleasurable designs in all creation.
8. We can deduce that God is also a God of order because of the order and precision we see in His creation.

9. We know that God possesses unfathomable intellect and a loving, caring personality by looking at the complexity of His creation and the life-sustaining environment.
10. The earth was much like heaven, with only love and beauty, before Satan and sin entered it.
11. The Genesis account of creation contradicts the theory of evolution by declaring that there was no death before Adam's sin and death resulted from sin. Evolution declares that everything, including human beings, came into existence through natural selection, a process of the death of the weakest and survival of the strongest.
12. Evolution contradicts Christianity because Christianity teaches that death came into the world as the result of sin and Christ died to forgive and take away our sins. Evolution teaches that there is no sin and death is not the result of sin, but a natural part of life.

Chapter 10

1. John saw twelve gates in the New Jerusalem.
2. New Jerusalem will be in the shape of a cube.
3. The length, width, and height of New Jerusalem will be fourteen hundred miles. Some Bible translations say fifteen hundred miles.
4. The city and the new earth will be lit by the light of God's glory.
5. The walls of the city will be built on twelve foundations.
6. The predominant material of the city will be transparent gold.
7. All the construction materials of the city will be transparent to allow the light of God's glory to shine through them.
8. The gates will be made of pearl.
9. The crystal-clear river will originate from the throne of God and the Lamb.
10 The trees bearing fruit each month suggests that there will be passage of time in the new heaven and earth.
11. People in heaven and the new earth will probably not eat meat because there will be no death there.

Bibliography

Alcorn, Randy. *Heaven*. Carol Stream, IL: Tyndale House, 2004.

——*In Light of Eternity*. Colorado Springs: Waterbrook Press, 1999.

——*Life Promises for Eternity*. Carol Stream, IL: Tyndale House, 2012.

Barclay, William. *The Letter to the Galatians and Ephesians*. Louisville, KY: Westminster John Knox Press, 2002.

Barton, Bruce B., et al. *Life Application Bible Commentary: 1 & 2 Corinthians*. Wheaton, IL: Tyndale House, 1999.

Blamires, Harry. *Knowing the Truth About Heaven and Hell*. Ann Arbor, MI: Servant Books, 1988.

Brown, Daniel A. *What the Bible Reveals About Heaven*. Ventura, CA: Regal Books, 1999.

DeStefano, Anthony. *A Travel Guide to Heaven*. New York: Doubleday, 2003.

Enns, Paul. *Heaven Revealed*. Chicago: Moody Publishers, 2011.

Evans, Anthony T. *Are Blacks Spiritually Inferior to Whites? The Dispelling of an American Myth*. Wenonah, NJ: Renaissance Productions, 1992.

Funk and Wagnalls Standard College Dictionary, text ed., s.v."pleasure."

Graham, Billy. *Angels: God's Secret Agents*. Garden City, New York: Doubleday, 1975.

Graham, William F. Jr. *The Heaven Answer Book*. Nashville: Thomas Nelson, 2012.

Green, Michael. *Tyndale New Testament Commentaries: 2 Peter & Jude*, revised edition. Grand Rapids: William B. Eerdmans, 1999.

Grudem, Wayne. *Tyndale New Testament Commentaries: 1 Peter*. Grand Rapids: William B. Eerdmans, 2002.

Habermas, Gary R., and Moreland, J. P. *Beyond Death*. Wheaton, IL: Crossway Books, 1998.

Hanegraaff, Hank. *AfterLife: What You Really Want to Know About Heaven and the Hereafter*. Brentwood, TN: Worthy Publishing, 2013.

Holt, Rackham. *George Washington Carver: An American Biography*. New York: Doubleday, 1943.

Kalman, Bobbie. *The Life Cycle of a Butterfly*. New York: Crabtree Publishing, 2002.

Kreeft, Peter. *Heaven: The Heart's Deepest Longing*. San Francisco: Harper and Row, 1980.

King, Martin Luther Jr. *Stride Toward Freedom: The Montgomery Story*. New York: Harper Collins, 1958.

Lewis, C. S. *The Problem of Pain*. New York: Macmillan, 1962.

Lutzer, Erwin W. *One Minute After You Die*. Chicago: Moody Publishers, 1997.

MacArthur, John. *The Glory of Heaven*. Wheaton, IL: Crossway Books, 1996.

——*Revelation: The Christian's Ultimate Victory*. Nashville: Word Publishing, 2001.

Marshall, Howard. *The IVP New Testament Series: 1 Peter*. Downers Grove, IL: InterVarsity Press, 1991.

McGee, J. Vernon. *Revelation*. Nashville: Thomas Nelson, 1991.

Phillips, John. *Exploring Galatians: An Expository Commentary*. Grand Rapids: Kregel Publications, 2005.

Prior, David. *The Message of 1 Corinthians*. Downers Grove, IL: InterVarsity Press, 1985.

Rhodes, Ron. *Heaven: The Undiscovered Country*. Eugene, OR: Wipf and Stock Publishers, 1996.

——*The Wonder of Heaven: A Biblical Tour of Our Eternal Home*. Eugene, OR: Harvest House, 2009.

Scudder, Horace E. *The Complete Poetical Works of Henry Wadsworth Longfellow.* Mattituck, NY: Amereon House, 1920.

Sheets, Tim. *Heaven Made Real: The Best Is Yet To Come.* Shippensburg, PA: Destiny Image, 1996.

Smith, Chuck. *What the World Is Coming To: A Commentary on the Book of Revelation.* Costa Mesa, CA: The Word for Today, 2001.

Syswerda, Jean E. *Is Heaven Real? Meditations on Scriptures About the Afterlife.* Grand Rapids: Zondervan, 2011.

Tada, Joni Eareckson. *Heaven: Your Real Home.* Grand Rapids: Zondervan Publishers, 1995.

Tan, Paul Lee. *Encyclopedia of 7,700 Illustrations.* Rockville, MD: Assurance Publishers, 1992.

Wade, Nicholas. *Your Body Is Younger Than You Think. The New York Times*, August 2, 2005.

Walker, Sally M. *Fireflies.* Minneapolis: Learner Publications, 2001.

Washington, Linda. *Everything the Bible Says About Heaven.* Minneapolis: Bethany House, 2011.

Wellman, Sam. *George Washington Carver: Inventor and Educator.* Uhrichsville, OH: Barbour Publishing, 1998.

Wiersbe, Warren. *Be Wise: A New Testament Study (1 Corinthians).* Colorado Springs: David C. Cook, 1982.

Wilson, Mark. *Wonders of Creation: Human Life, Crown of Creation.* Vol. 6. DVD. Chicago: Questar Inc, 2005.

Other Books by
Dr. Kenneth E. Sullivan
www.EmergeCurriculum.com

Stand: A Handbook for Building Strong Disciples

Emerge Commentary on The Book of First Corinthians

Emerge Commentary on The Book of Galatians

Coming in 2015: Emerge Commentary on The Book of James

www.ingramcontent.com/pod-product-compliance
Lightning Source LLC
LaVergne TN
LVHW051551070426
835507LV00021B/2517